PRAISE FOR *13,760 Feet*:

You get a "two-fer"; an insider's gritty view of the stress, torment, humor and joy that is reality for those who love to fly, and intertwined with the flyer's story, you get an uncommon insight into an outwardly confident and skillful man's tender inner self pushed to an emotional brink.

    HUGH SCHOELZEL | VP at TWA and Mark Berry's Chief Pilot
    (Lots of planes from a vintage 1909 Bleriot to an F-100 to a B-747)

After a couple of decades (plus) of writing and editing aviation material for publication, the routine and rigorous demands of constant deadlines does tend to dampen spirits from time to time. But once in a while, an unsolicited manuscript shows up, which, after laying dormant and neglected until a rare idle moment presents itself, makes the daily grind all worthwhile. Such nuggets from a previously unknown and unpublished author is a fulfilling discovery, and makes it all worthwhile. Moreover, Mark Berry sharpens the edge of his already finely drawn writing with his imaginative body painted artwork and own song-writing skills. Well done Mark!

    JOHN WEGG | *Airways* Magazine Editor-in-Chief

As an airline pilot, Mark L. Berry is trained to be precise, methodical, and unemotional. That's what makes his memoir — *13,760 Feet* — all the more interesting. In his quest to continue the healing process through sharing his experience with others, Berry gives the reader many gifts through his expressive, detailed, and heart-wrenching story of love and loss. You don't have to be a pilot or long-distance traveler to appreciate this love story.

    IAN J. TWOMBLY | *AOPA's Flight Training* Magazine Editor

A sensitive, intelligent, and touching rendition of a tragic story, told by a sensitive and intelligent man who is also a good craftsman with words. There is a great deal inside this written record of a nightmarish personal journey that creates an unerringly compelling effect. This book is not only about that heartbreaking personal experience, it is also about the resulting emotional aftermath — a long, arduous and significant journey — that often needs to come after life has dealt what is seemingly a knockout blow to our senses. *13,760 Feet* is a poignant and amazingly candid tale.

    THOMAS BLOCK | Co-author of *Mayday* with Nelson DeMille, and author of *Captain* and five other novels

Your prose is resonating with truth, wisdom and tons of humor. Usually I have a lot to say about any book. This one stunned me into blissful silence as I devoured one page after another. It's so beautifully and lovingly written, that it should be read many, many... Every word hits the mark and every sentence an illumination shining from within you out... This is a very empowering book.

    DA CHEN | Best-selling Author of *Brothers, China's Son, Colors of the Mountain,* and *My Last Empress*

Straight from the airline pilot's seat, Mark Berry has written an eloquent memoir that takes readers inside the cockpit and, through intimate memory and original song, one of the world's most devastating flight disasters. An irresistible read for frequent flyers and frequent readers.

LARY BLOOM | Editor, Columnist, and Author

Mark Berry's journey is a dissection of career and self. The duality of aviation: unfettered joy juxtaposed against the crushing reality of loss, unfolds in front of the reader. Set at a unique point in the history of commercial aviation, it gives the reader a view of the glory days of aviation and their demise. *13,760 Feet* is an introspective view of an industry and a man; both on the edge of existence

LELAND 'CHIP' SHANLE, JR. | Author, Airline Pilot, Former Navy Test Pilot, and Documentary Leader

Captain Mark L. Berry's debut memoir, *13,760 Feet*, will make your heart jump. From the pilot's cockpit, we travel alongside his excruciating personal losses and the world's losses from the destruction of TWA Flight 800. Interweaving riveting scenes with original song lyrics, we rattle along this ride of unthinkable tragedy. Ultimately, this intimate memoir lands us in a place of joy and triumph. You will be moved to tears by the twists and turns of this compassionate retelling of one courageous pilot's journey. Powerful.

DEBORAH HENRY | Author of *The Whipping Club* – Selected for *O Magazine* July Summer Reading Issue

Mark L. Berry tells a vivid and heartfelt story about loss and recovery. His memoir, *13,760 Feet*, deftly takes us on a journey through the demanding minutiae of piloting that we, as passengers, take for granted while simultaneously transporting us into a profound emotional journey.

JIM SHAHIN | *Washington Post* Smoke Signals Columnist

Captain Berry wisely dovetails his excruciating psychological odyssey with the fascinating journey of his own airline career. An eye-opener for any landlubber, he presents a bird's eye view — warts and all — of the gritty, sometimes comical, reality of those daring young men and women in their flying machines. From his shoestring-budget gambit to launch his career by becoming a "Pilot of the Caribbean," to his misadventures as a naive B-727 Flight Engineer based in Germany, Berry's book could easily double as an entertaining, Ernest K. Gann–infused how-to manual for the airline pilot wannabe.

ERIC AUXIER | Airline pilot and author of *The Last Bush Pilots*

13,760 FEET

13,760 Feet

My Personal Hole in the Sky

MARK L. BERRY

A TRANS WORLD AUTHOR, LLC PUBLICATION

A Trans World Author, LLC Publication
St. Louis, MO, USA

Print ISBN: 978-0-9897869-0-4
E-Book ISBN: 978-0-9897869-1-1

Typography by John D. Berry

LOOK FOR TWO NOVELS BY MARK L BERRY:

Pushing Leaves Towards the Sun
Street Justice

CONTENTS

THERE ARE thirty-four companion songs associated with this book, and you can hear them all in their entirety on my website: http://marklberry.com/memoir

Or hear them along with my memoir's associated photos: http://marklberry.com/memoir/memoir-photos/

This book is dedicated to Susanne G Jensen
June 23, 1965–July 17, 1996

...and the eternal memory of the passengers
and crew who were all lost on TWA Flight 800.

ACKNOWLEDGMENTS

SOME OF THESE CHAPTERS originally appeared, as stories in slightly different form, in the following publications:

> *Airways*
> *AOPA Flight Training*
> Connecticut Newspapers – *Greenwich Time, The Advocate,*
>   *The News-Times*
> *Epiphany*
> *ERAU EaglesNEST*
> *So...Stories*
> *The Stoneslide Corrective*
> *The Story Shack*
> *TARPA Topics*
> *Under the Sun*
> *Write This*

The author gratefully acknowledges and thanks each of these publications; with special thanks the Editor-in-Chief John Wegg at *Airways* magazine where over a dozen chapters have appeared.

After demonstrating a passion for writing fiction, many friends and family who read my survivor's guilt novel *Pushing Leaves Towards the Sun* recommended that I tell my true story, and I resisted. It was Dr. Michael C. White, Fairfield University's creative writing MFA director, who gave me the final push to write a memoir rather than another novel as he accepted me into the low-residency MFA program. This is that story.

As you and I cruise together, I'd like to announce that you're sharing my flying experience solely from my perspective and imperfect memory. This isn't journalism; it's my personal journey. In many cases I've contacted the people mentioned for clarification or their view of events. Any errors are unintentional. In some cases I've altered the crew manifest (changed the names), as it's not my intent to harm anyone in the telling of this tale.

DREAMS OF FLYING

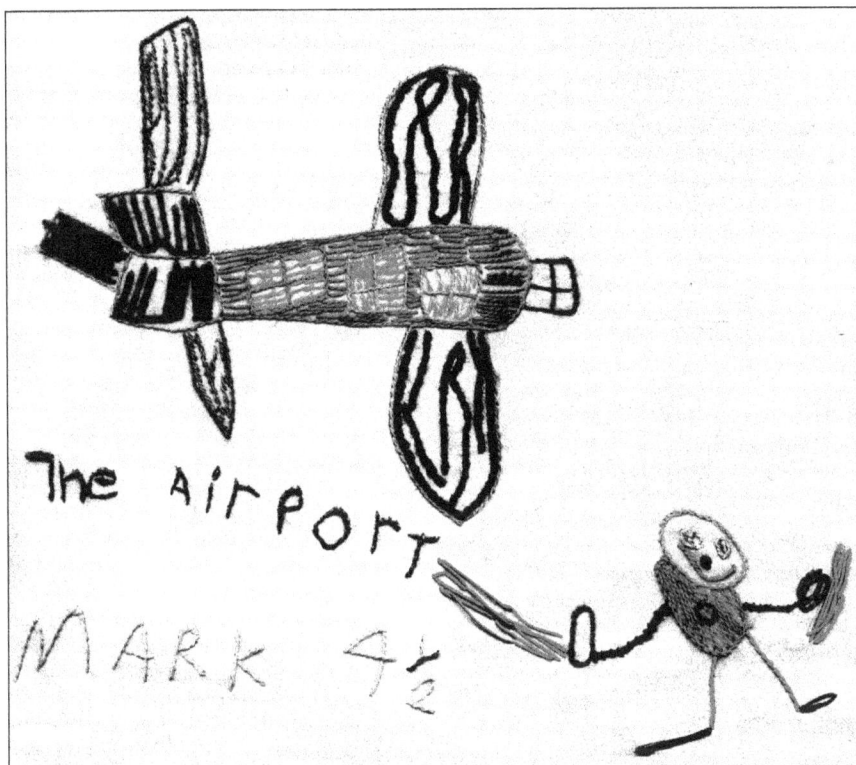

EVEN AS A LITTLE BOY, I knew I wanted to become a pilot. I still have an Official Junior Captain certificate from National Airlines, signed by a Captain P Lowman, that I was given on a flight to Florida when I was only three-and-a-half. At four-and-a-half, I sewed this orange wand-waving ramp guide man directing an airplane with yarn on stretched canvas. His head looks like a marshmallow, and I think the doughnut on his chest is supposed to be his belly button. I have no idea why I thought he would be working shirtless: maybe because I remembered Florida as a hot place. The airplane came out slightly better, albeit with wood-framed picture windows. My schoolteacher mother apparently trusted me with a sewing needle at an early age — probably because it kept me quiet, and out of her incredibly long, straight brown hair. My flying life is depicted in that early art, and it has been anything but what I'd imagined.

– MARK 47 (AND A HALF)

INTRODUCTION
BY AIRLINE PILOT/AUTHOR KARLENE PETITT

Karlene is a Seattle-based major airline pilot, advocate for aviation safety, and author of the aviation thriller FLIGHT FOR CONTROL. *She hosts a blog, Flight To Success, at: http://karlenepetitt.blogspot.com*

WELCOME TO THE JOURNEY of an ordinary man — an airline pilot. He carries in his hands a daily responsibility not taken lightly. Like most pilots he is focused and prepared for any emergency. But when an unfathomable airborne calamity blows apart the core pieces of his life — scattering his airline's flagship, his coworkers, and his fiancée across the bottom of the Atlantic Ocean — nothing could prepare him for the aftermath.

While no loss is more tragic than the next, when it happens on an airplane the impact becomes a tremor of pain that cracks souls worldwide. Our airline family is torn to shreds, and we're faced with the painful challenge of fitting our own pieces back together in order to go on. Tears leak through the holes for years, and some never make it back. But as a pilot, when it happens on your airline and the love of your life is ripped from the world, this challenge is magnified to a pure survival level.

Airline pilots connect the world through a tapestry of unity while crisscrossing the oceans and continents. We are a family of thousands. Our contrails blanket the world, providing a sky-written assurance that our passengers are being safely carried to their destinations. On a rare occasion control is yanked from our hands when the unexpected happens. Such an event occurred on July 17, 1996, when a Boeing 747 exploded in full view of my aircraft.

I am an international airline pilot who watched TWA Flight 800 disappear from the twilight sky as my 747 began a similar trans-Atlantic flight from JFK International Airport. We had expected to trail them all the way to Paris but never had the chance. While so many of us have been impacted from this horrid airborne travesty, Mark L Berry has a unique experience.

His journey of survival is an amazing tale that anyone faced with loss can use to heal his or her own life. To all airline employees, families, and friends who have been touched by an accident, this is a journey of understanding after the unexplainable happens. Flight deck dwellers will laugh while reading Mark 's challenging career path — one that reflects so many of our own journeys while chasing that almighty captain's seat. Flight attendants will appreciate the shared stories on the road. Everyone will cry as Mark's heartfelt story rocks our world and touches our hearts. We all retain the power and capacity to carry on, even when our lives have been destroyed. But sometimes we need a flight plan to get us there.

Welcome aboard to a journey of a life, love, and loss — a story of adventure and aviation. You are invited into the secret world of an airline pilot. Once there you will see the humor, passion, and strength of those people that hold your life in their hands. Most pilots fly at least Mach .75 — three quarters of the speed of sound — but we are human. When we hit an emotional wall, the question is not whether or not we will survive, but how. I believe it is better to have loved deeply for a moment than not at all — and that conundrum is rooted to the core of Mark's tragic experience. His love lives here in beautiful prose, and symbolically at *13,760 Feet.*

    — KARLENE PETITT

13,760 FEET

1 | TWA FLIGHT 800

Aluminum Parachute

AN ONSHORE BREEZE stirred as the mercury began its slow descent from near the top of the thermometer glass, barely cooling from the afternoon high of over 90 degrees, and the sandy beaches shook off the day's glaze a little faster than the ocean. Some high-altitude cirrus clouds traversed with the imperceptible speed of a clock's minute hand, almost like they were an atmospheric afterthought. I've flown thousands of flights into New York's major airports and admired Long Island's southern shore so many times that I could paint it as it must have existed on the evening of July 17, 1996.

The sky was that deep shade of blue you only see at dusk during summer, in the moments just before the sun finally sets. After a full day of absorbing radiation, heat, and light, the ocean set up a low shimmer above the steadily rolling waves as the atmosphere tried to reclaim what the golden orb had tirelessly delivered while passing overhead. The sea and sky seemed to be shaking a thousand hands along that stretched horizon. The distant colored sails of leisure boats jibed and tacked — small irregular triangles bending and pulling their water-skimming vessels. And above them were departing aircraft — some fanning out for a variety of domestic destinations, while the European-bound flights cued up offshore like a string of marching ants on an invisible fishing line, all heading for the North Atlantic track system with an entry point somewhere far off near Newfoundland.

A recent departure from JFK International Airport joined the procession — a double-decker red and white Boeing 747 with four under-wing engines, each producing roughly 50,000 pounds of thrust during climb-out. From the shore, it appeared as a Cross of Lorraine: a single line for its body with two lines across it — one larger to represent the wings, and a smaller one for the tail — such as a stick figure a child would draw. Inside the plane's windows, too far away to see, were 230 passengers and crew. And although I knew several of them, someone special to me was in seat 3-2 in the forward first-class section: my fiancée Susanne Jensen.

Air travel was a regular requirement at both of our jobs, and Susanne and I always looked forward to it. She could hear the aircraft's inner workings from her upfront seat, and through her time with me she had some idea of how and why it all functioned. The gentle vibration after takeoff as the landing gear retracted and stowed, followed by the hum of jackscrews retracting the flaps for the aircraft's acceleration, reminded her she was now safely on her way to Paris. I'd shared part of my professional aviation training with her and explained that most aircraft accidents happen in the first eight minutes after takeoff or the last three minutes before landing, when the aircraft is close to the ground. With the world getting smaller outside — dwellings turning into doll houses and then further reducing to pillboxes, trees shriveling to matchsticks, and people shrinking to mere dots as her flight climbed — she would have already reclined her seat and most likely taken off her high-heeled dress shoes with a smile of satisfaction, happily unaware that anything was about to go fatally wrong.

At 10,000 feet the flight attendants would have just been given the signal to unbuckle, rise from their retractable jumpseats, and begin their service, but there wouldn't have been time to wheel the dull aluminum carts out into the aisle. Susanne would now be reading reports and notes from her briefcase, mentally preparing for her multilingual financial meeting in the morning, or chatting with my coworker and friend Captain Gid Miller, deadheading on this flight and seated across the aisle to her right. If she instead looked beyond the seat to her left, her view out the pressure-retaining, double-pane window would have faced north across the water at a steady string of Long Island's strands — Atlantic Beach, Long Beach, Lido Beach, Point Lookout — with the slowly setting sun behind her casting lengthy shadows. She may have recognized Long Beach as it went by, where I had a crash pad when we first started dating, where we'd consummated our relationship in spite of my former roommates' taunting and good-humored pressure, and where she'd subsequently visited many times.

TWA Flight 800 had taken off about an hour late, but some of my off-duty pilot and flight attendant friends might have still been packing up the beach volleyball net by the shore, although they'd now be far too small to identify from Susanne's vantage. With a US Air flight overhead, her 747 was restricted from climbing above 10,000 feet until adequate aircraft separation was obtained. More seaside communities — Jones Beach followed by Fire Island — would have slipped by creating a beautiful moving view from the largest successful commercial aircraft of its day — one I'd hoped to eventually command. But Susanne's Long Island sightseeing ended without warning at Smith Point near Moriches, New York.

So many witnesses reported seeing a streaking flash of light; that's what shakes the perfect summer evening's tranquility when I imagine what happened. The sky is suddenly stained with exploding smears of red and orange airborne violence. A glowing fireball spreads out from Susanne's 747 like a grenade. At 8:31pm near the longest day of the year it was still daylight, but not for much longer. The only red in this image should have been the pair of painted red stripes that ran the length of the aircraft's 230-foot fuselage and the red tail displaying TWA's slanted, white-letter logo. The only orange should have been the impending sunset.

Whatever caused TWA Flight 800's center fuel tank to explode, that initial blast would have instantly shoved Susanne and everyone else onboard twelve feet upward and seventeen feet to the right, according to William Donaldson, an independent researcher and retired U.S. Navy commander. The Suffolk County medical examiner's office announced that the probable cause of death for almost everyone onboard was a snapped neck. That's the feel-good report for victims' families so that we imagine our loved ones departed this world quickly and painlessly — and the bulk of the passengers were seated in the main coach section where this probably was the result.

But because first class, in the nosecone of the aircraft, broke off and didn't remain with the rest of the now burning wings, fuselage, and tail, I can't get this image of Susanne out of my head: she's freefalling for what would have felt like a lifetime, lap-belted to her mostly blue seat styled with a single narrow white and two wide red vertical stripes. She's in pure panic while flopping about violently, gasping for breath from the sudden decompression and deafened by the explosion and resulting wind noise — only to finally die with her eyes wide open when impacting the water at roughly triple highway speed in what would later become known as the yellow debris field.

My only consolation is that, without being able to turn around, she never saw behind her the giant hole where the rest of the aircraft should have been — an oblong oval opening to the tumbling sky, bordered by torn cables, shredded aluminum aircraft skin, sheared beams and spars, and accented with sparking severed wires. And I hope she couldn't comprehend what was actually happening if she lived long enough to ride this nearly three-mile-high, free-falling hell-ivator all the way down to the ocean's surface and then sink to 140 feet below, where her body would wait to be recovered.

She's gone. In hardly more time than I can hold my breath, her life was over, and mine was torn inside out. The 747 that went up whole and came down in 876 pieces invaded every part of my life.

Moving on from real-world disaster isn't so easily imagined. I can't just paint over the images in my brain of the streak of light, the burning jet fuel, the now lifeless bodies, and the splintering aircraft. The woman I loved, nestled in the safest, most sacred place in my professional aviation world, was eradicated out of a clear evening sky without so much as a hint of a warning.

Six days later I couldn't turn away from the news; it was everywhere. *The New York Times* reported, "At the Ocean's Edge, a Wrenching Farewell," and the *Connecticut Post* printed an article, "Ocean of Tears." Even standing with Susanne's family knee-deep in the receding tide — floating a rose for her out to sea, along with a crowd of other mourners — was a spectacle captured by cameras, microphones, and a fleet of high-powered antennae trucks. Gone forever was the love of my life, torn from the sky while in the trusted and competent hands of my fellow employees — my mentors and my peers. The red and orange fireball that consumed her life also burned its way into my core existence. I'd lost everything, and even my airline didn't know what to do with the pilot whose fiancée was on that flight.

As the days and weeks and months without her stretched on, I looked for solace within the familiarity and fraternity of the cockpit — the only thing with meaning I had left, and what I came to know as my aluminum parachute. It wasn't much, but going to the cockpit was something tangible for me to hold on to, and a reason to get out of bed. After I buried Susanne, I buried myself in my work.

> *When all else fails*
> *When those I love die*
> *From sudden stops*
> *After falling from the sky*
>
> *My aluminum parachute*
> *Is better than gold*
> *A place to re-compute*
> *That never grows old*
>
> *There's a place I still go*
> *There's a place I belong*
> *Forward of the front row*
> *The source of the siren's song*

The night of TWA Flight 800's demise — the night I lost Susanne in that very personal hole in the sky and my life without her began — occurred over sixteen years ago. Wrestling with her loss has been a long unwelcome adventure. The earliest steps toward my emotional recovery only manifested after I finally started writing lyrics — first in the form of fiction as I developed companion songs within my debut novel, *Pushing Leaves Towards the Sun*, penning them from my protagonist's perspective while trying to address my own issues of survivor's guilt — and then more recently in nonfiction form as my friends, family, early readers, and eventually my grad school encouraged me to tell this story. My story. Susanne's last story.

I'm not much of a musician, and people who have heard me sing have nearly threatened to file restraining orders if I attempt another off-key performance in their presence. But my fascination with songs has always focused on their words. I don't know what part of my brain or heart is tickled by writing lyrics, but that's where my personal struggle — and professional aviation disaster journey — began.

> *My aluminum parachute*
> *Is better than gold*
> *A place to re-compute*
> *That never grows old*
>
> *My window with a moving view*
> *My office in the wild blue*
> *My sanctuary in the clouds*
> *Where I'll always think of you*

NOTE:

The lyrics to all thirty-four companion songs are infused into this memoir where they appear as vocals in the audio read-by-author version. They are double-indented, italicized, and printed in gray rather than black. Feel free to read or skip them, as you prefer, while reading this print version.

I suspect the lyrics will have more meaning after you have listened to the associated songs but will be distracting until then. Multimedia is a rising format and not yet widely accepted as I'm writing this.

2 | THE BEST DAY OF MY LIFE

Under the Tiny Bridge

HOW DID I FALL IN LOVE with a Scandinavian gal born across the ocean, the same ocean that would later claim her? Susanne moved from Copenhagen, Denmark, to Cos Cob, Connecticut, with her mother and first of two brothers when she and I were almost ten years old in 1975. Her youngest brother would later be born here. Her mother thought it would be a good idea to socialize her in the last few weeks of fifth grade before summer break. My family hadn't moved across town yet: we were about to. It would be that fall and sixth grade before Susanne and I would actually meet at North Street Elementary, but she told me about sitting among her new classmates and not being able to speak a word of English. I can picture her mother assuring her in Danish before each school day that everything would be OK, that she would make new friends and learn the new language. Then she wasn't able to understand another word from anyone — classmates, teachers, anybody — until the bell rang at the end of the day. Her mother must have dropped her off and picked her up because she couldn't even ask for help to get on the correct school bus.

I wish I could tell you that we became friends that fall when our lives crossed for the first time, but I was too wrapped up in a boy's world — fighting for a reputation and struggling for a place in the pack. We would have had so much more time together if I'd noticed her back then, but girls weren't up on my radar yet, even long-blonde-haired, blue-eyed beauties from a foreign land.

In junior high our friends overlapped, but we were all too busy trying to grow up. The first dance I attended was in eighth grade, but I was still too shy to do more than watch my football teammates — the offensive linemen — break a folding table they tried to use as a stage while playing air guitar to the Rolling Stones. I occasionally sneaked glimpses at the girls dancing together, but I was still a nerd — Dungeons and Dragons occupied too much of my time. Susanne was a fair-haired elf living in my neck of the woods, but I was far too in tune with fantasy and role-playing, and I carelessly overlooked her existence in the real world.

Back then Greenwich High was the size of some college campuses, hosting twenty-five hundred students over three years — sophomore through senior. Susanne and I rode the bus together until we each learned how to drive. Her family and mine lived not more than a couple miles apart on winding, back roads originally blazed by livestock around the time of the Revolutionary War. The closest we came together was my time as her mother's paperboy. Her two Irish Setters chased me up and down her street as my blue one-horsepower Puch moped made more noise than speed. It wasn't much, but newspaper home delivery would later serve as the catalyst between us. I didn't know it then, but we would live nearly parallel but untouching lives — each of us going off to college (she to U-Conn for a business degree and I to Embry-Riddle to learn how to fly), then each would find jobs overseas in Europe (she in Ghent, Belgium, and I in Berlin, West Germany).

Both of us returned to the northeastern United States (she back to Connecticut, and for awhile I settled on Long Island's southern shore in the shadow of JFK International Airport), and it would take a dozen years for our tracks to cross again at the horizon. The place where parallel lines meet is the vanishing point. The place where our two parallel lives met was a fifteen-keg party at Stamford, Connecticut's Cove Beach. Susanne and I were made for each other, but we weren't childhood sweethearts, and our early life wouldn't make a very interesting made-for-TV afterschool special. We each had to find our own way in the world before we were destined to share our accomplishments, dreams, and goals together. Like most things in life, the timing had to be right, and it couldn't be forced or rushed.

That magic day on May 13, 1995 — just over a year before TWA Flight 800 ended Susanne's life — between the viewing and burial of my friend and TWA mentor Captain Ken Cook, was not a time I was looking to meet a future spouse. Although it's a cliché that people are more likely to find a relationship when they're not looking for it, that's what happened for me.

Ken lost his battle with pancreatic cancer and was buried near his home in Madison, Connecticut. My Long Island crash pad was a long drive away. To make the commute to Madison for the two days of services easier, my friends, who were renting a duplex in my hometown of Cos Cob, Connecticut, offered me their couch. Arriving straight from the viewing of Ken's open casket, I shuffled in with my travel bag. I was emotionally frozen. The weight of depression from losing someone who meant so much to me both personally and professionally narrowed my unfocused gaze and slumped my posture, and the gang immediately felt my somber mood.

Handing me a beer from their kegerator, Simon said, "We've got just the thing to cheer you up. Tonight is the cove party."

"I sooo don't feel like a party, guys. You go have fun."

Glenn added, "As if you have a choice." The others laughed.

Dieter said, "Better grab him now before he has time to think about it."

Dave grabbed one arm. Glenn, grabbing the other, said, "Your only choice is whether you go to Stamford Cove Beach in my boat or in Simon's car."

Simon and Glenn were friends of mine from elementary through high school, and Dieter and Dave were their roommates and had also become my friends. I didn't have the fight in me to challenge four against one. "At least let me get out of my formal clothes," I pleaded. "I'm not getting in a Boston Whaler wearing a pressed shirt, tie, and leather shoes."

The cove party turned out to be an annual event for U-Conn graduates living in Fairfield County. I was introduced to the sponsoring individuals, and they proudly pointed out they had fifteen kegs to serve, as well as several fifty-five-gallon drums cut in half and made into giant charcoal grills. There was no shortage of food or alcohol, but I felt like a freeloader. In an effort to contribute, I asked, "Can I make a donation to this impressive event?" while peeling a twenty from my money clip.

"No," my new host responded. "Put your money away. We're not charging — just selling T-shirts to cover our costs."

"Great. I'd love to buy one."

"Oh, we sold out this afternoon. Enjoy the party."

Left on my own in a crowd of happy people, I watched my friends mingling and drinking. It made me feel like I was at the Playboy mansion without a bathrobe. I really didn't want to bring this party down with my brooding, maudlin presence. I was also impressed the hosts weren't trying to make a profit from their friends — the kind of capitalist mentality that's usually ingrained in young Fairfield County entrepreneurs. So, when I offered to do a bit of cooking on the huge homemade grills, to feel like I was contributing and also to pass the time, I was handed a spatula. Soon I was flipping burgers, searing them with crosshatched grill marks, and serving them onto handheld buns stretched out from people three deep in the hungry crowd.

I was blissfully content — until I noticed through the swirling charcoal smoke a longhaired extremely blonde gal walk by a few times. She had an air of familiarity that intensified with each pass, even though she was wearing a handkerchief tied over the top of her head and sporting expensive sunglasses. If I could travel back in time to relive my life from any moment, this would be the one. As she settled into a conversation with a girlfriend, I began thinking I might know her. After all, I had grown up nearby, although it had been twelve years since I'd graduated high school. My initial reaction was curiosity, to see if I could solve the puzzle of who she was.

It occurred to me that she might be the Danish gal who rode the school bus with me and lived near the house where I grew up. When my soggy brain finally recalled her name, to test my memory recall, I handed off the spatula and walked over to where she was now engrossed in a story.

When somebody is walking directly toward you with their course established for a collision and their gaze focused and not scanning, you notice. It's different than when someone is casually walking toward you. Both girls lowered their sunglasses and gave me what I learned was their defensive look and posture as I approached.

"Susanne?" I queried.

"Yeah?"

"Susanne Jensen?"

"Yeah."

"I'm Mark Berry. I was your mother's paperboy."

Astonished by what she considered an opening line, she asked, "Are you for real?"

Susanne's friend Amy decided to leave us to our own devices. "I can't touch that," she said. "You're on your own, girl." She walked away, but like a good wingman, she returned every five or ten minutes to check if Susanne needed an excuse to bail out of our conversation. Susanne didn't.

I later learned Susanne was meeting a date at this party. Amy was ready to run interference as necessary. However, it was the one time in my life when the cards already felt played.

After the beach party broke up, we shot pool at Jimmy's Seaside Tavern. Susanne asked me to hand her some Blistex, and I told her I didn't have any. She smiled and said, "Yes you do," — and she was right. She had somehow slipped some into my pocket. After that night, I'd find Blistex in the pockets of every pair of pants I owned — all put there while I was wearing them. I called her a stuffpocket. Blistex was her addiction, and I became her mule.

Dating Susanne meant almost an hour-and-a-half drive from Long Island to Connecticut. I made it as often as possible, staying at my friends' house in Cos Cob between get-to-know-you happy hours and dinners, but from that first real encounter, I knew my life was already changing. It would be the other guy — not me — who lost Susanne's interest. It scared me that this felt so real. I was so acclimated to my independent, worldwide airline lifestyle, but I hung on for the ride, and it would be exactly one year later when I'd jump onboard ready to offer a permanent arrangement.

After we'd been dating awhile, Susanne finally decided to go down to Long Island and spend a long weekend at the beach with me. My roommates and friends wanted to meet her. My buddy Berto saw an opportunity for a prank. I'd made the mistake of telling him I was falling in love with her and that sex could potentially screw it up. We hadn't slept together, not because of prudish values, but because of inflated expectations. That's when Berto started leaving literature about erectile dysfunction in my mailbox at work, as well as voice-mail messages like "Don't worry about performance anxiety; I'm sure it can't happen to you."

When Susanne finally arrived on a Friday, the tension was obvious, as she'd be staying the long weekend until Tuesday. My roommate Duncan said to her, "Since you two aren't sleeping together, you can sleep in my room." That's just what I needed — her to know that our sexual history, or lack of it, was a discussion point around the house. I told Susanne, "You don't want to sleep with him; we lock his cage at night," and moved her bags into my room. We locked eyes until I stepped out and closed my door between us, allowing her privacy to change for the beach. We both knew that was the last time we'd be on opposite sides of a bedroom door.

That evening Berto's prank calls came rapid fire, and it was still a time before I was sharing with Susanne insider details like Berto's friendly harassment. He was determined to give me too much pressure to perform. I could have shut my phone off, but his persistence made me laugh, and I used the ringing as background music. As important as this moment was for Susanne and me, I also look back with a nostalgic feeling about how close my group of friends were. Nothing was sacred and we were inseparably woven into each other's lives.

The day after Susanne and I shared something so good that it still stings with longing to recollect, while we were relaxing with the pre-coital tension successfully relieved, I had her call Berto and deliver an unexplained message: "Houston, we have ignition; the boosters have fired and orbit achieved. P. S. You're a real bastard." She probably had a good idea what the message was about. She was intuitive, and it didn't feel right hiding anything from her even if I tried, but a series of margaritas that evening allowed me to explain the joke in detail to her — in front of my roommates, who were rocking in their seats while still balancing their salt-rimmed, long-stem glasses, never spilling a drop. The attitude around my house and throughout my close circle of airline friends was, "No slack given; none expected." Everything was fair game for a personal attack. Susanne took no offense. She laughed the hardest.

Once our relationship became serious, I was shipped to St. Louis to fly

McDonnell Douglas MD-80 aircraft, and then back to New York a few months later to crew the Boeing 767. TWA kept changing the overall flight plan, and as a result, I took advantage of every training opportunity. Susanne had had enough of traveling to see me by then and wanted me close by, so I settled down with her in Connecticut in a temporary arrangement while I began house-hunting — first without her, then with her as the serious dial cranked up even higher.

I absorbed every detail about her and learned that even this beautiful woman had an Achilles heel, almost literally. She didn't like her feet. High-heeled shoes and sports had given her calluses, and it was the one part of her body she didn't like to show off. I didn't agree, and I showed her by kissing her feet and sucking on her toes. When I first tried this, she said, "You're crazy," but she said it in a tone of approval that turned me on.

Another time her friend Amy told me I'd really done it. "Done what?" I asked. It turned out my crime was that I'd given her a silver belly chain.

"She looks so awesome in it," I said in my defense.

"Of course she does. She slimmed down from a size ten to a size six before she met you. She's self-conscious about her weight. That you'd want to emphasize her stomach was the greatest compliment a man could give."

Who knew that the way to this gal's heart was through her flat stomach and her knobby feet? I just called it as I saw it and was glad I was accidently making her happy.

The best day of my life was May 13, 1996, the day I proposed to Susanne, one year to the day from when I encountered her at the cove party. As the planned proposal date approached, Susanne was scheduled for a business trip to Paris and Oslo. Her official title was Portfolio Analyst — Portfolio Development & Support, although these international accounts came with a promotion to manager. I still have her business card. That's a fancy way of saying that she maintained GE's financial interests after another division invested in a manufacturing company, often on foreign soil. She'd completed GE's in-house MBA equivalent and was being groomed for higher positions. We'd discussed that we both wanted to continue working after we had kids. Both of our careers were important to us. She loved her job, and I assume she was great at it from the feedback her coworkers have given me. Fortunately, I was able to shuffle my days off to accompany her to Europe.

In my family, proposals have some history. When my dad told me the year before that he was going to propose to Faith, who has since become my stepmom, I told him to take pictures. "How am I supposed to do that?" he asked. He planned to do it in church because he had met her at a religious retreat.

"That's your problem," I said.

He brought a camera and arranged with someone in the pew behind him to be ready. When he and I caught up later, he delivered the goods—pictures of his proposal.

When I informed my dad that I planned to propose to Susanne, he told me to take pictures. I asked him, "How am I supposed to do that?"

"That's your problem," he replied.

Susanne had suggested we make an adventure out of this business trip. She'd leave two days early, attend her meetings in Paris, and once I arrived, we'd drive to Belgium and Amsterdam, and then she'd hop over to Oslo for another meeting and rendezvous with me in Copenhagen to visit her Danish family. I had my own secret plans for this journey. She and I both flew over to France on TWA a couple days apart.

On my way to Europe to meet up with her, sitting in what I call the Captain Kirk chair, alone in the forward portion of the middle row in first class, I made a tactical error. "I'm on a proposal mission," I confided to the flight attendants.

Word spread at mach speed among the crew, and soon all twelve working cabin flight attendants surrounded me and sang, "Another one bites the dust." It was like an airborne scene from a TGIF restaurant after a birthday announcement, complete with air guitar. The pre-engagement party over the North Atlantic was a surprise, but maybe I should have expected it. Flight attendants love any occasion that brightens their trip, especially an engagement, and we shared this moment as an airline family.

The champagne flowed, and I ended up wearing what missed the glasses. A blur of smiling uniforms were handing overfilled flutes to the other first-class passengers they had recruited into our soirée. They let the corks pop to the ceiling, which the pilots could probably feel under their feet. The cockpit in this jumbo was the front part of the upper deck. One flight attendant attempted to wipe off a little dribble from my sport coat with club soda, the in-flight cleaning cure all, but another said, "He's going to Paris to be with his new fiancée; let him wear a little French bubbly." I was intentionally over-poured, although I can't claim to have put up a fight.

I was lucky I didn't lose the rings. I passed around the brilliant-cut, full-carat solitaire set on a white gold band. The ladies all kissed it for good luck, although I think they made that tradition up on the spot. "How did you afford that on a TWA salary?" one asked me. I interpreted her question as a sign that she was impressed and hoped Susanne would be as well.

I explained about the comfort fit of the band, insisted upon by my jeweler. It was supposed to be all the rage, but it didn't leave room for any engraving. I wanted to commemorate Susanne's and my encounter twelve years after high school. While I was sipping champagne, I explained about our initial reac-quaintance at the beach gathering between Captain Cook's final services, and the reason for the inscription *The Cove Party 5/13/95* on the accompanying three-band roll-on ring. They all knew and respected Captain Cook and were glad something good came out of his loss—his wife insists that Ken was looking out for me and helped arrange Susanne's and my encounter from the great beyond —but the good would be short-lived. These rings would ride on this exact flight just over two months later adorned on Susanne's fingers. This was a Boeing 747 and TWA Flight 800—daily service between JFK and Charles de Gaulle. Prior to it becoming a national disaster, it was the ultimate setting for celebration, and a place that symbolized both my professional success and the apex of my per-sonal relationship with Susanne. I was living a lifelong dream, and could never have imagined this could turn into my worst nightmare, for even a nightmare has to be imagined. What the summer would bring was in no way conceivable.

Drunk, jet-lagged, and giggly, I knocked on Susanne's door at the Concorde Lafayette hotel after riding through the Parisian streets on the crew bus with my still-celebrating fellow employees.

"Are you for real?" she teased as she stood in the doorway wearing a bleached white, hotel-monogrammed bathrobe and still trying to squeeze the water from her blonde hair. These four simple words have many memories now associated with them and another use to come.

I kissed her with my booze breath and she gave me a mock look of disap-proval when we pulled apart. Both her eyes and her lips were smiling. I was excited to see her, hugged her hard, and held on a long time—one of the things she later told me she should have recognized as a sign that something was up. She smelled of floral soap, and I wanted to hold on to her fragrance as I finally crawled under the down comforter for a much-needed nap after the all-night ocean crossing. She was radiant — fresh out of the shower and getting ready for her last Paris meeting. She put Colgate toothpaste on her Crest toothbrush and crawled in beside me while working the bristles up and down and side to side. I reflected that we'd independently chosen those same oral hygiene prod-ucts as she next poked her foamy toothbrush into my mouth and told me, "I want a real kiss before I have to go to work." I couldn't argue on principle, and besides, she'd already begun working my molars and incisors while it was her turn to giggle.

We shared everything now, and I felt guilty that I was keeping a secret from her, even if it was to create a special once-in-a-lifetime moment. I was ready to get down on a knee sometime on this trip—when the timing felt right.

I'd explored Paris before, bumbling around with a combination of slowly spoken English, finger pointing, and hand signals. But Susanne spoke fluent French — opening the city far wider than I'd been able to do on my own. Or maybe it is the city of love, and it took both of us to unlock its true splendor. After a wonderful night together in the Latin Quarter dipping bread in fondue cheese, listening to a guitar-playing musician sing in a variety of languages, and watching the canal boats slip by on the River Seine, It almost felt like the perfect moment, but it wasn't the thirteenth yet.

Susanne and I rose early the next morning and rented a car to visit where she'd lived during her first two years with GE Capital in Ghent, Belgium. I'd spent much of my first years with TWA at satellite bases in West Berlin, Frankfurt, and Munich, Germany, and also in Rome, Italy, and Vienna, Austria. We both felt a sense of home on both sides of the Atlantic, and being anywhere with her felt as warm and fuzzy as the hotel feather bed.

Amsterdam was supposed to be our next two-day pit stop, but the Schnapps House in Ghent sucked us in an extra night. They make their own spicy brown mustard, served in clay jars, and we must have each dipped a couple hundred matchstick fries while tasting it. We washed them down with Flanders beer and, of course, shots of schnapps. We didn't wake up until 5:00 p.m. after our night of drinking. We missed checkout, late checkout, and even a call from the hotel manager who asked, "Are you checking out?" Unable to flee the gravitational pull of the Schnapps House, we returned a second night, but only to feed our hangovers with more mustard-dipped delicious fries and, of course, a little hair of the dog.

We finally arrived in Amsterdam on May 13 with no plan, though I had a diamond ring with a white-gold band along with its inscribed silver companion jingling and calling me from my pocket like Poe's "Tell-tale Heart." They had the weight of Frodo's one ring, and I was tempted to call Susanne "my precious," but I didn't want to creep her out. I'd hidden these proposal accessories in an aspirin bottle before getting off the airplane, and I almost lost the surprise when Susanne went looking through my shaving kit for a hangover remedy. By sheer luck I was one step ahead of her and she didn't find the rings. Now we only had the one night to explore Amsterdam because we were each scheduled to fly out the next day — she to Oslo for her next meeting and I to Copenhagen to stay with her natural father and other assorted relatives while waiting for her to finish up the business part of her trip and join us. I had my own important business to attend to first. I needed an artistic strategy, something memorable, a moment of planetary alignment. Instead, I was totally winging it. Important to me was the cove party anniversary date, not the location, but now I was on the lookout for the perfect spot.

Dinner was nice, in the quiet back room of a restaurant I can't otherwise remember except for an open fire in the middle that was warming a giant hammered-copper kettle. We carved up tender medium-rare steaks and drank a bottle of Merlot. We looked into each other's eyes that were reflecting the dancing flames, and it was romantic, but nice just wasn't enough. I held off the temptation to make that our magic moment. Passing up a perfectly acceptable location, on the night I'd chosen to propose, gave me doubts. Was I chickening out? Or was there really such a thing as the perfect time and place? I had no doubts about Susanne. I knew she was the one, in that way people ask about and that there is no way to actually describe. But the rings still sat in the bottom of my pocket.

We meandered around the city, over endless bridges, and back and forth across canals. Eventually we stopped at a pub she described as cute and popped in to shoot a game of pool. She was very good. I didn't have to let her win—I had to struggle to sink some of my balls in the pockets before she ran the table. I miss the picture I took of her that night stretched over the pool table and facing the camera—her two matching gold bangles dangling from her left arm to the dark red felt, almost interfering with her pool cue as she lined up her shot. I lost that picture along with thirty dollars in my wallet when I was held up at gunpoint years later. I rip my house apart looking for that negative every time I move, but it has never turned up.

We held hands while we gawked at the gals in the windows of the red light district. Most of them looked South American and a long way from home, which surprised us, although some looked Eastern European. None seemed to be Dutch locals. Susanne pointed out the turquoise lace that one gal was barely wearing. "You can get that for me. My birthday is next month."

"Do you think she'll come to Connecticut for you if I ask her?" I joked.

These were working girls, but to Susanne this was a stroll through Victoria's Secret with live models instead of mannequins. She really was window-shopping. I did later buy her as close a match to that gal's outfit as I could find at our local mall. Susanne looked best in any shade of blue, and I often fed her wardrobe with gifts in any hue of that primary color.

We wandered through the diamond district. Susanne started pointing out the different cuts of stones. "Look, Mark, this one is brilliant because it reflects the light back through the top facet. No other cut does that, although the princess is beautiful just because of its shape." I'd spent the last couple months learning all about the five Cs — carat, color, clarity, cut, and certificate, but I pleaded ignorance and let her explain them to me. I didn't know how long I could keep a straight face, so I told her it wouldn't be a true trip to Amsterdam if we didn't take a canal cruise. There was a boat launch near our hotel, and I recalled riding in Glenn's Boston Whaler to Cove Beach exactly a year before. The water began feeling like it was calling me. I cut our jewelry tour short before she caught a whiff that jewelry might be in her immediate future. Susanne had amazing intuition, and when she felt something coming that she couldn't quite explain, she often said, "I can smell it." She later confessed she didn't smell what was coming this time, which made me feel successful.

Our timing was perfect for a wine and cheese departure with over a dozen other tourists — the candlelight cruise.

> *I followed my gal to Amsterdam*
> *We took a cruise through Amsterdam*
> *It's the way to see true Amsterdam*
> *Where Vincent Van Gogh drew Amsterdam*

The announcer was young, probably working his way through college. His name was Kevin. He had short dark hair, and he pointed out all the sites of interest in English, German, and Japanese.

> *The cruise began*
> *In three dialects*
> *The guide informed us*
> *Of what would be next*

We headed for a unique footbridge early in the tour that I thought looked familiar. At the last moment we made a sharp left turn and didn't go under the Magere Brug. I asked Kevin, "Aren't we going to see that?"

> *The Tiny Bridge loomed ahead*
> *I asked if we'd go through*
> *But sir, shall I ruin*
> *The end of the tour for you?*

He had intentionally not called attention to it, but now he replied, "Sir, that is the Tiny Bridge where Vincent Van Gogh painted many of his famous works, but you don't want to ruin the end of the tour, do you?"

At that moment it clicked. I knew when and where I was going to ask Susanne to spend the rest of her life with me, but we still had a lot of cruising to do first. Kevin continued with his trilingual tour. We saw the gabled architecture, looked under the seven bridges, and paused alongside the Anne Frank house.

> *Anne Frank's House*
> *Was on the right*
> *We imagined her hiding*
> *Day and night*

Throughout our meandering along the watery maze of canals, I kept glancing ahead, on the lookout for the Tiny Bridge to reappear. I kept Susanne's and my wine glasses full and requested a second bottle to keep up with my jittery guzzling. Susanne later reflected on how nervous I was, but she didn't smell it at the time.

> *The rest of the cruise*
> *Was only a blur*
> *I knew now*
> *Where I'd propose to her*

At last, the location of my romantic moment approached. Kevin was busy announcing our arrival. I reached inside my pocket, the one not holding the rings, and removed my Olympus compact camera.

> *Then finally*
> *Up ahead*
> *The bridge appeared*
> *And the guide said*
> *Lovers who kiss*
> *Under the bridge*
> *Will share their lives*
> *In a happy marriage*

Kevin said, "Lovers who kiss under the Magere Brug will stay together a lifetime," just as I reached out with my 35mm memory maker.

"Come here, please," I asked him.

"But sir, I hardly know you!"

Susanne giggled, and I blushed. I told him it was to take Susanne's and my picture, and he complied with the knowing smile of having pulled off a good joke.

As Kevin put down his microphone and prepared to use my camera, I reached into my other pocket and produced the silver roll-on ring. I told Susanne, "We've been dating a year now, and I want to commemorate it. The inside of this has an inscription on one of the three intertwined bands."

While she was busy trying to read inside the first ring, I pulled my chair away from the table, got down on a knee, and presented the engagement ring as we slipped under the bridge. I pulled her hand to my heart, looked her in the eyes, and asked, "Susanne, Susanne Jensen ... Will you marry me?"

She stalled momentarily, reprising her words from the night on Cove Beach. "Are you for real?"

I put the diamond ring up to, but not onto, her finger. "You haven't answered me yet."

"Yes," She whispered.

"I don't think I heard you, and I know they didn't hear you in the front of the boat."

By this time all fifteen or so people onboard were watching, and our captain put the boat into reverse to hold us under the bridge. She repeated, "Yes," and with tears forming in her eyes, I slipped the ring on her finger and we kissed.

> I asked her
> Will you marry me
> And she asked
> Are you for real?
> I held her hand
> Close to my heart
> And I kissed her
> To seal the deal

Kevin clicked off a four-shot sequence that I was able to share with my dad. I also later learned that the Tiny Bridge was Kevin's personal translation for the Magere Brug. It's more commonly referred to as the Skinny Bridge, but it will always be the Tiny Bridge to me, because that's the way I remember it described that night with Susanne. Its legend also came true. Susanne and I did stay together a lifetime — hers. I wish I had asked for more, as that was merely another two months and four days.

Susanne was very excited, and after we kissed a dozen more times, she started reflecting on all the odd things I'd done that should have given her a clue this was coming. Her mother later told me Susanne had confided she'd wait for me forever. I'm glad I didn't make her wait. Never before and never since have I been so happy I'd done something right. It would be hard to live with myself if she'd never known how much I loved her. Instead, it makes me feel good every day I remember that for the short time following our moment under the Tiny Bridge, she lived knowing how strongly I felt.

On the remainder of the ride back to the dock, Susanne wanted a telephone to call her mother and friends back home. Our cell phones were analog back then and didn't work in Europe, and we weren't carrying them. She asked, "You planned this proposal on a boat so I couldn't call anyone afterwards, didn't you?"

"This is our time," I replied. And I had her all to myself for about an hour before losing her to the phone in our hotel room. I caught a lot of cold looks from her as she announced our engagement to our world back home, because they already seemed to be informed. Prior to leaving for Europe, I'd asked her mom, told my dad and her boss, plus confided in a few close friends that I planned to propose on May 13, to give me enough pressure not to chicken out. She eventually connected with a few of her girlfriends who were surprised, and watching her finally be able to break the news is now another of my magic memories.

3 | MANGLED MAUI JIM

I WOKE UP EACH MORNING in a bed Susanne and I not only picked out together but that she'd returned and traded up three times — each mattress exchange requiring men in a truck to swap them out. A Restonic Silkience Luxury Plush queen eventually earned her approval. Susanne had huge knots in her trapezius muscles, and we'd done everything to try to help her with the pain, from arranging a new ergonomic workstation, to buying a massage table, to finding the perfect mattress. Now I slept on the quilt-top without her in the finished basement of her mom's house — the temporary arrangement we'd made while house hunting. I was so close to being able to carry her across the threshold of our new home. Now her mom, her youngest brother, and I were struggling to live on with a common loss and totally unable to come to terms with it. I didn't know where to go or what to do. My chief pilot told me to take off as much time as I needed, with no indication of how long that should be.

One morning the deposit check that I'd written toward our impending house closing came back in the mail with a sympathy note. The mortgage application was returned in a similar attempt at compassion. But no condolences could take away the fact that the home in which we were going to build our future was gone — swept away like Dorothy's house in a Kansas tornado. I felt stranded and alone in my new reality with the future I planned with Susanne now forever out of reach.

Weeks after TWA Flight 800, Susanne's personal effects were returned by the FBI. The flotsam had been logged and cataloged and separated into plastic bags. None of her stuff was covered in blood or ocean-floor mud, but nothing was washed, pressed, or folded either. I suppose that each passenger's belongings had to be returned by some sort of regulation, or out of my airline and the government's combined sense of obligation, but most of the items only emphasized the harsh reality of her final moments. Idealistic notions of her being in a better place dissolved quickly and thoroughly while her family and I silently poked through the contents, our faces blank. There was a faint scent of low tide

—an unappealing smell to most people, but one I longingly associated with the New England shore of my youth. But now I understood the source of the odor: decay, as the ocean's contents lay exposed in the open air.

Everything seemed to be accounted for—a miracle recovery of mostly useless stuff from under a hundred and forty feet of salt water. Her uncle eventually made cufflinks from the Danish, French, and U.S. coins in her purse. Her engagement ring was returned to me. She'd barely had time to have it resized to fit perfectly on her finger. Even that expensive item would have best been left on the ocean floor. At least it was insured. What woman is going to want to wear it now, even if another woman one day enters my life? After the hundreds of millions of years Susanne's diamond probably spent buried in the earth, I hope it doesn't mind the fifteen years and counting that it has been locked inside a safe. I haven't had the urge to offer it to anyone else—or the compulsion to sell it—and the five grand it cost prevents me from returning it to the earth at her grave.

But it was the mangled pair of Maui Jim sunglasses that undid me. Susanne had bought them several weeks before this trip and spent a fortune on them. Actually, the pair she initially purchased cost close to $300, and she was embarrassed when she told me about her extravagant purchase. We were new at disclosing financial information to one another—but recently engaged, we were learning how to plan our future together, and more immediately, save for our dream house. With every penny accounted for, the sunglasses had been a questionable extravagance, and without my asking, she exchanged the over-the-top pair for the Maui Jims—still expensive, but not as much. Thin orange-hue frames with slightly reflective lenses protected her North Sea blue eyes; she looked gorgeous in them. I told her they'd be great in the cockpit, assuming we were now sharing everything, and she replied playfully, "No way, you'll just break them. You lose or break every pair that you own." She was right. I'd long since stopped buying Revos, Serengeti Drivers, and Ray Bans and instead owned a constant stream of the best sunglasses $20 could buy. My military friends picked them up for me at the BX (base exchange) whenever they'd go shopping on base—balancing my need for quality at a disposably cheap price. Susanne and I were in love and engaged. We shared everything, but those Maui Jims were strictly hers.

Now I stared at those damn sunglasses. Snarled, mangled, smashed: they were the physical record of what Susanne went through as the aircraft split in the middle and the first-class nose cone she was strapped to made an uncontrolled nosedive from two and a half miles high. The Maui Jims couldn't have looked worse if they'd been run over several times by an overloaded semi. These sunglasses wouldn't be protecting anyone from harmful ultraviolet rays ever again. I don't know why I didn't throw them out right away, along with her toiletries and ruined clothing. I put the sunglasses on her bedroom dresser with the rest of her personal belongings — the stuff she hadn't taken with her or the sentimental things we didn't immediately pitch. The dresser became an unintentional shrine of jewelry, hair clips, the silver belly chain I'd given her when we'd started dating, watches, and accessories — all things that had once amplified her beauty and that now magnified her absence. Small things like her blue hairband that was no longer going to hold her French-braided blonde locks after I twisted them for her. Bandanas, which she called wig jams, sat folded and collecting dust. These had kept her Danish mane from bleaching almost frosty white from too much sun, and one of them was the one she was wearing on Cove Beach when we re-met. The ring I'd used to find her size while buying her engagement ring turned out to be a hand-me-down from her mom, and not the perfect fit I'd hoped for. At least these items weren't damaged, although they still hurt to look at.

I finally couldn't take it anymore, but instead of chucking those sunglasses in the garbage, I took them to the optics store where she'd bought them. They'd made her so happy and, I reasoned, if the store would replace them, I would wear them for her. Maybe they'd become the first pair I wouldn't lose or break. I know now that I was looking for any way, however small, to still hold onto her.

I walked in and put the sunglasses on the counter. I didn't bring the clear FBI evidence bag. That much I had at least thrown out. "You don't know me," I said, "but these belonged to my fiancée. Perhaps you remember Susanne Jensen? I think she was here a few times shopping before she picked these out."

Susanne's name caused the salesperson, a forty-ish lady wearing readers at the end of her nose, to pull back almost imperceptibly. She hesitated, examined the sunglasses without touching them, and then looked at me as if I were a trick-or-treater and she was trying to identify my costume. Finally she replied, "I read about Susanne in the local newspaper. I'm very sorry."

"These sunglasses were very important to her. I'd like to replace them with the manufacturer. I'm sure they're still on warranty."

She poked at them with a pencil, as if touching an article of the dead would bring some kind of curse on her. Finally, she said, "I'm sorry, but no. This damage isn't a fault of their workmanship. I'd like to help you but I can't." It looked like it hurt for her to turn me down, but she did.

On the scale of losing Susanne, a pair of sunglasses, even an expensive pair, was nothing, but still deflating. Buying another pair didn't even occur to me. There would be no connection to her that way. Since the moment I had seen the wreckage on TV and realized there were no survivors, I was riding the fragile edge of emotional control. I fought to keep my face unreadable, walked out onto the street, rounded the corner onto Sound Beach Avenue, and shuffled along until I encountered a trash container. Holding the remains of the Maui Jims over their soon-to-be final resting place, I said, as if to Susanne, "And you think I don't take care of my sunglasses? Look what you did to yours." It was a spontaneous release, but it hurt to hear myself talking out loud to her. I imagined I heard her laughing one last time. Then I let go of the tangled mass of metal, plastic, and glass and turned before it landed in the trash on whatever else people had discarded that day.

In a matter of weeks, I'd had enough of my emergency leave of absence. I needed to work, where I could focus on flying and keep my mind active. But TWA was no sanctuary — on the hundreds of faces I encountered, I saw tight lips, downcast eyes, and locked jaws. Two hundred and thirty passengers and crew had died suddenly, and all at once. Everyone was grieving and nobody was solid enough to offer support. We were all still rowing a lifeboat that had clearly sunk to the bottom — and we were collectively holding our breath instead of letting go.

4 | TIGHTY-WHITIE DEEP-SEA DIVERS

Tighty-Whitie Deep-Sea Divers

DANIEL SLOUCHED left or right every time my father let go of him. It seems he didn't want to, or couldn't, sit up straight in the chair. My dad was trying to take a photograph of this historic family event. I was three years old and my new baby brother Daniel was dressed in a white christening gown, way too big for him, that contrasted against a black-leather reading chair in our living room. The walls were painted dark orange, a reflection of my parents' decorating tastes back when America was racing the communists to the moon and drafting soldiers to fight in Vietnam, and Timothy Leary was telling the counterculture to turn on, tune in, and drop out. This is my earliest childhood memory, my only memory of Daniel, and my first experience with death.

> *I remember my first brother in a white christening gown*
> *It's the first memory I had, but then he wasn't around*

Not many days after Daniel's christening, I woke up to discover my parents weren't home. Ms. Baker sat in our dining room. She was lean with straight, shoulder-length, jet-black hair. She greeted me with, "Good morning."

"Where's Mom and Dad?"

Mrs. Baker's lips were naturally puckered into a pre-kiss, but more in a way like she was thinking really hard. She took an extra breath before she answered me. "They had to take your brother to the hospital."

"Can you make my breakfast for me?"

I clearly wasn't getting the big picture. Ms. Baker poured me a bowl of cereal. I can't remember exactly what kind, but the little corn-based flying saucers in Quisp would be a good guess — *the crispy flavor is out of this world*. Her numerous bracelets and bangles dangled as she reached across the table.

"I want to pour the milk myself." I'm sure I spilled — nobody cared — except maybe my dog Crayon, a seventy-pound German shorthaired pointer with dark brown spots and patches. He hovered close for whatever left the table. What parents but mine would let their three-year-old name the family pet? Even standing on all fours, Crayon was as tall as I was, and he could crane his neck to put his nose up on the table if Dad wasn't around to command, *No begging.*

My parents had raced out of the house sometime that morning before I'd woken up. Something had happened. Daytime babysitters were rare, as my stay-at-home mom usually took me with her if she had to go somewhere. Mom gave up her public school teaching position when I was born. Ms. Baker had never been invited into our house before.

This was 1968. Mrs. Baker was divorced, and her son introduced me to several uncles who came to visit during the era of free love. My parents were hardcore Episcopalians. They were obsessive — never missing a Sunday mass — and attended or taught Bible study during the week. Ms. Baker didn't fit into their perception of a good Christian influence, but in times of crisis, whole communities bond, and in this case the nearest available neighbor was sent in to keep an eye on me during this family emergency.

I think Ms. Baker received word confirming Daniel's passing when one of my parents called from the hospital. I remember an off-white rotary phone mounted on the kitchen wall with an impossibly long, coiled cord for the handset that could stretch all the way into the dining room. I'm sure it wasn't their intention to pass the burden of telling me onto her, but somehow I picked up on it. We sat around the table after she hung up the handset — its cord re-twisting but magically not knotting. With most of my cereal consumed by either Crayon or me, I asked her, "Where did Daniel go?"

Her comprehension of the horrible news probably compelled her to dig the pack of cigarettes out of her purse and push one into a black extension holder. I can picture Ms. Baker slowly and forcefully smoking that cigarette. This was before President Nixon signed the Clean Air Act. Secondhand smoke wasn't even a concept yet, and our walls were probably so orange thanks to lead paint. Ms. Baker took a big drag before her reply. She was polite enough to blow the smoke toward the kitchen. This was a long pull and a lot of smoke, but finally she said, "To heaven, my dear."

"Where's heaven?"

Again she sucked, and this time the smoke magically came out of her nose. She looked at me for what felt like a long time. "It's where little babies go when they're not ready for this world."

"Can I go there and see him?"

She had long, candy-apple red fingernails. With the thumb of her free hand resting on the table, she began tapping her remaining fingers: pinky, ring, middle, index—repeat. "Someday, Mark. But let's hope not for a long time."

I was still in the misguided years of cartoons—where death only lasted an episode. Jerry, in his perpetual quest to outwit Tom, would blow up, burn up, chop up, or electrocute-into-a-skeleton the hapless feline predator, and I would laugh. This would happen at least twice every half hour of cartoon opiate—a regular occurrence in my midday, small-screen schedule. I turned on our television at ever opportunity—my interpretation of Timothy Leary's cultural advice.

I wasn't old enough to read yet, but in the margins of *Mad* magazine, Spy vs. Spy revealed endless sinister plots through pictures—most involving black bowling ball-sized bombs with cord-like fuses. I was certain that death was only a temporary condition to be celebrated—not feared. I knew Daniel would reappear after a few of my young life's pages had turned. I barely knew him, but he was my little brother. I loved him unconditionally, even if he was still too young to sit up straight on his own.

> *The baby sitter told me he's gone home to the sky*
> *I didn't understand it and I didn't know why*

Some combination of Lego, Lincoln Logs, and puzzles kept me busy. I was really good at spreading all the small pieces across the carpeting. When Mom and Dad finally walked in the front door, they were both really upset and Mom was crying. Did I make too big of a mess on the floor? They didn't have Daniel with them. Was he still in Heaven?

Years passed before my parents tried to describe crib death to me, and only after I brought in the mail containing a letter from a charity with SIDS in its name. "Nobody really knows how or why it happens," wasn't a very satisfying explanation, but research is still being conducted today. From what I've read, it has to do with infant apnea. I do know the emotional impact death has on a family now. Death-days mark the milestones of my life more powerfully than birthdays, beginning with Daniel. I was old enough to understand when my mom passed away not many years after I graduated from college and first flew a jet. And then there's my fiancée Susanne's death in 1996 not long after I proposed.

There is no love like that of a parent for a child, and as an adult I've seen Susanne's mom suffer her daughter's loss first hand. But why does a baby stop breathing in his sleep? I've got no clue—medically or philosophically. Big Bird didn't have an episode for that: "This episode has been brought to you by the number 3 and the letter B, and sometimes little babies just aren't ready for this world. Sorry for the loss of your little brother, Mark," wasn't something Sesame

Street was approved to air during my childhood. It was a new show, and they were still learning how to teach me. When Mom and Dad came home with our first color TV — possibly their unconscious attempt at retail therapy during the aftermath of Daniel's death — I was surprised to learn Big Bird was yellow.

The rest of my third year is a blur but still a guide for my modern life. I think I just looked forward and started attending nursery school. That's the kind of advice my dad surely gave me: "Knuckle down, eyes forward, the past is history, and we can't change it."

Ever practical, ever positive — that's my old man, even with his heart carved out. He's still stoic and forward thinking. His only salve: VSOP cognac (that makes it easy to Christmas shop for him). At three I hadn't begun drinking yet — although ironically, as an adult, I occasionally put mixed drinks in plastic sippy cups while at crowded parties in order to not spill when bumped. Instead, I buried myself in my work: playing in the leaves (after raking them for a quarter), trying to parachute with an umbrella (perhaps my earliest flying lesson, a premonition for my future, and — surprise, surprise — it didn't work), slamming my thumb in the car door (physical pain still hurt more than emotional pain at this point in my life), finger painting (something I still do, albeit with live nude models as the canvas — a hobby my current significant other hopes I'll eventually outgrow), struggling left-handed with right-handed scissors (the safe kind with rounded tips for much less effective eye poking), and singing "London Bridge" with new classmates (loud and off-key; some things never change). Then came the arrival of my new baby brother, Timothy.

The night Timothy was released from the hospital with Mom and Dad, I was playing deep-sea diver with my friend Glenn and his two brothers, Chris and Greg.

> *A year has gone and I'm at my friends to play*
> *And we're on an ocean expedition today*
> *We'll swim right down to the bottom of the sea*
> *All hands on deck come diving now with me*
>
> *We're deep-sea divers*
> *We're deep-sea divers*
> *I don't know where my dad is but he took my mother*
> *And they left me here to play while they made me a new brother*
> *We're deep-sea divers*

We were jumping off one of their beds into the imaginary ocean of their blue-green shag carpeting as if we were splashing off a ship, all wearing our tighty-whitie underwear over our heads while peeking out of the leg holes.

Then my mom walked in the room with a blanket in her arms
We were bouncing on the bed and sounding the ship's alarms
Here's the treasure that you're diving for, my dad said to me
Welcome your new baby brother. We named him Timothy

That must have been the moment my parents began successfully practicing birth control. After Timothy, no more brothers or sisters arrived wrapped up in blankies. With one son wearing his briefs like a diver's helmet, another recently passed away, and the third just getting his first look of what life in the Berry clan was going to be like, my parents had enough on their plates. A picture of us would have made a great print ad for the pill: *Have enough family and not enough practice?*

My parents really had to put a lot of strength and love into rebuilding our family after losing Daniel. I'm proud of them. Shortly after I lost Susanne, well-meaning friends tried consoling me by saying that losing a child is worse than losing a soul mate. I cringe whenever I even attempt to imagine a deeper loss than what Susanne's death put me through, and I know my parents had to bear it. While they were grieving after Daniel died and praying every day that their new son wouldn't suffer the same inexplicable fate, I was blissfully caught in my own childhood moment of undersea adventure, and the arrival of another bundled-up baby was confusing: Why did my parents make another brother for me? Was this one going to stick around awhile? Why couldn't Daniel learn how to breathe? With my cotton diving helmet, I can breathe under the sea!

These aren't just tighty-whities that I'm wearing on my head
I was peaking out a leg hole and jumping on the bed
Our cotton diving helmets let us breathe under the sea
Jump off the bed into the shaggy green sea

We're deep-sea divers
Tighty-Whitie Deep-Sea Divers
We're diving to the bottom of the shag rug so green
And the bathtub is a bubble bath machine
We named the bed Calypso, it's a Yellow Submarine
We're deep-sea divers

5 | AN UNWELCOME RETURN

FOR MY RETURN TO DUTY as a 767 first officer, during what remained of the summer of 1996, I chose an easy trip as the relief pilot—the eater in TWA-speak. Essentially I was the third pilot on a two-pilot crew. My major duties would include the aircraft exterior preflight, aligning the IRS navigation units, and then transmitting trans-Atlantic position reports once en route. I'd be able to watch the movie in the first-class cabin during my break and enjoy the elaborate multicourse dining service, hence the third pilot's nickname. It should have been an easy getaway—a welcome relief from all the chaos inside my head and everything that reminded me of Susanne inside her mother's home—but I never made it off the gate.

Working in first class and attending to the cockpit for this trip was a petite flight service manager named Meg whose lapel-pin collage rivaled any war veteran's chest-ribbon display. TWA flight attendants wore mini flag lapel pins to represent the foreign languages they spoke. Meg was Asian, I think Chinese, with short straight black hair, and she was uber-multilingual.

Meg and I had flown together many times and we always got along, although I knew bitter flight attendants who didn't like her. This anger was the residue from a strike that happened before I was hired. Those who held a grudge called her The Black Widow, though I doubt they had the nerve to say it to her face. I don't know the circumstances, but she had confided in me that she had lost two husbands to unforeseeable accidents. She was intelligent, compassionate, and always cheerful, and yet she had experienced darkness of her own and knew the territory.

When Meg walked into the 767 cockpit and saw me sitting on the jumpseat finishing up my preflight inspections, she immediately gave me a huge hug with all of her ninety pounds. When she stepped back in tears and said, "I'm so sorry, Mark," the captain threw me off the trip.

It happened that fast. The son-of-a-bitch in the left seat couldn't be bothered to find out how important it was for me to be back at work. I gave him a look of disbelief, but I know now that he must have been so insecure with his own grief—thirty-eight fellow employees and dependents died on TWA Flight 800 while either working or pass riding—that he couldn't handle adding mine to the cockpit mix.

"I can't have you upsetting my crew," he explained.

"Someone shows me some sympathy, and for that you won't let me do my job and go flying?"

"I'm going to have the chief pilot replace you. You should be home."

I asked him to reconsider. "I don't want to be home," I said. "It's Susanne's home and she's gone. I need to be doing the one thing in life that I have left—flying airplanes. I want to help take this bird to Milan."

"No Mark, not today. I'm doing this for your own good."

"The hell you are." I suddenly felt as if I were a thousand feet under water and wanted to scream against the pressure. My core impulse was to drive my fist through his thick skull—something that would have made my dad proud and my chief pilot not so much—but I didn't. That would be the anger phase of grief hitting me with its full force, although I hadn't had any counseling about that yet. Instead I picked up my crew kit and my overnight bag and walked out of the cockpit and exited the airplane. I walked past the boarding passengers in the Jetway, through the terminal tunnel, and out to the crew bus stop. I wore my inexpensive military-style aviator sunglasses, and I was now crying underneath them.

Without thinking, I rode to TWA's Hangar 12 parking lot, but I didn't know where to go after that. I put my bags in the back of my light blue Chevy S-10 Blazer and then sat in the passenger seat, not prepared to drive anywhere, staring straight ahead at a sign I had affixed to my dashboard above the glove box. The sign had come from a tag sale somewhere, but originally it was from a commercial airplane. It advised, "Life Vest Located Under Your Seat." I had no such easy answers.

I pounded my left fist into the sign—my rage desperate to find some avenue of relief. The dashboard was somewhat spongy, although it was sporadically cracked and dried out from years of exposure to the sun, giving way only enough to prevent me from breaking my hand. But it was still solid enough to shoot pain up my arm from the impact. I hammered my fist again and again. It felt good to fight, even if I was acting no more rationally than Don Quixote battling a windmill. Eventually I tired and looked at my knuckles. They were raw like my dad's—a lifetime brawler. He was also missing a knuckle where his head had smashed his hand that was still holding onto the steering wheel during a near-fatal car accident back while I was struggling through elementary school.

I still had all my knuckles, but thinking about my dad made me suddenly embarrassed about the tears that were rolling down my cheeks. In contrast, my raw hand and aching arm reminded me that the urge to fight through adversity was a gift passed down from father to son.

6 | SORTED BY SPEED

Outside of School

I COULDN'T HELP THE TEARS whenever I was reminded of Susanne, as hard as I tried to hold them back. Even today, sometimes just thinking about her — and that she's gone forever — brings that all-too-familiar sinking feeling, and the waterworks sneak to the surface. I don't like crying. It's not manly, and my dad never respected it while I was growing up. We're extremely close now, like best friends. But we shared a lot of father and son moments while I was learning early life lessons, and I still turn to him when I need a reminder. According to his mantra, crying is never an acceptable solution to any adversity, pain, or grief.

I didn't make the long drive from New York's JFK up to Massachusetts to see my dad, although I needed him after I was thrown off that trip for attempting to return to work too soon after Susanne's death. I should have. It took me a long time to ask for his help. I'm stubborn that way, but that's also the way he made me. Stoic, self-sufficient, solid — these are terms I learned over the years from Dad's *How to Become a Man* playbook. Eventually, I hopped a flight up to see him. My cockpit duties were suspended, but I still had pass benefits.

Riding in any car with my father is our best personal time now that we're both adults, as long as catching up doesn't interfere with his driving. After he picked me up from Boston's Logan Airport, he was in the middle of a story while behind the wheel of his Mazda when I interrupted, "Look out!"

The unwashed SUV swerved away from us while honking. The occupants were a blur through the salty, dirt-covered windows, even though the filthy glass was close enough to reach out and write WASH ME with my finger. Dad swerved back into his highway lane with a quick jerk. I heard the inertial reel lock with a snap as it did its job, even as my head almost hit the passenger side window. Dad slowed to let the vehicle's startled driver pass us on the right. "Blind spot," was all Dad said.

After a brief silence, which I used to readjust my tightened seatbelt, Dad continued with his childhood summer camp story as if nothing had just happened,

"I just broke his nose. The big baby acted like he'd never seen blood before."

I'm not sure the stereo in Dad's car even works, because we never turn it on. I relish the moments we spend together and make the most of them, especially as a captive audience while on the road. He had been telling me about his first day at sleep-away Camp Pemigewassett sometime in the late 1940s, when accidentally sharing a lane with another car on Interstate-95 momentarily interrupted him.

"Some kid wet his bed, even before I arrived. He thought he could just switch mattresses with mine and get away with it. I walked in, and every kid was staring at me. I knew something was up as I put my bags down beside my bunk, even before I smelled the urine. It was easy to pick out the face of guilt and fear among my unfamiliar cabin mates. It was a face that just needed to meet my fist before introductions."

Dad has always been a bruiser. Dad's killer instinct is inherent in every aspect of his personality. He likes to remind me how tough he is and how I should be. I envy his fortitude, but I sometimes question when tough becomes ruthless. That's our biggest difference; he acts, while I stop to consider my options. He's always first, fearless, and relentless. I inherited his DNA, but somehow missed the blood-craving gene. For him, there's no backing down—*flight* isn't an actual choice in the primitive *fight or flight* conditioned response to threats. He's like Rorschach in *The Watchmen*, and Ajax in *The Warriors*. I think I disappointed him when I was young because I didn't instinctively think with my fists first. As his oldest son, I was expected to be a bruiser too, and never cry.

The story of my childhood fighting wouldn't win me any Oscars for best performance in an action film. As the only first-grade boy in a combined first-, second-, and third-grade class, I was a soft target for the upper classmen of Dundee Elementary—and it didn't help that I was also young for my grade with a September birthday. It seemed the entire class had to test their pecking-order position against me. Walking to and from school became a dangerous event, often involving circuitous routes through the woods to avoid potential confrontation. The threat, "I'm going to beat you up after school," was a recurring theme.

> *Those guys are just jerks*
> *Their parents don't love them*
> *So don't take their bait*
> *When they call you a fem*

A year of physical development was a huge deal if it meant I had to fight someone from a grade or two above me. Six-year-olds typically don't fare too well against seven- or eight-year-olds.

Whatever you do
Don't let them see you cry
Let them punch you
And beat you 'til you die

I wish I could tell you I was the exception — the Jack Reacher of my day. I wasn't — and the biggest sin I could commit was to come home crying. My dad expected me to win. At the very least, he expected me to earn respect. Almost daily I fought off name-calling, wedgies, being spit on, and a general pack mentality that I was slow to break into.

'cause they were waiting for me when the school day let out
The first one who saw me, let out a big shout
"There he is. Let's get him, that wise-acre fem."
I ran for the woods but I failed to outrun them

Sports were finally a way for me to earn acceptance among my peers and fight less. In small numbers we played Cream the Carrier or King of the Hill. In larger numbers we played two-hand touch football in the street or tackle football in the grass. Anyone who didn't want to play tackle on anything softer than asphalt was a fem, the ultimate term of disrespect in my neighborhood back in the 1970s. If someone took a hit that left him gasping, for instance if he were tackled on the point of the football, then two players had to sit out — the injured and one player from the other team to keep the sides even. The game wasn't actually going to stop just because somebody felt a little wounded. Several plays later, the conversation usually went something like this, "Tough it out. Don't be such a fem. Get back in the game or we'll give you a wedgie. I think I hear your mother calling you, momma's boy."

Playing through the pain taught me to tough it out. Eventually I earned enough credibility to avoid being picked on regularly. Nevertheless, even as a new pack member, there were still more battles to fight.

Cecil moved onto my Connecticut suburban block all the way from Georgia. I was in third grade and he was in fourth. He must have had his own parental coaching because he was ready to fight for a position among his new peers. Most of the kids I played football with in my neighborhood were older than me, so I still must have looked like the softest target. Cecil called me a fem, an insult I had to answer to or lose what hard-earned respect I had—it was automatic.

He hammered me with a few good punches for no good reason and I hate to admit it, but I ran home crying. I barely made it to my room where I thought I'd find sanctuary, but Dad smelled weakness like guard dogs can smell fear. It felt like he grabbed me by the scruff in his powerful jaws, and then he dragged me right back out of our house, across the neighborhood lawns, and straight into Cecil's house uninvited. I was scared and confused, and I tried to break free. I was still on my feet, but Dad was now hauling me by the arm. I pulled against him and begged him to let me go, but there was no fighting his two hundred and twenty pounds of solid muscle or his unbreakable determination not to raise a wimp. I thought Dad was supposed to be on my side, not throw me back into battle to get hurt some more.

Dad told Cecil to beat me up again in the hall between their family bedrooms and kitchen while yelling orders to me: "Keep your arms up to block. Keep your head in the fight. Lead with your right (Dad and I are both left-handed). Keep your feet moving. Whatever you do, don't you dare cry!"

By today's standards, Dad's actions would probably cause him to be arrested. To use Susanne's line — I can smell the metal that he's forged from — Dad's desire to raise only strong offspring is very real.

Dundee Elementary sits in my memory with scattered books, dented metal lunchboxes, broken thermoses, ripped clothes, skinned knees, bloody noses, and unauthorized tears. So on the first day of sixth grade, as I entered North Street Elementary after we moved across town, the school Susanne began attending after her move from Denmark, I looked around Mr. Hardvall's classroom and tried to guess who it was going to be — who I was going to fight to establish my new reputation.

> *Whatever you do*
> *Don't let them see you cry*
> *Even if they punch you*
> *And beat you 'til you die*

The bell rang after first period. We were scheduled for English composition next. In the hall, as all three sixth-grade classes mingled for the classroom exchange, Stuart Helgeson grabbed my sleeve and said, "At lunch, you and me are going to go." My blood pressure peaked and I almost cold-cocked him right then and there, I was so wired for a fight. The crossing classes wedged between us and we all settled into our newly assigned seats, but word spread with viral speed and everybody began sneaking peaks at me—the new guy already set to be tested on day one. After verb conjugations and attempts to identify subjects and predicates, our classes switched again, and this time the kids all gave me a wide berth in the hall. I wasn't the local favorite. I was clearly the unpopular visiting team. Nobody wanted to associate with a condemned man, if in fact a sixth grader could be honored with such an adult term. Although I was feeling isolated, I was also excited—yet anxious—for my opportunity to climb into the ring and earn a little respect this time.

Back in Mr. Hardvall's class, I didn't learn anything the rest of that morning. I watched the clock. At 12:15 p.m. our combined lunch hour and recess was scheduled to begin. The weather was windy but still warm, with green leaves just starting to turn their last-breath radiant colors. When the bell finally rang to start the now fully anticipated lunch break, nobody went straight to the cafeteria. They all gathered behind the school on the foursquare, basketball, and tetherball courts—where painted pavement opened up to the jungle gyms and further away, the baseball diamonds and the schoolyard's perimeter fence. I used that walk through the hallways, and then through the staring spectators outside, to psych myself up. I told myself: *He's just a big fem.*

Stuart led me to the middle of what felt like the entire student body, which parted to let us inside the giant huddle. I half expected the principal to step in as the referee and start the fight with the school bell. I clenched and unclenched my fists. I felt my heart rate increase and fought to maintain control over my breathing—in through my nose and out through my mouth. That was the practical advice my dad had given me, and I heard him in the back of my mind coaching: *"Break his nose or at least make it bleed. If you don't make the first guy suffer, you'll have to face every other kid in your new class as they try to kick you to the bottom of their pack. Just remember this: Hit first and hit hard; whatever you do, don't cry; and don't stop swinging until you decide it's over."*

Whatever you do
Don't let them see you cry

Stuart grew up to become a walk-on starting wide receiver at Penn State. He became a United States Marine. He competed in Eco-Challenge races across the Australian outback. I mention this because even in sixth grade he was athletic, and this was not going to be an easy fight for anyone—especially not as the new kid with everyone watching and rooting against me.

I closed within two steps of Stuart, ready to throw my first punch. I wanted him to step into it and I wanted it to count. My blood was pumping. All I needed was for him to take a single step toward me and I would start the fight with all the fury I had—no leading jab, but a surprise roundhouse left. I wasn't going to hold back in any way or wait until he hit me first.

> *Even if they punch you*
> *And beat you 'til you die*

The whispering crowd silenced as Stuart pointed into the distance and spoke. "We're going to run around that backstop, then to the far baseball diamond, around the entire school, and the first one back to this half-court line is the winner."

"What?"

"We need somebody to say, 'One, two, three, go!' Are you ready to race?"

It came as a shock that at North Street Elementary, the pecking order was sorted by speed, not by fighting.

I raced for all I was worth—pumping my fists to add power to my pounding legs. Stuart started the long race at a full sprint and never seemed to slow down. I let the sweat drip into my eyes and tried to ignore the shouts for my demise. Even the teachers cheered for Stuart as we ran by. I think my little brother Tim, who was in the second grade, was the only one who yelled my name. I came in second in a two-person race, but I didn't care. I finished winded, but not with the wind knocked out of me. It was my first bloodless and bruiseless battle for respect.

My dad was born with the killer instinct. I had to learn it. Life would still throw many more challenges my way, but they would be emotional and intellectual ordeals rather than the kind solved with raw knuckles.

Susanne was in the audience of my race that day with Stuart. Behind the school—past the baseball field backstops—stretched the fence that separated our school from an expansive, non-denominational cemetery. That's where the girl I hadn't taken notice of yet is now buried. I had to be tough when our lives first overlapped, and tougher still now that she is gone.

7 | SPECIAL LEAVE OF ABSENCE

WITH NO HOME OR A JOB to go to after being thrown off my trans-Atlantic flight at JFK, I sat in the passenger seat of my Chevy S-10 Blazer in the Hangar 12 parking lot for a long time—parked, contemplating, trying to draw strength from my dad's early coaching. After my eyes finally dried and most of the international flights were in the air, I finally walked up the three flights of stairs to my chief pilot's office. I felt like I was already wearing out all of my friends with my gloomy disposition and I didn't know where to turn, plus I didn't know if I was now in trouble because I wasn't on my scheduled flight to Europe.

Captain Hugh Schoelzel—the JFK chief pilot and, as such, my boss—invited me in. Before he closed his office door, he told Helen, his secretary, that he was now in a meeting and was not to be interrupted by anyone. He offered me his chair behind his desk and then sat across from me where I'd expected to sit—in the chief pilot's hot seat. His switcheroo caught me off-guard, but it went a long way to try to assure me before he even said a word that discipline wasn't the direction this conversation was going to go. I still wasn't sure. We talked about TWA Flight 800, how it was affecting everyone—so many of the 230 victims were crew or family members of employees—and he told me I could talk about anything I wanted to and he would listen. "Am I in trouble?" I asked.

He reassured me I wasn't being fired, that I was on GMF hold—a special leave of absence designated by the general manager of flight—and was actually getting paid for the trip I was missing. He wanted me to take as much more time off as I wanted—all still with a paycheck. I tried to tell him I didn't want time off.

"Mark, you're not alone in this. It feels like I've been to more funerals since July 17 than in all the time before. I've lost close friends, crewmembers with whom I've shared this fraternal career with, and I'm hurting inside too. I know this is magnified for you. Numerous people have inquired how you are doing, and I want be able to pass along good news, and to that effect I also want you to talk with someone."

I didn't know what he meant by that. It was scary enough talking with my boss while I felt impossibly deep in an emotional deficit. My career, whatever was left of it, was in his hands, and I wasn't in any position to make an argument on my own behalf.

"One funny thing happened out of all this," he told me. "I know it's hard to appreciate subtle humor in times like this, but six of us management pilots chartered a King Air and flew up to Captain Schneider's funeral together — all in full uniform to be pallbearers. When we collectively climbed out of the nine-seat light twin and stood in a cluster on the general aviation ramp while waiting to unload our own bags, the aircraft fueler walked up to us in his oil-stained overalls and asked: *How many of you airline captains does it take to fly one of these little things?*"

I could imagine it and tried to laugh — the scene must have looked like a clown car act — but I'm sure I barely cracked a smile. More power to Captain Schoelzel for trying to bring humor to such a dark situation. He used whatever smile I did give him as his cue to open the door and walk me down the long hangar corridor to an office I'd never entered before, where Johanna O'Flaherty gave me a series of welcoming hugs. It only took a glance to see that this little office was the nucleus of our airline's disaster recovery effort, and this woman was the atom in the center of that nucleus.

After a brief discussion about my feelings — the single subject I was least comfortable contemplating, much less verbalizing — Johanna arranged for me to see the company's contracted psychiatrist for some straight talk about life, death, and dealing with both. She wasn't pawning me off; she was prioritizing and sending me to who she described as the top dog. I felt triaged and sent straight to surgery. An appointment was made for me to go to his Long Island office the following week.

8 | THE MAJORS

My First Solo

WITH NO FLYING DUTIES to perform, I had time to reflect. One of my childhood goals was to play professional baseball; I was born with the initials for it after all: MLB. At eight, I was a starter in the nine- and ten-year-old league and I had a mean fastball with a natural rising screwball action. I spent plenty of time pitching to those backstops that Stuart and I raced around, and I tried to keep batters from knocking the ball over the perimeter fence and into the graveyard beyond. As a lefty, I could throw it inside the plate to right-handed batters, and it would ease over the inside corner. Every strike appeared as a brush-back pitch. When I could control it, that is, and therein lied the problem. I threw harder than my peers, and some of them had the bruises to prove it. My nickname was Beanball Berry.

I should have stuck with pitching—lefties are always in high demand in the big leagues—but I also loved to bat. Pitchers didn't play every game unless they were also awarded a second position and therefore didn't spend as much time at the plate. Pitchers typically bat ninth, and I wanted to bat in the front of the lineup. Instead of improving my throwing accuracy, I focused on my hitting. By the time I moved up to the Junior Babe Ruth League at age thirteen, my coach moved me over to first base so I could stay in the line-up every game. I accepted my coach's wisdom and left pitching to my teammates who were learning to throw fancy pitches like curves, change-ups, and sliders. My pitching reputation didn't fully go away after I forfeited the mound, though. At my ten-year high school reunion, I thought Will Wilson was approaching me to shake hands and say hello. Instead he said, "Hey Beanball, in fourth grade you hit me in the back with your uncontrollable fastball. I still remember it."

"That's Captain Beanball to you." It was good to be remembered, but not as the kid with the wild arm. He didn't need to know I was still merely a first officer at my airline at the time. Reunions are great for glorious self-declarations of success.

As I was growing up, the baseball funnel grew tighter as all three of my town's junior high school teams graduated into a single high school. Being good wasn't good enough. I didn't make Greenwich High's roster. My major league baseball dreams were crushed about the time I was learning to drive.

High school became my soul-searching time, and like almost every other kid, I had to face the future as Mom and Dad made plans to kick me out of their nest. That's when I asked for flying lessons at a nearby airport in Westchester, New York.

After an introduction and a handshake, Glenn Larson became my first flight instructor. He asked me, "Shall we check the weather?" as he walked me over to an area set up as a multi-use office. Lots of machines were buzzing and humming. I remember watching weather reports spit out on tickertape, and instructor Larson read official-sounding words from the gibberish shorthand. A glass door beyond the flight-planning area revealed a ramp filled with single-engine Piper Cherokee airplanes. Behind them were a multitude of colored lights and a maze of pavement. As we walked to tail number 1945-Hotel that would be our aircraft for the next six-tenths of an hour, Instructor Larson handed me a small clear cup and taught me how to sump the wing tanks free of water. AvGas spilled on my hands, and the flying bug soaked into my soul. I could smell my future in the sky as I held the cup up to my face to see the separation of AvGas and the little bit of water I'd drained from the tank. We opened the cowling and checked the oil level, verified the tire inflation and remaining tread, tugged on the flight controls, and everything I touched on the plane felt like first-kiss excitement.

On this introductory flight, in addition to the four fundamentals—climbs, descents, straight and level flight, and turns—we flew over my house for a new aerial perspective of familiar surroundings. Trees obscured it, but we saw the neighborhood churches and schools, including North Street Elementary. I was awed by the whole experience until Instructor Larson put me back to work learning to operate the aircraft. My logbook includes radio communication in my initial entry. Communicating with New York's extensive air traffic control system was something I'd have to learn by doing. He taught me to unkey the microphone if I was going to say uh. Better to let someone else talk than announce to the world that I was standing on my tongue.

After Instructor Larson landed with me following through on the flight controls—we each had our own interconnected control yoke and rudder pedals, but we shared a single throttle between us—I tried taxiing the airplane back to the ramp while he kept our wheels on the pavement. Mom picked me up; I was old enough to take flying lessons but still only possessed a learner's driving permit. It was obvious to her that I was onboard with this new activity, so she bought me a logbook for Instructor Larson to sign and a primary flight book that I still recommend as a first read for flight students: William Kershner's *Student Pilot Flight Manual*.

My enthusiasm earned me a trip to Daytona Beach to visit Embry-Riddle Aeronautical University with my dad, my first and only campus tour, and I decided on the spot that's where I wanted to go to school. Afterward, we extended our trip to the Florida Keys for the scuba-diving mini-lobster season and flew on Provincetown Boston Airlines—whose single pilot delivered us to Marathon Key. I won the golden ticket: I was able to ride in the copilot's seat. I wore a set of heavy headphones that completely covered my ears and tried to make sense of the radio communication. I wondered what all the cockpit buttons and knobs did, much as many of my passengers wonder about them today.

I didn't have any clue about the job market back then, but my dad had some understanding because he was a businessman. With no formal aviation training yet, he was already studying the industry from a financial viewpoint to see if learning to fly would offer me an opportunity to obtain a reasonable return on the required educational investment. As I returned the borrowed headset to our pilot and stepped out onto the tarmac for the walk into the terminal, my dad grabbed our bags and asked me a serious question. "If flying Cessna 402s around the Keys is as far as you advance in your career, will you be satisfied?"

I was post-airborne euphoric. The flight up front was better than any home run I'd ever hit. For me, flying was just about the flying. Earning a living was still an abstract idea. I was still in high school and hadn't paid rent or any bills. I think Dad was trying to prepare me in case my flying career got stuck like my baseball ambitions. My view was idealistic and I said, "Hell, yeah!" That was good enough for Dad.

Airplanes fascinated me as a small child. Now I sized this metallic winged creature up with a serious gaze, as if it was an opposing pitcher and I was a fan suddenly invited to don a uniform and step up to the plate to face it. I'd turned the corner and found a new, more obtainable career goal than baseball, although Embry-Riddle accepted me as both a flight student and a baseball player.

As high school ended, I couldn't wait to learn how to fly. Six days after my high school graduation, I planned to drive my loaded my car to Daytona Beach in order to start college with summer school. My coach was crushed because my senior Babe Ruth baseball league was still only midseason through our schedule. I was batting over six hundred after nine games against my high school's pitchers, who were spread around the league for additional playing opportunities.

My parents miscalculated their annual vacation and left me as the man of the house as high school ended. I walked across the stage in my cap and gown and then threw a high school graduation bash for three hundred friends; all the while my folks were sailing in Greece. Piss-poor planning on my parents' part, and I was long gone by their return.

The first letter I found in my new university mailbox was from Mom and it began, "Dear Mark, Why is our lawn growing flip tops this year?" This was before the tabs on beer and soda stayed attached to the cans after opening, and I hadn't stuck around town long enough to collect those shiny little discards.

After Dad cleaned up my mess and made me feel guilty because our dog cut his paws on the sharp aluminum hidden in the grass, he decided to check out what it was that I saw from the cockpit. He bought an old Piper Cherokee 160B — the same aircraft type used during my first flights at Westchester County Airport — to take his lessons in during weekends. He was running a manufacturing business. It was the beginning of the computer age and his company was developing scuba-diving computers back when they were big and clunky — the size of a paperback book with the weight of a softball. This began our friendly rivalry: Who would earn his private pilot's license first and take the other one flying? The loser would have to buy clam chowder on Martha's Vineyard, Nantucket, and Block Island as we planned to make a cross-country chowder run during my next visit home.

Most of the family flying was shared only between Dad and me. My brother didn't have any interest in aviation, although he recently surprised me by skydiving. Mom went with us once but screamed louder than she did at Yankee games. Her friends called her Pat, my dad called her Trish, and the stadium ushers often called her over to have a talk about her unbridled enthusiasm. She was a true fan and always at the verge of being ejected. She had the world's longest brown ponytail that she pulled through the back of an adjustable baseball cap, and she cheered and jeered like nobody I've ever met. She loved attending baseball games — both the pros and mine. Maybe that's why a career on the mound seemed so appealing during my impressionable years. Mom's attention was very focused at the games.

One afternoon at college, my scheduled training flight was rained out. That's something that flying airplanes and playing baseball share; they're both subject to delay and cancellation due to foul weather. As I returned to my dorm, I was doused with water from all directions. The parking lot flooded during extreme afternoon thundershowers, and the battle of the dorms was happening with wastebaskets and water balloons. It was all kinds of fun until my instructor showed up looking for me and was also doused and soaked in the process. Instructor David Esser told me the rest of his afternoon flying was cancelled, but since I lived on campus we could go up when there was a break in the weather.

"Awesome," I said. "Just let me change."

"No," he said. "If I have to fly wet, so do you. And by the way, your friends are all crazy."

"I know, isn't it great?"

Off we went to the small southern runway at Daytona Beach Regional Airport in a Cessna 172 Skyhawk — a bird we sarcastically called the mighty Chickenhawk, but we really revered it with affection. It has a high wing with diagonal support struts running down to fixed, not retractable, landing gear. Inside there is room for two pilots and two passengers behind a single engine in the nose that powers a two-bladed propeller. Our school's aircraft are all painted white with light blue and a single dark gold stripe, and all of the registration tail numbers end in ER for Embry-Riddle — pronounced Echo Romeo in the phonetic alphabet over the radio.

> *Startin' the engine*
> *Instructor just watchin'*
> *He's just relaxin'*
> *Lettin' me try*
>
> *To handle the throttle*
> *The flaps and the radio*
> *Rollin' for takeoff*
> *He's lettin' me fly*

Three times Instructor Esser and I went around the traffic pattern together, and then he told me to pull over onto the local fixed base operator ramp — a facility for general aviation aircraft.

> *Three landings later*
> *We pulled over*
> *Under beautiful weather*
> *And a clear blue sky*

I was confused because Embry-Riddle had its own ramp where we parked our airplanes. He hopped out, but before he reclosed the door, he said, "Now go back out and do what we just did three more times. Remember, the airplane will be lighter without my weight in it, but you can handle it." With that he closed me in that little cockpit, walked into the building attached to the hangar, and was gone.

I later learned this was the old school method—the human version of being kicked out of the nest. No dwelling about soloing—I was just made to go out and do it without warning.

I was both scared and excited as I looked over at the empty seat beside me. I was hyper-aware now, and even noticed that Instructor Esser had courteously secured his seat belt and shoulder harness. I restarted the engine and read my checklist out loud. Releasing the brakes was the deciding moment. With just a nudge to the throttle, I was rolling and on my way on my own.

> *I'll never forget*
> *My first solo*
> *Instructor hopped out*
> *And away I go*

I taxied out only to find the airport was just turned around. The wind had shifted, and takeoffs and landings were now operating in the opposite direction. I briefly considered turning back to retrieve my instructor. Was I qualified to do other than what he'd specifically told me to do? The urge to solo took hold of me and I rationalized, *I need to be flexible. Adapt, isn't that what pilots do?* I wondered what Instructor Esser thought when I taxied a direction other than expected. I don't know what the aviation equivalent of Beanball is, but he was probably thinking it. Perhaps he was wondering what else he was qualified to do if the FAA ripped up his license. As a solo student, I was flying on his ticket.

> *I'll never forget*
> *My first solo*
> *Up in the air*
> *Up all alone*
>
> *No one to ask*
> *No one to talk to*
> *No one to blame*
> *My oh my*

I was really flyin'
I was really tryin'
To keep from diein'
Durin' my first landin'
I was really sweatin'
No time for contemplatin'
Put it on the runway
On my first try

I wasn't signed off for touch and goes—every landing had to be made to a full stop with a lengthy taxi back for another takeoff. Air traffic picked up as darkness approached and day-flight-only students returned from the local practice areas. It was a double Ray-Ban shade of dusk when I taxied back into the FBO ramp to pick up Instructor Esser. He was wired on iced Pepsi, his favorite vice, and was still holding a giant cup of it. I was wired too—I had just soloed! He sipped while letting me taxi back to the school's ramp to park the plane. I tried to be smooth on the controls so he didn't spill.

We went up to Instructor Esser's desk, and he grabbed a pair of scissors. Several other instructors and fellow students watched as he cut the back off my T-shirt, still wet from the water war and now also mixed with my sweat. I was initiated as a fledgling pilot in the true aviator's tradition. He signed my now priceless shirttail with the airport name, runway, and date: 8-9-83. First solo is the monumental milestone, even with so many more ahead. The shirttail was a trophy like none I'd ever earned before, because it marks the day I can forever look back and recognize myself as a pilot. I sent it to my dad with thanks for his support. A few weeks later his arrived in the mail, and I hung his solo shirt up proudly in my dorm room. Coincidentally, we were scheduled to solo on the same day, twelve hundred miles apart, and we were both rained out. My soaking wet instructor made up our flight right away, while it took my dad two more weeks to reschedule.

From that point on, Dad continued learning to fly, but he couldn't keep up with my pace since I was learning full-time in a total-immersion aviation environment. I went home for the winter holiday and went flying with Dad soon after I'd earned my private pilot's license. As we buckled into our seats, I asked him, "Who is the pilot in command?"

He had to think about it for a second. I was the only one with a license, even though it was his airplane. He replied, "You are."

I felt the urge to enforce my new authority. My eighteen-year-old mind needed the ego feed as much as we really needed to establish who had the final word over the safe operation of the flight on our long-awaited chowder run. He was the owner/operator and I was the pilot in command — our roles in the cockpit were now clearly defined — and for the first time I was in charge of my father. I consoled him with the fact that letting me fly his plane was putting my college tuition to immediate good use.

He made good on his debt, and we became clam-chowder connoisseurs throughout New England. The pre-departure discussion came in handy on our return to Danbury Airport where he kept his plane. We asked for runway three-five. The approach to that runway is nestled through a cut between two prominent hills. It's an arrival that's breathtaking during the colorful weeks of fall foliage but still exciting anytime. After touching down and rolling out, Dad told me to turn off onto the crossing runway eight. I told him, "No," and tried rolling through the intersection with a goose of power. Dad applied the brakes and we stopped in the middle of the intersection, but I refused to turn onto the other runway. There was a pregnant pause as I tried to move the airplane and Dad tried to keep it stopped. In this small cockpit, both of us wearing puffy down jackets, Dad's and my shoulders almost touched but we were having trouble making our minds meet. The tower announced over the radio, "Seven-One-Whiskey, roll through to taxiway Alpha. The aircraft on runway eight is waiting to take off."

Dad was thinking about the shortest taxi time back to our parking area. He wasn't experienced enough yet to keep the whole airport operation in mind. He released the brake and I taxied to the next exit from our landing runway. We doubled back on a parallel taxiway and then waited for clearance to cross runway eight once the departing aircraft was airborne, and then I delivered us back to his tie-down spot.

We threaded the ropes through the underwing and tail-ring mounts in silence before hopping into his car. We didn't drive far, because we did what most pilots do after a flight — we debriefed over a beer at the nearest pub. Every flight is a learning experience, and sometimes it just takes a look back from a nonmoving seat to see the big picture. During that and other debriefs, Dad also helped me see that major-league ambition didn't have to mean striving for Major League Baseball. I was able to wind down my baseball dreams as a second-string first baseman playing for the Embry-Riddle Eagles while starting my flying career and resetting my focus toward becoming a major airline pilot.

9 | THE ROAD BACK TO THE COCKPIT

Learning to Breathe Again

LIKE A GOOD PILOT, I arrived on time at the psychiatrist's office (that TWA sent me to) for what I thought was grief counseling. Dr. Oshiro's office on Long Island was expensive-looking and neat — an oversized desk, diplomas, and plenty of open space. The overall effect was "prime of career success with a hint of Yankee fan."

After introductions, he got right down to business and made me count backward from one hundred by sevens. I started out thinking the countdown would be short. After seventy-nine, I paused and took a deliberate breath, hoping this short display of cooperation would satisfy him.

He nodded his head slightly and gave me a welcoming wave that I instinctively knew meant he wanted more. His facial features remained rigid underneath his short black hair. Reluctantly I continued, "Seventy-two, sixty-five, fifty-eight..."

I tried to stop several more times, but he stared blankly at me from over his manicured fingertips, palms pressed together, so I continued. He didn't let me stop until I reached minus twelve. I don't know if that was symbolic of how far I would have to fall emotionally before hitting bottom, but that's where he took me — through the floor of positive numbers and into the negative. I've heard that police challenge questionable drivers with recital of the alphabet backward as a sobriety check, but decreasing numerical leaps was Dr. Oshiro's test for cognitive thinking. Brain function was not my problem. Nevertheless, he was just warming me up.

"Mark, why do you think you are here?"

"Obviously, I didn't volunteer. This was TWA's idea. I didn't do anything except try to do my job, and I got grounded. I'll be honest; I'm pissed off about it."

"It is good that you are being honest, and I will be honest with you. Do you know your career is now in my hands?" For a split second I envisioned him as President Harry S. Truman, a wooden plaque with *The Buck Stops Here* displayed on his desk. Then I returned to reality and our regularly scheduled program. He was serious. Ever since Susanne died, everything had taken on a surreal quality. "You cannot go back to fly until I allow it. How does that make you feel about our meeting today?"

"Even more pissed off."

"Yet you are here. I have nothing on my schedule except to speak with you for the next two hours. Your airline feels it is important that we spend some time together and investigate your feelings."

Two hours? I had figured forty-five minutes, max. In fact, after passing the countdown test, I thought I'd be out the door with a back-to-work pass in ten more minutes, tops. *Investigation* is the word that really made me mad and more than a little nervous. People are *investigated* for things they've done. I didn't do a damn thing except receive the news that Susanne had died. My job was now in jeopardy and my mental health was in question. As a pilot I felt I could fly through anything, even emotional trauma. Most of us are hard-wired that way.

"Tell me doctor, why do I have to have my head examined because my fiancée died?" I asked. "What did I do? Exactly nothing, that's what. The woman I love most in the whole world died, and because it's on one of my airline's airplanes, I'm not allowed to fly them anymore? What kind of bullshit, vindictive logic is that?"

"Mark, that is what we need to explore," he explained, inching his chair away from his desk, crossing one leg over the other as though he were David Letterman's next guest. "You have been delivered a great wrong. Life isn't fair, and you do not need me to tell you this. But if you want to examine your situation, look at it from your chief pilot's point of view. The airline knows you are suffering, and I can see that in you right away — it is in your face, your flat affect, the mask that tries to hide your feelings — but would he be doing his job to provide safe air travel if he did not first offer you all the help at his disposal before returning you to work?"

I leaned in and squared my shoulders in what would be an aggressive stance, except that I was sitting. "So this is a liability issue then? My chief can't let me fly until someone signs off on me? He's worried about the airline's insurance premiums more than the needs of one of his own pilots? I'm an employee, and I've now lost more than anyone can ever be expected to suffer on my company's aircraft, and right now I want to — I need to — go out and go flying." I thumped his desk to punctuate my point. "I've had enough taken away from me. I'm not giving up my wings too."

"If it makes you feel any better to look at it that way, then yes, I am the one who must risk deciding if you are OK to fly. Someone has to be liable for you, and your company is paying me a good sum of money to take that responsibility. Is that not what you also do? Do you not accept the responsibility of every passenger's life when they board your airplane? So you and me, we are the same in that regard. We are decision-makers, and others accept our judgment as part of our job. Other people look to us to act in their best interest, but let us look at this another way. You receive a checkride occasionally, do you not?"

"Twice a year—once in the simulator and once on the line while flying passengers. Also every time I upgrade or transition into a new seat or aircraft type."

"Well, then, you are not so foreign to this concept. Consider this discussion to be an oral checkride, just like you have to do with the FAA when you learn a new airplane."

I began feeling conflicted. Part of me was still angry that I had to face his tribunal at all. Another part of me admired the way he was asserting his authority with references I could relate to. I sat back to think this through. "You seem to know a lot about my job. Are you a pilot?"

"I am a licensed psychiatrist; that means I have been to med school, not flight school. But I am also a Zen Master in Japan and the chosen authority for your airline's mental health. You are not the first pilot to sit across the desk from me —far from it, in fact. And, I have sent a great deal of them back to work—when they are ready."

"I'm ready now. I've told you that."

"You are only ready when I have made that call. We have much to talk about."

"So what are you planning on doing next, making me count backwards using only prime numbers?"

"Would you like to do that?"

"Hell, no."

"Good, because there are other ways." He pointed to a glass case full of every assortment of pill I could imagine. It looked like the Lite-Brite toy I played with as a child, with little colored dots of various sizes and shapes. Except these must be prescription narcotics and other mind-altering capsules. I had no interest in a trip down the rabbit hole.

"I'm not taking any pills. You can forget about that. I already told you I didn't do anything and I'm not going to be drugged for any reason. Even my job isn't worth that."

The only pills I'd taken were sleeping pills the first couple weeks after the crash—over-the-counter Unisom that my friend Chip recommended. Before I tried them I couldn't relax; I just stared through the night. If I did sleep, I think my eyes were still open. I wasn't going to admit any of that to Dr. Oshiro. All I wanted was his signature on the proper line and to be done with this interrogation. I would cooperate in order to graduate, but I was careful not to give him any excuse to label me unfit to fly.

"Well, now you know why you were sent to see me specifically. If I give you any of the drugs in this case, as I often do with my non-pilot patients, you cannot fly while using them and for a good deal of time afterwards — in many cases a minimum of one year."

"To hell with that idea."

"Exactly, Mark. That is why for pilots there is another way. We must break through your subconscious block, but without using drugs. Do you know how we can do this?"

"Sorry, Doc — no clue. I'm sure you're going to tell me though."

"Not exactly. You are going to tell me. What is the one thing you can do while you are awake or while sleeping?"

"Think about sex."

"Very clever. I knew your mind was working, but think again. This is a physical thing. We all do it without thinking, and we can control it when we do. We are both doing it right now."

He followed up that statement with an exaggerated deep breath. I almost laughed when it occurred to me this was like an open-book test. He was feeding me the answer.

"Breathing."

"Precisely." He made a one-finger silent snap in the air, like an orchestra conductor signaling a cymbal strike, to emphasize his point. "I would like to teach you how to do it better, more deeply, with your chest and your gut. My American medical degree taught me how to change the chemicals in the brain, but I prefer the natural Eastern ways if my patients are willing to work hard at learning them. It is your choice. Would you like to learn how to restore your emotional balance through breathing, or with a prescription?"

I let my face droop with an almost sleepy expression, as if I'd just sat through a record-length lecture. "OK, give me the yoga lesson and send me back to work."

"Mark, you may be skeptical, but keep in mind that we both know you are deeply grieving. It is now part of your life. I need you to learn to do it well. When you fly, you feel it and you fly well. Everything in life that you do, you must do well. When you shit, a primal need, shit well."

This caught me by surprise, but he was serious. He continued, "To accept your life again as it is now, you must learn to grieve well." He was staring at me to make sure I received his message. "I want you to take the next few weeks to learn and practice breathing exercises. Call me if you have any questions or concerns, then come back and see me. I do not need you to be free from grief to return to flying. I only need to know that you are on your way."

"I take it you aren't letting me fly to Europe this week."

"No, but I am prescribing my breathing workbook. I am going to show you the basics now to get you started; read what I have written and let your internal journey begin."

I saw a doc to resolve all of my outbursts
He made me count from 100 by 7s in reverse
He knew I needed help to learn to grieve
So he said he would teach me how to breathe

I'm just trying to learn to breathe again
Trying to live another day
I'm just trying to learn to breathe again
As I try to find my way
And I'm just trying to learn to live again
Trying to end this slow decay
I'm just trying to learn to breathe again
To get this pain to fade away

10 | ATTRITION AND LESSONS LEARNED

Black Firebird

FRESH OUT OF HIGH SCHOOL, was I really ready for college and an aviation career? Aircraft crash prevention was covered extensively throughout my flight training, at every level. Dealing with the aftermath of a fatal crash, however, was not a subject my university offered back when I was learning to fly, although there was a brief lesson on attrition during undergraduate orientation.

"Some of you won't make it." The speaker was addressing the incoming freshman class, and that included me. We were a small group because it was the summer session. In less than a week, I'd graduated Greenwich High School —home of the Cardinals—and became part of the newest flock of Embry-Riddle Eagles. I was working my way up the wild-bird pecking order, at least as far as mascots were concerned.

"Look to your left and to your right. Remember the faces you see. One of them won't still be here at graduation. One in three of you will fail or drop out." I knew the speaker was talking about the difficult course work that awaited us. As it turned out, he underestimated—neither of my first two university friends would make it past their freshman year. Lip would fail and Ken would bail, but all three of us were still beaming with toothy grins on day one. What I didn't see coming was that sometimes friends and family would actually die. Attrition means death sometimes.

More useful advice followed: "Pay attention to these next four years of school. Fifty percent of your education will come outside the classroom." I didn't know what he meant by that yet, and I doubt the speaker had a specific lesson in mind, but one was headed my way at high speed.

Following our formal indoctrination, summer classes soon began at my aviation university in Florida. I was starting my education early, before the fall rush, and I was eager to take advantage of the predominantly sunny weather that bode well for flight training—but distractions also abounded.

One morning Lip broke into my dorm room by pounding on the window near the locking pin, and once inside, he kicked my bunk. I was hung over. Lip,

Ken, and I had been up late, and we'd pounded way too many speed-rail screw-drivers at a trendy beachside nightclub's free-drink night. I had collected and moved the stir sticks from glass to glass and still lost count of my total intake. That much of the previous evening I could still remember.

"Fuck off," Ken said from across the room, but it was too late for me. My bunk was nearest the jimmied window, and Lip already had me in a chokehold and was barking orders. "Put your sneakers on; we're going for a ride." I had no idea how useful the sneakers were about to become. Flip-flops were the rule in the Sunshine State.

> *Early one morning, he happened to stop by*
> *Yelled in my window "Lets take her for a ride"*
> *Breakfast was calling as I crawled to the car*
> *My head hung over from drinkin' at the bar*

Lip had left his black Pontiac Firebird running out front. Nobody would dare drive off with his wheels. He'd seemed to instantly develop a fearsome reputation. Maybe it was his excessively loud conversational tone, the devil-may-care way he'd ripped the lower portion off all of his sleeveless T-shirts, or the pseudo jabs he threw at anyone he passed, just to watch them flinch. Maybe it was the scowl he wore even while smiling.

Lip's 1983 Firebird was trimmed with tinted T-tops that he carefully stowed in felt restraints mounted under the rear hatch, and a golden bird-of-prey emblem that stretched across its hood. The fresh wax job was already glistening in the rising Florida sun, reminding me to grab my sunglasses. I was hoping Lip would drive us to a greasy breakfast joint: Denny's, Village Inn, IHOP —I didn't care which one.

> *That new Firebird was his pride*
> *Midnight black, with black inside*
> *Gold bird of prey across the hood*
> *He's always washing it and shining it good*
>
> *Lets have some fun and take a little ride*
> *Just a speed run to the airport's other side*
> *We took off so fast I was glued to my seat*
> *Engine's howling whine, I feel the heat*

Instead, Lip drove the long way around the airport to the nearly endless, straight, deserted perimeter road. On the way, he rambled about how his transmission was occasionally slipping, his odometer was about to roll over 12,000 miles, and his warranty was about to expire, while he eased the speed up over 80 m.p.h. As a fledgling pilot, I wasn't averse to speeding, and the wind pouring in through the open T-tops helped me imagine what flying must have felt like in an open WWI cockpit. Manfred von Richthofen, a.k.a. the Red Baron, had his Fokker triplane; Lip, albeit on wheels rather than on wings, had his precious black Firebird. As the stereo blasted over the incoming air noise, I empathized with David Byrne of the Talking Heads when he sang the line, *You may ask yourself, well, how did I get here?*

> *From a distance I could see the Village Inn*
> *My stomach aching and I'm feeling sick & thin*
> *I saw it in his eyes, shoulda thought the worst*
> *It caught me by surprise when he slammed her in reverse*

Still traveling at nearly triple-digit speed, Lip muscled the automatic transmission lever into reverse without warning. I heard a metallic grinding clatter that wasn't part of the song, and then a violent thud. The car fishtailed. Through the windshield, the firebird emblem on the hood looked like it was jinking for some invisible serpentine prey as we danced with both edges of the road, and all four skidding tires screeched as if inspired by the wingspread, hunting emblem. I was thrown side to side while restrained in my now locked seatbelt. I'm no mechanic, but I think the transmission seized—exactly Lip's intention. He managed to stop on the right side of the road—mostly facing the correct direction. The air stank of burning oil and rubber, and there was a mix of gray and blue smoke. The pavement marked our progress over the length of our stop as if painted by a child just learning cursive writing. Or maybe the tires had spelled out lunatic in a long-lost foreign tongue. One thing was for sure—the Firebird, which miraculously remained upright, wasn't going anywhere under it own power.

This is where the importance of my sneakers came in to play. I asked him, "Why the hell did you do that? Were you trying to kill us?"

> *Engine screamed I'm sorry, tires squealed and smoked*
> *We suddenly came to a stop and he finally spoke*
>
> *"You don't think I wanted to walk back to the dorms alone, do you?"*
> *I want to keep this car, I want it like new*

It's a long walk back and that's why I brought you
Sorry about breakfast, I hope lunch will do
Thanks for the company, I can see you're not amused

I couldn't believe he'd dragged me into this mess just to become a hiking companion. Also, as an aspiring pilot, I felt that deliberately damaging any vehicle was sacrilege. I asked, "Why trash your new car? I thought you were in love with your Firebird."

"It's not new anymore. The warranty is almost toast. Didn't you hear anything I've been telling you? My dealership didn't believe my transmission was slipping, and I want them to replace it, not me in a few hundred more miles."

You see my warranty is up in just a few weeks
I'll have to pay out of pocket to fix all the leaks

"You're crazy, you know that?"

He stared at me with a toothy grin that mirrored the one he'd worn during our indoctrination speech. His jaw protruded, and both his upper and lower lips curled out in the first hint of a snarl in spite of his smile. It didn't require much imagination to guess how he'd developed his nickname. When Lip's lips finally moved, he said, "Well, now you're crazy, too," and we started walking.

Hung over, dehydrated, tired, and shaken up, I couldn't stop thinking that this must be part of that *education outside of the classroom* my orientation speaker promised. Was I cheating death while he was cheating on his warranty? We walked past the long, tangled black rubber lines in the road made by his tires —a symbol of this event that lasted beyond my eventual graduation. And many years later, the biggest challenge of my airline career would also occur outside of the classroom or the cockpit, and attrition would again be the subject. Was I supposed to accept attrition as an inseparable condition for learning to fly?

He never returned for the second semester
He probably went to jail or is some big investor
When the pages of life turn with time
and memories of friends turn to rhymes

Refreshing my mind of a dangerous time
That airport run is still burned in my mind
And that black Firebird, black as night
A symbol of my youth, before this boy took flight

11 | KEEP THE GIANT EMERGENCY LIFE RAFT INFLATED

Keep the Giant Emergency Life Raft Inflated

ON MY SUBSEQUENT VISIT to Dr. Oshiro, he quizzed me on his breathing exercises, and we practiced some together. Although I was still skeptical, I didn't want to continue feeling the depression I was hiding, so I'd read his book from cover to cover and tried to breathe along, sometimes with my chest, more often with my abdomen. In through my nose, then out through my mouth, I was instructed to feel my Ki energy.

I was still very angry but now also a little distracted. I felt like the distraught passenger who crewmembers are trained to assign hand-pump duty once everyone is safely inside the life raft after a ditching. It's a small bellows pump that's stored in the survival kit, and although it barely produces tiny sips of air, it's supposed to keep the giant emergency raft inflated. Its purpose is as much psychological as it is functional. The ranking crewmember in each raft becomes the raft commander once we're in the water. He or she is supposed to give this tedious task to the passenger creating the biggest disturbance, or the one most in denial, as a form of exhausting distraction. The genius is that this takes the most upset person's mind off the critical survival situation. He or she doesn't have time to worry about drowning, freezing, starving, or sharks while pump, pump, pumping away to keep us afloat. In my case, my gut and lungs became the emergency bellows, and my breathing exercises became my distraction from the feeling of absolute loss.

> *I see a giant yellow life raft*
> *In the crisis of my dreams*
> *No matter how hard that I pump it*
> *The more pointless that it seems*

The doctor was looking for a change in the expression on my face. If I was in emotional pain, he would see this as a sign of progress, and he wanted to see that instead of the flat affect I was previously hiding behind on my first visit.

In my head
The giant yellow raft was leaking
In my head
Water was spilling over the side
Oh In my head
The captain handed me a hand pump
In my head
I couldn't accept that she had died

"I feel like shit," I told him, "but I'm shitting well, and I want to go back to work."

"Very well, Mark. You have a long road still ahead, but I think you are willing to continue making each required effort that the mysteries of life deliver."

I felt as if I were listening to his Zen-master persona more than his M.D. degree, but I only needed either authority to sign me off. I smiled when he asked me, "Shall we call your chief pilot, share the good news, and schedule your return to the cockpit?"

Doctor Oshiro already had the phone in his hand. "Captain Schoelzel, I think Mark is perfectly OK to fly now." The doc knew I wasn't happy having to prove myself worthy of doing my job. He looked at me as he addressed my boss. "Do you want to give me a try and see how you do with an evaluation in my office?"

I started to laugh, and then I put my face in my hands so the sound wouldn't travel through the phone. Looking back, I think that phone call was staged in order to give me confidence as I returned to work. I didn't see the doctor smirk— he too could master a flat-affect appearance. I didn't realize how much healing I had yet to do. At the time I just saw this call to my boss as my pilot's license and airline ID being handed back to me.

Keep the giant emergency life raft inflated
Keep the giant emergency life raft inflated

In therapy
The hand pump was my breathing
In reality
It did more than keep me alive
In therapy
My breathing was my reminder
In reality
She would have wanted me to survive

12 | TEACHING IS A LICENSE TO LEARN

Teaching is a License to Learn

BACK AS A seventeen-year-old primary flight student, I was still making the transition from the hijinks of high school to the seriousness of college. After Professor Esser cut my shirttail, Mary became my Embry-Riddle flight instructor for the next course from post-solo through my private pilot's license. As she prepared me for this next level of aviation responsibility—a license that would allow me to fly without supervision and even grant me the authority to carry my own passengers, though not for hire—she rapidly grew tired of telling me that my hand belonged on the throttle from takeoff through 1,000 feet of altitude to keep the power from sliding back.

We'd discussed this in the cockpit before—over the wide variety of noises that makes conversation challenging. The cockpit is right behind the four-cylinder engine, much like in a car. But mounted to that engine is a six-foot spinning propeller that we look through while we fly. Sitting behind the prop wash adds a vaguely lawnmower sound to the engine noise. Next, the only significant ventilation in a Cessna 172 is provided through outside air scoops. Drive at twice the highway speed limit and then open a couple of side windows about a quarter of the way down for a similar effect. And Florida is hot, so leaving the vents closed is not a practical option. To defend against this onslaught of sound, we roll up small, cylindrical foam plugs and let them expand inside our ears. Then we make sure to face each other while speaking, and we shout. With the effort it takes for an instructor to impart wisdom during flight, Mary did not enjoy repeating herself.

Shortly after rotation in a Cessna 172, when I used both hands to pull back on the yoke, she asked, "Where does your hand belong?"

"Right here at the end of my arm."

This was not the response she was looking for. It earned me a lecture about treating her with respect, taking my training seriously, and on and on and on. The foam earplugs did nothing to defend me against this emotionally delivered lesson. It didn't help that my flight partner in the back seat couldn't stop laughing. I eventually had to admit she was right, but I remember feeling at the time that her reprimand was overdone in both length and volume.

Two years later I was sitting on the other side of that four-seat, one-hundred-and-sixty shaft-horsepower trainer and it was my turn to instruct. I'd made it through commercial, multi-engine, instrument, and certified flight instructor courses. I was assigned to teach advanced instrument training and commercial maneuvers. Many of my students would fly with me one day and then fly solo for a day or two to practice what I'd taught them.

> *My students and I sit side by side*
> *Sometimes it's a turbulent ride*
> *Sometimes new ones get terrified*
> *That's when I have to stay dignified*

I was at my desk — one of eighty identical metal versions spread around an open, circular instructor room — giving a last-minute briefing to Jim and John before our flight, when up walked our head mechanic with a look of fury in his eyes. He slammed down an aircraft clipboard that served as its logbook, which rang with all the subtlety of metal on metal. He had both my students' and my attention. "Look what your smart-alec student wrote in my clipboard!" He used his thumb to implicate Jim while looking at me and then continued, "Here, I'll show it to you."

> *Keeping a cool personality*
> *It's harder than it appears to be*
> *While flight instructing daily*
> *Teaching is a license to learn*

The mechanic picked up the clipboard, opened it, and then handed it to me. Having released some of his anger in the act of slamming my desk, he read out loud from memory what I could see was an entry from the day before, "Auto-pilot lands hard and the number three laser ring gyro is out of tolerance." Jim and I looked at each other, but the mechanic continued, "He may think it's funny making up stories, but writing up a hard landing in my logbook, even as a joke, requires me to do an airframe and gear inspection. The logbook isn't a coloring book, and our aircraft aren't toys. If he can't get that through his thick head, he can learn to fly somewhere else."

I waited to see if he was done. It looked like he'd continue if I didn't intervene, so I said, "Jim, what do you say to the man?" I hated making him feel like a child, but it seemed necessary to acknowledge the mechanic's point. I didn't just want him to go away, I wanted him to go away happy that he'd been heard loud and clear.

"I'm sorry, sir."

The mechanic opened his mouth to speak again, so I cut him off. "Well, I hope that just about covers the proper way to fill out a logbook. Lesson learned, don't you think?"

The mechanic said, "Don't let it happen again," and turned to leave. He reached three paces away and then turned and came back. I worried he had more venting to do. Instead he reached down and grabbed the aircraft clipboard from me, turned to leave again, and did his best storming-away impersonation. I had worked with him before and this was uncharacteristic of his nature. The logbook write-up must have really pressed a nerve.

> *Every mistake that a student can do*
> *Is a chance for me to learn, too*

Jim looked like a defeated man, and he seemed as if he expected me to add another chewing out to his day, right before we needed to go out and fly. Not much learning was going to happen that way, so instead I asked, "What's a laser ring gyro?"

The bad cop had left. Since I have a hands-across-the-throttles relationship with my students in the small Cessna cockpit, I was more than happy to accept my role as the good cop. It hadn't been so long ago that I was getting myself into trouble for inappropriate comments, though mine were verbal and Jim's written. Plus, I couldn't stop wondering what a laser ring gyro was. In addition to being a tension breaker, my question was a sincere request for information.

> *Keeping students from crashing me*
> *Giving advice and acting naturally*
> *While flight instructing daily*
> *Teaching is a license to learn*

I never asked what advanced aviation magazines Jim was reading or if he had a parent in the airline industry. I just knew that I still had a lot more to learn. My job was to find the best way to teach my students and keep my eyes and ears open for information that they were also able to teach me. I learned lessons that day on how to manage upset people, how to balance the stick and the carrot as learning tools, and I even picked up some advanced technical knowledge.

And I was getting paid for the experience.

And just an FYI, so you don't have to deface a logbook to find out, laser ring gyros are internal components with no moving mechanical parts that provide the guidance for inertial reference systems. Basically, they allow an airplane to know where it is without any outside navigation signal from the ground or a satellite. Cessna 172s obviously don't have them, at least not university trainers. But that didn't prevent me from learning about them while teaching in one.

I show students the proper procedures
How to handle the throttles and mixtures
How to plan for unexpected encounters
And how to emergency land into pastures

Keeping students from crashing me
Giving advice and acting naturally
While flight instructing daily
Teaching is a license to learn

13 | REALIGNMENT

SEVERAL DAYS after meeting with Dr. Oshiro, with chief pilot Shoelzel's blessing, I was back in my TWA Boeing 767 cockpit — a glorious 335,000-pound machine made for crossing oceans with only two engines.

One of the first things I did as I arrived for my flight was to align the aircraft's IRS navigation units. Their internal laser ring gyros needed to be turned on ten minutes before the aircraft is moved in order to align themselves with the rotation of the earth. I know that record players are rare these days, more so than in 1996, but imagine one with its needle tracking through a vinyl groove. Even though the record is spinning at the same steady speed, exactly like the earth spins constantly on its axis, the needle has longer to travel the further it is from the center spindle. That same concept applies to our location on the surface of the earth. The IRS navigation units feel how far they travel in the first ten minutes after being turned on, and that's how the aircraft knows what latitude the flight is starting from. Enroute points — that the aircraft will follow all the way to the intended destination — can then be loaded from the paper flight plan.

The earth kept rotating and the sun kept rising in spite of my impossible wish to go backwards in time. I struggled to feel my own internal reference system attempting to realign.

Word had spread that I'd been thrown off a trip and grounded, and that had one positive effect. Senior captains, pilots who had been flying for our airline since I was born, began calling me at Susanne's mom's house — my home number listed with the airline — during my absence. They all wanted to be the first to fly with me when I returned. A single captain's actions had made me feel unwelcome, and a whole lot of them went out of their way to encourage me back to work. Even with all the good will offered by my coworkers, it felt infinitely harder to become a functioning crewmember again than it did when I left college to make my way in the airline world originally.

14 | ST. THOMAS UPSIDE DOWN AND SPINNING

Island-Hopping Dream

"YOU'LL STARVE in the Caribbean," my boss said. The chairman of Embry-Riddle's flight department squinted at me in consternation as I turned in my resignation letter and showed him my one-way ticket to San Juan, Puerto Rico. He'd offered me a raise to continue flight instructing through the summer; instead I was leaving. We both knew I didn't have enough flight time to be hired by any of the regional airlines in the continental United States. I hoped the island-hopping air carriers navigating the gentle weather in the Lesser Antilles would be more open to a persistent rookie pilot craving the airline life. My now former boss was right; hungry days did lie ahead. I didn't know it yet, but I also hadn't taught my last flight student.

I was barely twenty years old and had packed all my worldly possessions into my 1975 Ford Mustang II, now affectionately known as *The Rustang* from all the time it served me on Daytona Beach, where driving on the actual beach is allowed, and sand and salt water had become intimately acquainted with my car's quarter panels and wheel wells. It was white with a tan roof and a crooked gray rear bumper — a junkyard replacement from a fender bender that I swear wasn't my fault. I couldn't see out my rear window or even the passenger side window, because my car was so full of stuff — books, clothes, leftover food, a fraternity pledge paddle, a TV, etc. — as I road tripped up Interstate 95 to my parent's house in Connecticut to unload everything before heading south on that one-way ticket.

After roughly twenty hours of driving, I was almost home. As a recent college grad, I was stupid like that, attempting to make the entire drive in one sitting. Like drowning within sight of shore, that's when it happened.

I'd left I-95 for the hillier, windy, and more scenic two-lane Hutchinson River Parkway. A blue, far-from-new station wagon with a young male driver was only doing fifty miles per hour in the right lane ahead of me. Like so many other times on this trip, I pulled out into the left lane and accelerated. His car disappeared from my view, obscured behind my burdened passenger seat, even before I pulled alongside of him. I kept my foot on the gas. My v-8 engine was strong but struggling with the heavy load and the steady uphill grade. I counted my usual five seconds — plenty of time to pass. My blinker was signaling my return to the right lane, and as I eased the wheel over, I heard skidding and then a horn trailing off behind me. The kid must not have wanted to be passed, and he'd stepped on the gas to block me. My confirmation of this would have been in the blocked rearview mirror. Finally his car appeared, headlights flashing, in my left side mirror.

He finally pulled close beside me — only inches away. His anger was clear even without the blowing horn and his extended middle finger. I laughed and then I shrugged. With my right hand, I patted the mountain of stuff piled up beside me. I watched his clenched teeth and flared nose loosen. Then his mouth formed the beginning of an oh as he grasped my situation.

It occurred to me that I'd need to improve my driving habits if I wanted to become a professional pilot. The other driver's temper had almost made us both pay for his unwillingness to let me pass, but I'd put us in that situation by over-loading my car, and I'd pushed my limit on fatigue as well — things to think about that also apply to airplanes. He must have realized his mistake, too, and stepped on the gas. His underpowered car pulled away in slow motion, its rattling pistons making more noise than power, giving me another good laugh and also lessons to think about. I stayed in the right lane until my exit.

Mom and Dad were glad to see me but not pleased about my clutter migrating its way into their house. Dad, however, still wears my *Big Daddy's Lounge Spring Break 1984* T-shirt, already two years out of date when he pilfered it from me. Mom pointed out that my vehicle was an eyesore in her driveway. She asked, "Don't any of your friends want to borrow your car while you're away?" Nice try, Mom.

In Frank Abagnale, Jr.'s book *Catch Me If You Can*, he regularly posed as an airline pilot to catch free rides around the world. This is a professional courtesy called jumpseating, and it's one of the big perks of the airline industry — free travel. Frank figured this out, and in the time before electronic record keeping, he was able to infiltrate this inner circle of aviators by impersonating one. In 1986, I had no intention of defrauding the system — I wanted desperately to become a legitimate part of it. Somehow I had to earn an airline ID. I was determined to return as a fully qualified airline pilot or spend the entire summer in the islands trying. I'd never sat on an airliner's jumpseat before, but I hoped that was the way I'd eventually come back home. Paying for a return ticket would mean failure.

I packed my bags
Left my winter coat
Went to find my wings
Left my folks a note
Bought a one-way pass
For S-J-U
Don't know where I'll end up
But before I am through
I'm coming back as crew
I'm only coming back
When I wear wings, too

I arrived in San Juan with more hope than money. The Luis Muñoz Marín international airport was very open air. With signs in both English and Spanish, it had the feel of an outdoor market. The sounds of cars arriving out front mixed with aircraft engines firing up out back on the tarmac, and between them were sandwiched a thousand conversations, footsteps, and computer keys tapping. The information desk volunteer guided me to a local bus.

My temporary housing was Ed's apartment — a friend of a friend from college. Actually, it was Ed's girlfriend's place, and I first met Barbie, a Georgia gal, when she answered the apartment door and I was standing there beside my suitcase — with two friends from Connecticut who had stowed away on the flight, a product of my going-away party that escalated a little out of hand. We were hovering at a level between freeloaders and bums. Fortunately both Ed and Barbie worked for an airline, and the vagabond lifestyle was not entirely new to them. They reluctantly agreed to put me up on their couch while I job hunted. My stowaway friends had to make their visit short.

We all stayed for dinner — peanut butter and jelly on toast and a pitcher of grape Kool-Aid — Barbie's southern hospitality shining through. "Sorry ya'll," she said, "fixin's are a little slim."

We were hungry, happy to have anything, and answered with a chorus of thank yous. My buddies told the tale of their stowaway adventure between bites. Barbie tried not to laugh, but her smile kept slipping through as the guys described their all-night going away party for me that was fueled by excessive drinking. This expedition eventually devolved into riding on the baggage carousel, outsmarting normally savvy ticket agents, and then hiding in the aircraft lavatory until pushback (that I swear I didn't know was happening at the time). Their misadventure was unplanned, and a lot of luck put my friends onboard with me. Much like in the movie *The Hangover*, many of the details were fuzzy.

Fortunately, we each still had all of our teeth, and nobody arrived with a face tattoo. A fictional account of this southbound journey appears in *Pushing Leaves Towards the Sun*, my first novel, available as a free audiobook. I recommend it for fans of the *Hangover* series.

After dinner, my buddies procured an alternate place to stay for a few days on the open floor of a friend's motorboat, absconding with half of the contents of my suitcase. I commandeered Barbie's couch and listened to my new hosts argue behind the bedroom door. I worried Ed would be thrown out along with me. If I had the resources to obtain alternative lodging, I would have, but I didn't. I wasn't sure how much longer my own tenuous welcome was going to last, so I needed to make every day of my job hunt count. I wanted an airline, any airline, to hire me so badly that I curled up under a sheet and pretended not to hear them fighting.

Ed and Barbie were struggling but were very generous with what they did have. When my friends were ready to leave Puerto Rico, I had to book and purchase their return flight on my starter credit card. Stowing away was a perfect storm of unintended consequences, and a repeat performance seemed highly unlikely to be successful. They elected not to attempt a sequel. Their tickets wiped out my $500 credit limit, and they tapped my pocket cash for airport food. They left me to job hunt with a half empty suitcase, far less cash than planned, and the memory of their stay on my first credit-card statement — as only sacred friends can get away with.

I visited every ticket counter and learned the location of every airline's backroom flight operations. I stalked chief pilots and paced from gate to gate to meet anyone wearing wings and stripes. Today I would have attracted the attention of Homeland Security with my extensive level of interest. In 1986, I was just an aviation-obsessed pest.

> *So I became an airport rat*
> *Begging to interview*
> *Every pilot that*
> *I ran into*
> *Is your airline hiring?*
> *I want to know*
> *Who will be acquiring*
> *More planes and grow?*
> *I want to be an F-O*
> *Copiloto quiero yo*

I shook hands with pilots at Crown Air as I tried to find out how to land a job in their nine-passenger Brittan Norman Islanders. They were friendly but offered little insight, except the names of various airline directors and chiefs for me to address in cover letters. I used Barbie's apartment as my stated address to appear, at least on paper, as a local. I didn't tell her this for fear she'd believe I was spreading roots in her living room. Ed flew nineteen-seat de Havilland Twin Otters at Eastern Metro Express where Barbie was also an agent, and they were trying to get me an interview with their director of operations, but its headquarters was over in St. Croix. Executive Air Charter flew Casa 212s scaled down to nineteen seats to avoid the need for a flight attendant (twenty seats or more requires one).

> *There are DC-3s*
> *And Briton Norman Islanders*
> *The Seaplane Shuttle*
> *And de Havilland Twin Otters*
> *Every island in the Caribbean*
> *Is connected by air*
> *But who needs another pilot?*
> *I'll take any job, I swear!*

My first choice was to fly for Aero Virgin Islands because they were flying aviation history — Douglas DC-3s. The other airlines' pilots snubbed them as Aero Pterodactyl, but I begged to be able to fly the thirty-passenger model of the Gooney Bird. Their base of operations was St. Thomas, and I sent messages to their chief pilot on every flight for days. I wondered how many hand-delivered notes it would take to attract his attention. It was my version of floating messages in bottles. Some contained my résumé and my recent experience as a flight instructor. Because of the raffle-ticket rule — *You must be present to win* — all of my notes expressed some version of "I am here in the islands and ready to go to work." I was doing everything I could think of to be noticed, short of jumping up and down and screaming, and that wasn't out of the question.

> *The hardest part about any job is getting it*
> *The hardest part of any dream is forgetting it*
> *And if my dream takes longer than expected*
> *And if it feels like I'm endlessly rejected*
> *I'm gonna do what I have to do*

There were a lot of DC-3s in San Juan that were amazingly still not retired. These classic airliners were serving out their remaining life in the snow-free, temperate climate of the Caribbean. I saw silver ones with "**** Four-Star Air Cargo" printed on their sides and dark blue beauties hauling loads for Borinquen Air. These birds inspired me to locate the doors of more chief pilots and keep knocking. My flight deck hunt was racing against the latitude changes of the summer sun — fall without a job would mean failure and a return to flight instructing — and both my lodging and my finances were running out far faster than the change of seasons.

Persistence paid off, and Aero Virgin Island's chief pilot finally sent word that he wanted to meet with me. His note included a jumpseat pass — the first I'd ever seen. I was to present this paper first to the San Juan ticket counter and then to the captain of a flight to St. Thomas. I couldn't contain my excitement and did the Toyota *Oh what a feeling* leap with my arms stretched over my head. I dressed in the best of my remaining clothes and added a necktie to look as formal as possible. Ed and Barbie advised me to shed the tie, that the dress code in the Caribbean was laid back and relaxed, but I ignored their advice. When I met the captain at the designated gate, I noticed he wore his uniform shirt with the collar open. Ed and Barbie were right. I had a lot to learn about local culture.

As the morning flights were loading, the captain led me into his ship from the main rear-boarding door. It was an uphill climb through the cabin, past the flight attendant, twenty-four passenger seats, cargo netting, radio racks, and into the cockpit. Where modern aircraft have plastic formfitting interior walls, this classic bird had gray quilted padding like the kind moving companies use to protect furniture. In many places I could see through to the exterior bare-metal skin. Tubes carrying wires looked bent by hand. Exposed wire was wrapped in black electrical tape. What was left of the worn interior paint job must have been applied in the original factory. In a word, this cockpit was *functional*. No attempt had been made to make it aesthetic, and I loved it even more for its pure sense of purpose.

DC-3s predate tricycle landing gear — a nose wheel in the front, followed by a pair of wheels under the wings that affords a more level attitude on the ground. This was a tail-wheel aircraft with two big forward wheels and a small castoring one in the back that allows for steering.

After the captain and the first officer climbed into their seats, they instructed me how to fold down the jumpseat into the cockpit doorway and fasten the five-point restraining harness. I felt like an umpire behind home plate. Short of being one of the pilots, this was the best seat in the house. From my perch in this great old bird, I marveled at the sheer amount of levers, knobs, instruments, and apparatus compacted into such a small space. There were nooks and crannies everywhere. This was not the ergonomic arrangement found in modern aircraft. I assumed that everything was installed where it had to be based on 1930s technology rather than situated in the ideal location for the pilot.

The first officer handed me a bulky black headset and plugged me in to hear what they and air traffic control were saying. Each of them had modern, green David Clark headsets with gel-pack ear covers — the kind that even ooze around the stems of sunglasses for complete comfort while muffling outside noise. The one I wore must have been issued with the plane when it was new. The ear pads were long past dried out and more sharp than padded. They did nothing to cut down on the engine noise once the wing-mounted radial pistons fired up. I could hear the pilots, but it sounded like a friend yelling in my ear from the front row of a rock concert while the guitar player blared away with full distortion.

I read a statistic that dust in human environments is composed largely of dead skin cells. If that's true, and if the great aviation writer Ernest K. Gann ever flew this particular DC-3, he might still be in here in some microscopic way. Surely some of his compatriots, who paved the way for modern commercial aviation, have left their DNA in this cockpit. Ernest K. Gann's memoir, *Fate is the Hunter*, is dedicated to three hundred and ninety-seven pilots whose wings were forever folded before its 1961 publishing date. This aircraft was made during an era when aviation wasn't considered safe by the general public, and those early aviators were true pioneers.

Ernest K. Gann delivered mail in DC-2s and DC-3s on Air Mail Route 21, between Newark and Cleveland, in the 1930s and 40s. He knew what it was like to fly these seventy-five year old birds when they were new. He wrote, "The DC-3 is an amiable cow, grazing placidly in the higher pasture lands, marvelously forgiving of the most clumsy pilot. Its immediate predecessor, the DC-2, is not such a docile beast although from a distance the unknowing can easily mistake one for the other."[1]

My own experience began with the unfamiliar nose-high pitch that the aircraft maintained with all three wheels on the ground. It sniffed the air curiously until we were rolling fast enough for the captain to raise the tail wheel off the pavement, lowering the head of this metal beast like a bull fully established in a charge. Then I finally saw the remaining runway out in front of us. During takeoff I sat silently, but I later asked and was told that the copilot would fly the leg back. They alternate. Everything about this cockpit experience was new to

---

1 Gann, Ernest Kellogg. *Fate Is the Hunter.* New York: Simon and Schuster, 1961. 28–29. Print.

me. The first officer used hand gestures in addition to his scratchy voice over the interphone to signal safe flying speeds: Vee-one (takeoff decision speed), Vee-r (rotation speed), and Vee-two (takeoff safety speed). Likewise the captain used an aggressive thumbs-up command to order the first officer to raise the landing gear.

Outside the seascape revealed its majesty with a surreal splash of the full-color Sunday comics. Framed through the forward rectangular windows like folded newspaper segments, no other medium can portray the natural over-lapping outlines of shoreline, horizon, and sky, yet maintain the clarity of the Caribbean luster. The light blue softened stratosphere, well above the reach of the DC-3, was sponged with puffy clouds ending at infinity where they joined the turquoise water — which changed shades with its depth and whatever was blurred below the surface. I imagined myself someday scuba diving the coral reefs and sandy bottoms. We passed smaller islands and the winding beaches of Culebra, Spanish for snake. The first officer pointed out his window as he gave me the tour. I could see the potential for living and flying down here to become paradise, if I could only land a job. I wanted this lifestyle with the relative urge of an adolescent just discovering the opposite sex.

Inside, power was adjusted and propellers were trimmed in an attempt to synchronize them. Out of sync, there's a steady wah-wah-wah that sounds like an out-of-balance washing machine in the spin cycle. In this very hands-on aircraft, both pilots were constantly making adjustments. The cockpit never fully cooled below crock-pot temperatures, even as we leveled off. Again I'm reminded of Ernest K. Gann's words as I appraise the captain in charge of this flight. "Minute rivulets of perspiration glisten along the side of his forehead. The rivulets meet where the earphones press against his flesh and form larger tributaries which finally join along the line of his chin and slide downward to his collar." [2] Now I understood why Caribbean pilots don't wear neckties.

The faint smell of burning oil from the engines and the musk of metal that has served faithfully long past its intended service life is probably not consid-ered a pleasant one, but to me it was and still is. I love all this moving machinery, alive for generations, that's graceful in spite of its age. This is exactly where I wanted to be. My jumpseat pass felt like a grand-prize winning raffle ticket.

After half an hour, the island of St. Thomas appeared as a dot on the horizon. We were cruising at 3000 feet. The first officer pulled a checklist from his flight kit, and we received clearance for a lower altitude. The captain reduced the power, and it looked like the first officer was working a pump near the floor.

2 Gann, Ernest Kellogg. *Fate Is the Hunter.* New York: Simon and Schuster, 1961. 2. Print.

Maybe he was priming the hydraulics to put down the landing gear? I thought about old-time wells — not the stone-lined shafts with a bucket on a rope, but the wells with wobbly hand cranks. Later, electric pumps took the arm work out of this effort. The DC-3 was old school for sure, but just how primitive were its systems? The Wright Brothers' first flight was in 1903. The DC-3 has been around for three-quarters of the aviation era. I was in a time warp — and loving it.

Two runways eventually appeared ahead. We lined up for the shorter one. The tower cleared us for a visual approach and the copilot acknowledged the clearance. I noticed the captain also acknowledged the copilot in what I later learned was looped communication. The captain touched down on one wheel at a time by holding a wing low into the wind — the right front main gear first, then the left main gear, and finally he flew the tail-wheel onto the runway as our nose again pointed to the sky in triumph. It was an impressive show. The longer runway reaching out into Charlotte Amalie Harbor was still under construction and covered in x's.

After the passengers disembarked, the lone flight attendant handed me off to a gate agent who escorted me upstairs inside the terminal. In a back office I finally met the Aero Virgin Island's chief pilot. He stood to greet me. Not many people are taller than me at six foot four, but he was. He looked athletic and strong, with a dark complexion, a cleanly shaved head, and a pressed uniform. We shook hands, and I handed him yet another résumé. He said, "I've been receiving these, thank you. Your interest in my airline is noted. I'm not sure when I'll be hosting another DC-3 ground school, but I'll be sure to keep you in mind."

"Captain, do you think you could loan me a manual so I could teach myself the systems ahead of time, anticipating your future need for a pilot?" Having come this far, I wasn't going to be dismissed empty-handed, and I craved a chance to learn the DC-3.

"Ah, Mark, the DC-3 systems are quite simple. You'll have plenty of time in class to learn them should the opportunity arise. In the meantime I have a more immediate need. I have someone I want you to meet."

In my eagerness to meet the chief, I hadn't noticed the dark-haired pale man, about my age, sitting in the room. Gary was a light-aircraft ground school instructor for the flight school the chief ran on the side. The chief tossed a single key on a chain to me and said, "Gary needs a spin endorsement to complete his certified flight instructor rating so he can take students up," and then he excused himself. A spin endorsement is one of the last steps to becoming a flight instructor, and the last thing in the world I expected to be doing here.

I was confused, but before I could wonder about the sincerity of the chief's DC-3 ground school opportunity, Gary had me out the back stairs and onto the ramp where the smaller aircraft were tied down. I decided to go with the flow. Maybe this little favor was a test of my résumé accuracy. I looked at this flight as a professional challenge and hoped the chief would be waiting to interview me upon our return.

We walked around a Cessna 172, the same kind of aircraft that I taught in at Embry-Riddle, except this one was only tied down under the wings. The tail tie-down ring had been ground down, probably by being dragged on the runway during over-rotation on numerous practice takeoffs and landings. I pointed this out to Gary and he said, "Don't worry about it. It's been that way a long time." I realized I was no longer in the sheltered world of my university where even the smallest repair was made right away by a team of mechanics.

Gary took us off and we climbed to 6,500 feet, which took a long time in the Caribbean heat. We stayed over the water east of St. Thomas, and I demonstrated the proper way to induce a spin and how to recover. First I slowly pulled the aircraft nose up into a stall, where the slipstream of air no longer flowed smoothly over the wings because the aircraft deck angle became too high, then I pushed in full rudder to start the plane rotating and the corresponding wing dropped out from under us, sending us into an upside-down, nearly violent gyration as we fell and twisted like one of our wings had been pulled off. The feeling from the cockpit is like an over-the-top amusement park ride. Seatbelts need to be tight, and it's best not to perform this maneuver on a full stomach.

Ocean, beaches, hotels, pavement, assorted sun-reflecting vehicles, steep tree-covered hills, and corners of sky became a swirling mish-mash soup of blurry colors, though still surreally identifiable. My firmly pressed foot on the rudder was causing this extreme motion, which seemed out-of-control, yet gracefully expected. Our aircraft was behaving according to unbreakable aerodynamic rules. A specific sequence of power manipulation, neutral ailerons, opposite rudder, and elevator movement would restore us to straight and level flight. I didn't expect to see St. Thomas upside down and spinning when I bought my one-way ticket to migrate down to the islands, but it was good to be at the controls of an airplane again and having fun.

We lost about 2,000 feet in a hurry but climbed back to 6,500 feet before starting each subsequent maneuver, and eventually I was satisfied that Gary could perform this with his own students. While spins have been the deadly descent of many disoriented pilots, they are a known condition. Once recognized, proper recovery technique can restore order to the aircraft if sufficient altitude remains. For this reason, every flight instructor must be able to recognize and recover from a spin, and that day, St. Thomas was the postcard-perfect backdrop for this lesson.

Gary landed in St. Thomas. I figured I should be sure he could do that successfully, since I'd be signing his logbook. As expected, he was a pro. When we returned to the office, the chief pilot was nowhere to be found. On his desk was another jumpseat form filled out in my name. My reward for performing this instructional duty was a free ride back to San Juan. I asked Gary if he knew when the next DC-3 ground school was going to be held. He was blunt with his reply. "The boss has been promising me a DC-3 training slot for a long time. That's why I'm managing the flight school for him. With this spin endorsement I can finally get my CFI and start teaching flight students, but I haven't seen anyone recently hired by the airline that wasn't a local. My guess is that he's stringing us along."

The ride back to San Juan was bittersweet. For the second time I sat in an airline jumpseat. This was likely to be my last time up front until I wore a pilot uniform. Now that I'd tasted the airline pilot life — observed what flying looked like from a skybox seat, smelled the worn leather, and touched the metal handled by generations — my craving for commercial cockpits was fueled to overload.

The trip to St. Thomas was exciting but a dead end. The DC-3 opportunity had just been a ruse to lure me to finish training the flight school's newest flight instructor. Or perhaps the chief pilot wanted an outside evaluation of Gary's ability. Regardless, it was still a new experience for me to teach outside of my degree-oriented university. I was young and hungry for flight time and opportunities, and a day in the sky beat a day handing out résumés.

I made it back to Ed and Barbie's couch and reported my job-hunting progress, or lack of it. I'm sure they wondered how much longer I was going to be their guest. They were polite, but I could feel the strain on their generosity. I considered sleeping on the beach to give them some relief and privacy, but nobody would hire me if I looked like a vagrant camper.

In subsequent days, I rose early to be the first one out of the house. I hated mornings, but hoped I could stretch my stay if they saw me as little as possible. I wore out the Luis Muñoz Marín Airport terminal halls with my pacing from counter to counter, gate to gate, and office to office. I ate *empanadillas de carne* on even days and *empanadillas de queso* on odd days in the employee cafeteria once I learned its clandestine location and the door entry code. These treats were meat or cheese fried in dough, and they were delicious and cheap. I brought home groceries for the refrigerator and gave Ed money for booze from the duty-free shop when his flights included an international destination in the British Virgin Islands. Pusser's was the BVI favorite rum, and we drank it straight or with Kool-Aid. He was still trying to arrange an interview with Eastern Metro Express for me over in St. Croix.

The hardest part about any job is getting it
The hardest part of any dream is forgetting it
And if my dream takes longer than expected
And if it feels like I'm endlessly rejected
I'm gonna do what I have to do
Still I'm gonna do what I have to do

I never thought the reason I'd obtain a job was because my new friends wanted me out of their house, but that's how I finally caught a break. A new hire de Havilland Twin Otter ground school was scheduled at Ed and Barbie's airline. Barbie was an operations agent and cashed in a favor to get me off her couch. The vice president of flight ops called me at her house and said I could sit in on the upcoming school. I wasn't actually hired over the phone, but I would be able to learn the Twin Otter's systems and the company's procedures.

There was an ultra-cheap inn right at the St. Croix Airport, and I was going to receive free turboprop training and a chance to be evaluated by an airline. I rejoiced in the hope and possibility of employment. I flew to St. Croix on a one-way complimentary ticket. It wasn't a jumpseat, but the captain left the cockpit door open, handed me an extra headset — not a new one, but a product at least younger than I was — and I bugged both pilots throughout the entire flight. I tried memorizing pitch and power settings. I asked about every island we flew over. I read the checklists over their shoulders, and I'm surprised they didn't unplug my microphone. I'm sure I was hyperventilating through the interphone into their headsets.

15 | HYDRAULICALLY ACTUATED

EVEN AFTER TWA RESTORED ME to flight status, the downtime between 767 trips was the hardest on me, especially while living alone in Susanne's mother's basement in Connecticut. My closest friend Warren invited me to move in with him and his fiancée Laura in lower Manhattan. We all hoped the city that never sleeps would help keep my mind off losing Susanne. Their Tribeca apartment bordered the West Village and Soho, and the three eclectic areas offered a plethora of things to see, do, and eat. They handed me a Zagat guidebook and told me to never let them hear me say I was bored. We lived just north of the World Trade Center where those Twin Towers still stood proudly over the financial district.

One day my buddy T came to visit, and I took him to my gym at Chelsea Piers as a guest. When we arrived, my indoor sand volleyball league was about to start a game.

"Mind if T joins our team?" I asked.

My teammates all agreed, we were a man short otherwise, but the referee said, "No."

"What do you mean, no?" I asked, "He's my guest today, and I'm not going to play if he has to sit on the sidelines."

"I can't allow any nonmembers in league play."

"There's no money involved," I pointed out, "or trophies, or even significant bragging rights riding on the outcome of this game. This league, as you call it, is purely for fun. We need a player; let him join us."

"No means no." He was a kid who looked like he was barely out of high school — maybe he'd just finished a growth spurt and he hadn't yet filled out into his lanky body — and he seemed to be on a power trip, so I stormed off. I was pissed. My fury multiplied exponentially. Under an emotional microscope my anger cells would have divided, subdivided, and then re-divided again. This minor setback upset me far more than it should have. Grief has an anger stage and I was neck deep in it. Actually, I was in well over my head. The slightest provocation had made my blood pressure rise like a hydraulic jack with a heavy hand pumping the handle, which felt like it gave me raging strength. Those stories we've all heard of moms lifting cars off of their babies after an accident, super power conjured from the adrenaline of a desperate moment—I felt it that day. Cage fighters and cornered combat soldiers should have that kind of rage, not me.

T followed me to the weight room. I put more weight on the bar than I'd ever lifted before and then easily bench-pressed it ten times. I was a lean 210 pounds and on my best days, I could barely do a single rep of my own weight. A football coach once told me that pressing one's own body weight should be the goal of every healthy male on the team. Two forty-five-pound weights on either side of a forty-five-pound bar totals 225 pounds, and I'd just pumped it ten times, seemingly without effort. "Ten more pounds a side," I yelled at T. He didn't know what weight I should be working out with, so he added the extra twenty pounds without questioning. I pumped it ten more times, and then I bolted upright as the reality of my accomplishment scared me. I didn't know what my blood pressure was at the moment, but it must have peaked. It was whatever my skin could contain without bursting.

My muscles wouldn't loosen. I felt like one giant knot, as if I were a puppet and someone had yanked on all my strings at once and then tied the slack so I couldn't hang loose anymore. I felt bunched up in a continuously painful way, but not from the weight training. It was purely psychological.

During this rage of power an image formed inside my head. I felt pressurized by a subconscious stream of yellow, the color of some antifreeze but without the greenish hue. I know this was all imaginary, but it felt so real. I could feel yellow fluid compressing through my limbs. I've seen a small hydraulic jack lift my Chevy Blazer and larger ones hoist two-ton trucks. I know that the flight controls of my aircraft are moved against the powerful air stream with three thousand pounds of hydraulic pressure. That's how I felt inside—hydraulically actuated—although aircraft hydraulic fluid is actually red, so I don't know why my imagination portrayed it as yellow. Perhaps it was a subliminal derivation of the phrase, "You're full of piss and vinegar," that my dad used to say when I was a kid. Regardless, I was convinced it wasn't muscles and ligaments that were moving my arms and legs; it was hydraulic leverage, and I couldn't shut it off or turn down the pump pressure.

Over the next year, I experienced that same feeling intermittently. One time, I held a solid plastic ashtray in my hand, and suddenly it burst into a dozen pieces. The fragments were sharp, but I didn't suffer a single cut. None of the friends I was with could bend or break one, even using two hands or stomping on them. I watched in horror as they tried. The restaurant manager didn't like it, either, but for different reasons. I felt as out of control as Bruce Banner when he turned into the raging Hulk, with just as little control over the anger. My buddy Warren still reminds me that I once vaporized one of his cordless phones. I didn't crush it; I suddenly bubbled with fury and gave it an expensive flying lesson that ended against a wall. Warren didn't laugh.

I lost track of time. The goals that had marked my calendar — Susanne's and my house closing, wedding, honeymoon — were all gone and I'd reverted to day-to-day living. My airline offered me more people to talk to and I made, as if on autopilot, the necessary appointments. I only went back once more to see Doctor Oshiro for a follow-up after he gave me clearance to return to flying, but I had his breathing exercises and occasionally returned to them when I felt the need.

What was left of my life was that I still had a job to do. I flew for a major international airline and had an open ticket to the world, but there was nowhere I wanted to be anymore. My life had traveled full circle from desperately craving that first island-hopping airline job to coasting vacantly between continents.

16 | PILOTS OF THE CARIBBEAN

Pilots of the Caribbean

Tryin' to Get Off-Island

AT THE INVITATION of Eastern Metro Express, my new home on St. Croix, U.S. Virgin Islands in 1985 proved that even paradise has a hidden orifice for eliminating waste. The condemned airport inn next door to the airline's flight operations was a *first-class* dump. *First* because it was the first place of lodging in terms of proximity to the planes, and *class* because that's where ground school was held and my entire class chose to stay. That it was a *dump* was exceedingly obvious even to the most casual observer. Worse still, it was located in the shadow of the island's actual rubbish dump. The inn's owner refused to stop renting rooms until the bulldozers arrived to level the place. Nobody knew when that would happen. Progress in the Caribbean moved slower than road kill.

Every pilot had to pay his dues while building flight time, and the regional airlines knew that sky-crazed junior aviators were willing to fly for nothing, just to get into a cockpit and convert jet fuel into black smoke and noise. When nothing is what you asked for, nothing is what you got, at least during training.

I was as hungry as any hopeful island hopper and overrun with enthusiasm when Eastern Metro Express let me sit in on a DHC-6 de Havilland Twin Otter ground school. For them, I was a no-cost item. At any other airline, we'd be considered new hires, but here we were merely potential new hires. This was an airline audition. I tried to be optimistic and look at this opportunity as an extension of college, without the need to pay tuition.

With a whopping $875 a month before taxes waiting for us if we were hired and after we were qualified and generating revenue for the airline, this airport inn met our three basic needs: cheap, cheap, and cheap. This was a food stamp-eligible salary even by 1985 standards, but the position still held a magical influence over me as the entryway to the major airline pilot-hiring pipeline. I tightened my belt and reminded myself that I wasn't here for the money.

Let's call the inn owner Hank. Like his hostelry, he was sleazy. He kept endless mono-gender porn running on the VCR over the bar. Hank's sarcastic answer when a new patron asked for a videotape change was, "What's the matter, don't you like sword fights?" However this inn and attached bar were the only hospitality available to those of us without transportation and living strictly on a beer budget. On the bright side, Lone Star bottles were only a buck apiece.

The rooms made for the pièce-de-résistance. They opened to a sidewalk and the empty parking lot, and that's what was good about them. There was no internal hallway, no business center, no workout room, but there was a pool — filled with a milky sludge. It could well have been the primordial slime out of which our amoebic ancestors first crawled. I shared my room with two other pilots. Three beds, our stools at the motel bar, and the room used for ground school constituted the limit of our existence.

I spent as little time in my motel room as possible. Before sleeping, I had to do a walk-around inspection of the pillow and sheets. Incredibly long millipedes, roaches the size of half dollars, and rats too clever to be seen but which could be heard chewing inside the walls, infested the accommodation. Placing a foot into a shoe without shaking it out first was a mistake I only made once.

Crawling out of bed one morning, still tired from the never-quite-feeling-safe-and-secure sleep that I'd managed to log, I slid my foot into a Timberland Docksider. Over-boiled linguini was the first sensation I felt, except it was also fuzzy and it moved on its own volition. The creeps, with a side of squish, is how my mind recorded it — except the foot-long, curled-up, multiple-footed milli-bastard didn't die. It crawled out of my shoe immediately after my foot made its hasty retreat. Letting out a screech that would have made any braces-wearing hysterical teenage girl proud, I smashed it with my other shoe and watched it splatter. The resulting cleanup made me skip both breakfast and lunch, not that I could afford the luxury of two meals in a row.

I have to shake the millipedes from my shoes
It's just a another part of paying my dues
But there's a runway just outside of my back door
That's all I care about, and that's what I'm here for

Behind the motel was the airport and that city landfill upwind. The sound of garbage-shoving bulldozers lulled me to sleep at night. Miscellaneous rotting smells blew in our perpetually open windows. The barely moving air of decay, accentuated by a ceiling fan that made more noise than provide any useful circulation, was preferable to roasting alive.

We did, however, have a view. If I looked past the parking lot, over the two-lane highway, and past the unused dirt racetrack, a sliver of ocean was visible. It was un-swimmable at this site, though, as the island refuse disposal site and the motel were sandwiched between the free world's largest oil refinery and the Cruzan Rum factory. Nice beaches were on the opposite side of the island, but they were a significant left-side-of-the-road drive away, even if a car could be procured.

All this could be overlooked for the chance to move up into the airline hierarchy. Commercial aviation was the seductive Siren's song that lured me through all obstacles and discomfort. An outsider might see this setting as a place of suffering, but I only saw opportunity. A four-year aviation education and the dream of becoming an airline pilot allowed me to wear blinders so that I only saw the goal straight ahead. If this is what it meant to pay my dues, I was going to do it with a big smile.

> *I'm a pilot of the Caribbean*
> *Just Another F-ing First Officer*
> *But I'm burning jet fuel and logging turbine time*
> *From the right seat of my Twin Otter*

I thought about my friends back at Embry-Riddle in Daytona Beach, still instructing, living on ten-cent oysters and washing them down each night with dollar Heinekens at the Silver Bucket. They were training U.S. Air Force cadets from their initial familiarization flight through first solo — the summer contract the school had procured with the military that I'd turned down, even with a raise. Better paying work for sure, but it was still single-engine reciprocating flight time for all involved. They would kill to be here, I reflected, barbaric conditions or not. This was the elusive first multi-engine job, and an airline one at that. It was the key to the kingdom of commercial flight. Compared to them, the two PT6A turboprop engines powering the Twin Otter that I was learning about put me on a career track well ahead of those still living comfortably back in Florida while keeping new students from crashing. I'd traded their $20,000 annual flight instructing salary, with an endless supply of students and the freedom to make their own schedule, for half that income with living conditions worse than camping, but it was a negligible price to pay. I'd never before flown an airplane big enough that I couldn't see on top of the wings while standing on the tarmac. Although the Twotters were old, the white with two-tone blue paint jobs were new. I performed every walk-around inspection with pride as if the aircraft were my own.

While most of my peers stayed content in their pristine and sheltered university world, I took a chance connecting the ports once roamed by pirates. My environment mattered not at all compared to the feeling of really making it into a commercial cockpit. I was still technically a flight instructor, but once I completed training, I could call myself a first officer. Soon I knew what beta-range was, and a host of other new terms as I learned my first turbine-powered aircraft. (Beta-range is when the pitch of the propeller is controlled by the power lever instead of the propeller lever, from flight idle to maximum reverse. It is a feature unique to turboprop aircraft engines.) I aced the ground-school exam, answering only one question wrong, yet I never heard the end of that single mistake from my roommate who scored a perfect one hundred percent. The exam determined our class seniority, so I received the number two slot. My snarky roomie called me junior, but we both would soon learn that the captains of this airline had other less complimentary names for us all.

We were collectively referred to as JAFFOS. In the 1983 movie *Blue Thunder*, the second person in the cockpit was described as a JAFO, which stood for *just another fucking observer*. So we became JAFFOS with *first officer* subbing for *observer* in the acronym. Disparaging qualifiers aside, the magic words first officer were printed on my very first airline ID, and that's all I really cared about. The ID came at the end of 2.6 combined hours of flight training and a checkride, all conducted on the same day by one pilot. Captain Leo Wood was the entire training department at Eastern Metro Express as far as I could tell. He'd given me the week of classroom ground school and the instructional flying. I knew I'd passed when he said, "Go buy yourself a uniform," with no indication where I might do that.

Leo handed me my first set of airline wings with the company logo in the middle — a white dove that doubled as the letter M against a blue oval — and then he shook my hand. I was sent to admin to smile for the laminated ID card with a shirt clip that I could have made myself at any office supply store. The one-dollar Lone Stars were on me that night.

Ed bequeathed a pair of epaulets and a white shirt to wear them on, after an urgent phone call. They arrived from San Juan via co-mail — a way of shipping company material between bases that was just one more small part of the airline world that was becoming unveiled to me. In his Brooklyn accent Ed said, "Don't even think of asking me for a fuckin' necktie, JAFFO."

This was the time of Tom Wolfe's *The Right Stuff*. That best-selling book had become part of the airline pilot culture's collective idea of what pilots are made of. We took pride in our suffering and meager wages as a right of passage in order to make those engines suck, squeeze, bang, blow, and screw (that's literally how turboprops work).

The de Havilland Twin Otter is a STOL (short takeoff and landing) aircraft with fixed — rather than retractable — landing gear that's made for harsh terrain. It's the off-road vehicle of regional aircraft. But the pilots I flew with in the Twotter were the real story. The lifer pilots drawn to this high-wing beast aren't looking for the fast-lane experience of jets; they're bush pilots and rugged individualists.

Four hundred years ago pirates roamed the Caribbean, and in the 1980s the same archetype prevailed—only they took to the sky instead. I'm not talking eye patches, wooden peg legs, potty-mouthed parrots, and yo-ho-ho-and-a-bottle-of-rum, but the island flying did seem to attract oddball refugees from all over the world. We were a rough, competitive, and sometimes predatory group, and I did my best to fit in without becoming trampled.

One captain at our base was called Two-Ton. He was a large mammal, and my peers weren't particularly kind when assigning nicknames. This was the mid 1980s and well before the politically correct movement, and sensitivity training wasn't included in our brief ground school. There was no shortage of testosterone among my cockpit cronies, and no pilot escaped hazing — especially an oversized target. Captain Two-Ton was the Eric Cartman of our clan, long before the cartoon comedy South Park was conceived.

Pilots boarded the Twin Otter through exterior crew entry doors on either side of the cockpit. This is an unusual configuration for a commercial aircraft. It was a big step up from the ramp, and there was a foot peg and doorway handhold to assist ascension to the flight deck. Like everything in aviation, it was built with the small-to-average person in mind.

I boarded our Twin Otters from the copilot's side — on the right — and watched the spectacle as Captain Two-Ton began his day. With both hands he hoisted his giant leg up to the foot peg, then grabbed the doorframe and the handhold while he started deep breathing like a skin diver about to attempt a record plunge. First he rocked his 4XL body to build momentum. When his arms, legs, and trunk were all orchestrated in the same direction, he heaved himself up, landing on the near corner of his seat, which shook the Twotter on its shock-absorbing landing gear. After folding himself into a position where he could reach the controls, he rewarded himself with a cigarette — the first of many throughout the day. The Twin Otter was unpressurized, so he flew with his cockpit side window partially open while he chain-smoked. I didn't like the secondhand smoke—a term I hadn't yet learned—but I counted the minutes I'd be adding to my logbook and passed the time with a forced smile.

The guy did have a huge heart, both literally and figuratively, but he was subtly abrasive. He often told me, "I've flown this airplane solo many times," implying that copilots weren't necessary. "Read the checklist to yourself if it makes you happy," was another passive-aggressive statement he used to show he preferred flying single pilot.

Captain Two-Ton liked to show off. Everything was a competition to him and he had to be better than his crew at flying, landing, navigating — you name it. His routine was to be bossy and demanding, while offering an endless supply of food to compensate for any harbored ill feelings. I steeled myself against careless comments and welcomed the salami and crackers, Gouda and French bread sandwiches, assorted chips, and salsa. Indeed, he was very generous with his victuals, and I was careful to always thank him for — and from — my full stomach. During level cruise flight, he would occasionally brag about deeds of daring, such as engaging the Beta-Range in flight (at a previous, foreign air carrier where apparently it was allowed) even though the practice was a strictly forbidden procedure in our flight manual. He explained that using Beta on short final approach allowed the engines to spin up to full reverse thrust by the instant the aircraft touched down. He boasted about how extremely short that would make his landings — tucking the aircraft into the tiniest unimproved runways further down the island chain from our scheduled service — and that he could measure his stopping distance in aircraft lengths rather than hundreds or thousands of feet. The risk factor for this procedure made it valuable only for combat operations during a war, which of course we weren't fighting. I believed him, although he could have been bluffing. Nevertheless, I didn't need to see a demonstration. My job was to watch and learn, but sometimes I thought we were playing scare the copilot.

Captain Two-Ton really did know the aircraft down to its last knot — its absolute limit. Flying with him was like participating in a test flight. As unorthodox as he was, he let me see how far the rugged bird could be pushed. He was also a master of the full flap takeoff — that another pilot was about to blow in a big way. It's only the luck of seemingly random scheduling that I wasn't the copilot on this upcoming infamous flight. We — the breathing baggage in the right seat — often had little choice but to sit down, shut up, and hold on.

On empty legs — ferry or reposition flights without passengers — captains sometimes took off with the flaps all the way down at 37½ degrees. This effect caused the plane to lift off using only a few hundred feet of runway with the main gear coming off the ground first, before the nose wheel. The nose-dipping skyward launch resembled a helicopter departure, and it was exciting even for an experienced pilot — especially so for a rookie JAFFO.

One day, a captain we nicknamed Glideslope tried this. At least that's what many of us surmised. Nobody but the two pilots onboard will ever know for sure, but we believed Captain Glideslope's nose wheel-steering tiller wasn't completely centered before he pushed the power up and began his dual propellers' bite into the moist morning air. When the aircraft began lifting and the main gear parted company with terra firma — and all of the airplane's weight was transferred to the nose wheel — the Twotter shopping-carted full left. I shudder to imagine the instantaneous stomach-sinking feeling he must have felt — like hitting black ice on a curving highway and suddenly facing the pavement's edge head on. The aircraft slid off the side of the runway and hit the orange and white glideslope shack at full takeoff power. It was a disaster for both the aircraft and the high-powered equipment on the ground. Luckily neither pilot was crushed or electrocuted. They both walked away from it, but Captain Glideslope didn't return to work.

Another captain we called Nap-of-the-Wave. If we had an empty leg, he flew it at fifty feet above the water, sometimes even lower. When an airplane flies at a height less than its wingspan, it floats on a trapped cushion of air producing what is called ground effect; or in this case, sea effect. I felt like we were trawling and I needed a fishing pole. He rarely flew above a whopping — for him — 1,000 feet even when we had passengers onboard, barely keeping us legal. Nap-of-the-Wave was a good captain to fly with while fighting off an impending cold — at an airline without paid sick leave — because maintaining a low altitude meant no substantial pressure changes and subsequently no impact to my sinuses.

Ranting Roger was one of the most senior pilots at our little airline. He always seemed bitter, but really he was a lot of fun. On empty flights with him, he made me put all the seatbacks down in the cabin — they could be pushed down flat like a lawn chair — and then he floated me in zero gravity. That's the true sensation of flying — hovering like an astronaut through the top of vertical parabolic arcs and then plopping down on the padded seatbacks as the aircraft leveled off and the pull of the earth's gravity took over again. I didn't have enough weightless time to try any flips or stunts; I simply soared like Superman with my arms stretched out. It was three-dimensional freedom like scuba diving, without the pressure of breathing under water. This little trick would get me in trouble at my next airline where I took this practice with me. But for now, I enjoyed flying Twin Otters and also floating inside them. There was nothing like flying an airplane, devoid of passengers, and seeing what it could do.

Regardless of the captain, my favorite place to fly in the Caribbean was Virgin Gorda, the third largest and second most populous of the British Virgin Islands. The airport was nothing more than a shack with a British customs officer next to a 3,000-foot crushed-shell runway.

The Virgin Islands and Puerto Rico
Just some places, that you know that we go
Beef Island on Tortola
The crushed-shell runway of Virgin Gorda

The first time I flew over Virgin Gorda, my captain asked me to look for any other traffic on approach. I asked, "Where's the runway?"

"You've never been here before?" he replied. "You're in for a treat."

"No, seriously. Where's the runway?"

He set up an approach pattern, and I thought he was pulling my leg all the way until we touched down — on what I thought was a beach. This is the type of flying that the Twin Otter was built for, and I learned to appreciate it. In contrast to the dark, underworld life back at the inn, this was paradise personified. Only a casual artist's brush could hope to capture this corner of creation to reveal its heart. Even the sun relaxed here in a folding lounge chair, pausing from its daily traverse, and this is truly where no necktie belonged, except maybe as a tool to dabble paint on canvas or as an omen nailed to the immigration checkpoint by way of a symbolic reminder that this is the antidote to civilization. Moisture hung in the air to give this marvelous utopia a permanent shimmer, a reflective shine.

Virgin Gorda is home to The Baths, a geological formation which makes this second only to Machu Picchu as the most beautiful place on earth. Delivery truck-sized warm, gray boulders appear to have been strewn and stacked across the beach by giants, making a warren of caverns and caves where the tide meets the shore. Bathers scramble under, over, and through this natural maze where a mermaid is more likely to be encountered than a Minotaur. Wooden ladders and knotted ropes help navigate the tricky parts. If ever there was a location naturally made for a centerfold or fashion shoot, where the sun, sea, sand, and stone feel divinely interlaced, this is it. The little restaurant up the hill from The Baths makes a killer frosty Bushwhacker too, for folks fortunate to find this island oasis on holiday.

The only time I actually flew while sick was with a captain whose last name was too long to pronounce. It seemed to have more letters in it than *Snuffaluffagus*, or even that railway station in Wales: Llanfairpwllgwyngyll-gogerychwyrndrobwll-llantysilio-gogogoch. We called him New Jersey instead. His accent was eastern European mixed with the Garden State.

We started before dawn. I became a bit achy and developed the cold sweats as the day went on. Before landing in San Juan, I filled a barf bag to the brim. Captain New Jersey told me to sit tight and he'd do everything for the remaining legs—perform the preflight, print the paperwork, handle the radios, and fly the airplane. We didn't have standby pilots, and he didn't want to lose any flight pay. I didn't realize I'd developed a 104-degree fever by the time we eventually returned to base. When I showed the thermometer to my chief pilot so he'd know I wasn't faking, he found another first officer to take my flights the next day, at a resultant loss of pay for me. If I wanted to make up the flight time, I'd have to go to the trouble of finding a pilot willing to surrender his trips.

Another pilot we called Mr. Gravity, and not just because his favorite Lone Star clinking toast was, "Don't take gravity lightly—it's a law." One night after the bar closed and we were all walking along the outside of the motel to our rooms, our inebriated toastmaster attempted to use a credit card in the lock instead of his flat plastic room key. Soon he was leaning against his door. His slouch deteriorated with repeated failed efforts. As we circled around him, one pilot announced, "He shoots, he misses, he shoots again."

Mr. Gravity finally collapsed against his door and slowly spun around while sinking to the ground as his feet slowly slid out from under him, also in slow motion. Our pilot commentator added, "No goal!"

In the last desperate moment of consciousness our door-denied hero dropped his credit card, looked us over, and pronounced, "Mean old Mr. Gravity."

The commentator closed out the event with: "Defeated by technology. Show's over, folks."

Like shameless deserting wingmen, we left him there. We figured he wasn't any worse passed out in the fetal position outside his door than inside his room with all the uninvited pests. We were a mutinous bunch bonded by our love for the air, the sea, and a carefree vagabond lifestyle with our futures tied to helms of galleons that took to the sky. Sometimes I felt more like a pirate than a pilot in the Caribbean.

As much of an adventure as island hopping turned out to be, I couldn't fly every day, so I traded trips to build extended blocks of time off whenever possible. I relished the travel benefit my Eastern Metro Express ID and accompanying union card provided, and I was eager to explore new territory, but the majority of jet airliners leaving the Caribbean departed from San Juan. Island fever quickly ran rampant in my veins and I heard a rumor that a freight carrier could transport me off of St. Croix in the quiet of predawn, if I stood outside of the airport firehouse and hangars in time for his nightly package pick-up. I decided it was worth trying.

St. Croix is beautiful
Someone said to me
It's more like a trailer park
In the middle of the sea

The hotel I'm living in
Has been condemned
One-dollar longnecks
Are my only friend

Tryin' to get off-island
In the middle of the night
Need to get off-island
Before morning light

Alone on the tarmac with my travel bag and my flight case (that was emptied of charts and filled with six underwear-wrapped bottles of Cruzan Rum—a perfect fit), I waited in hope for a ride as the distant sound of an airplane buzzed in the otherwise silent 4:30 a.m. sky.

I heard a rumor
I could catch a flight
With a mail plane in
The middle of the night

So I'm standing on the tarmac
With a flight bag full of rum
Here comes a couple of props
And I stick out my thumb

Tryin' to get off-island
In the middle of the night
Need to get off-island
Before morning light

The BN-2 Britten-Norman Islander that approached looked like a Twin Otter that had shrunk in the dryer—high wing, conventional tail, twin engines, and fixed landing gear. After the two Lycoming engines were shut down, a lone pilot shoved bags out of the plane, and it was quickly reloaded. As the work neared completion, I timidly approached the pilot and asked, "Sir, would you mind giving me a ride to San Juan?"

Tryin' to get to San Juan
To catch another flight
If I get to San Juan
I can make it home tonight

I was dressed in my uniform because I thought it helped me look like I belonged on the ramp, especially in the dark when the airport was mostly closed. The pilot recognized my wings and asked, "*Volando para*, um, you fly for Metro?"

"*Vámanos*," he said, when I replied that I did. The aircraft was big enough for eight or ten seats but they were all removed for cargo except the two in the cockpit. He was flying single pilot so the copilot seat was all mine. He fastened a net over all the loose duffle bags before climbing into his seat.

He started the engines, we taxied, and then took off in no time since we were the only ones awake at that hour. We made a sweeping left-hand turn and pointed northwest toward Puerto Rico. My new friend said, "Vieques is hot," while unfastening his seatbelt, no sooner than we cleared the hills north of the airport. He hopped into the back of the Islander and lay down on the netting. I think he was asleep before I realized I was flying. Recognition came slowly. First I was startled, then nervous as I grabbed the control yoke in acceptance of my new role as a working pilot. Next, I was hyper-aware as I needed to plan the flight and acclimate to the unfamiliar cockpit. I speculated that my sleeping pilot must have been up all night flying solo.

Vieques is hot, he said
So the ride won't be boring
Before I know I'm flying
He's asleep in back and snoring

It's just me and the sun and sky
And the endless blue sea
Sitting in the cockpit
I'm finally free

Vieques (pronounced *Vee-ay-kess*) is an island between St. Croix and Puerto Rico. Half of it was inhabited, and the other half was used as a practice bombing range for the U.S. military. When it wasn't being used, I'd flown over its lunar landscape. Craters of all sizes pockmarked the ground. When this airspace was closed for exclusive military use, it became a restricted area, and all other aircraft had to fly the long way around it. That's what the pilot meant when he said it was *hot*.

I chose the circuitous southern route and flew over the rainforest of Puerto Rico. El Yunque looked majestic in the sparse light creeping over the horizon — dark mounds reached to the stars that were fading as the night slowly washed away. Visibility was unlimited, but I eased the aircraft up to 4,500 feet to be sure to clear the highest peak. Unlit rainforest can be deceptive. I hadn't been trained on the Islander's specific systems, but it handled a lot like what I was used to in the Twin Otter. As I eased over the hills and descended toward the expansive city lights, I set us up for a long base leg that would lead to a single right turn to line up for landing. The sun was coming up in the east just in time to shine in my eyes as I turned onto final approach for runway ten, the southern of the almost parallel runways.

I really wanted the landing, but my conscience intervened. I shook the yoke and bounced the cargo around a little bit. This caught my new pilot buddy's attention as he flopped around in the netting.

"What? Huh? Oh, *sí*," he said as he struggled back to the captain's seat. "Thank you, *mi amigo*."

He pulled a pair of oversized, gold-framed, green-lensed Ray Ban aviator sunglasses from a leather pouch that was buckled onto his belt, a style that screams, *I'm a pilot!* These had ear loops instead of stems, the kind I hate to wear because they pinch my ears under a David Clark headset. He put a hand on the yoke and another on the throttles.

"Thank you, *mi amigo*," he repeated. I guessed that was his way of telling me he had control of the airplane again. Although I lost the opportunity to land an Islander that morning, it was my first time pressed into service as a relief pilot — a position I would later get used to on widebodies transiting the north Atlantic some years later at TWA.

After loosening the netting and dumping the duffle bags on the San Juan cargo ramp, my new buddy showed me where to stand to hitch a ride from this area of the airport to the main terminal on a baggage tug, fuel truck, or catering vehicle. I made it to Eastern Airline's gates in plenty of time for my choice of flights during the 7:00 a.m. push.

I don't know where I was ultimately going on that particular trip. My first likely stop was back to my university in Daytona Beach to trade stories of island flying for free meals from my fraternity brothers and former flight instructor coworkers. After that it was on to anywhere. I was a new wind unleashed upon the world and excited by that freedom. At the time I had no thoughts of settling down, saving money, building a family, or even embracing the responsibility of a girlfriend. I had a ticket to go anywhere, with adventures waiting for me to find them.

Tryin' to get off-island
In the middle of the night
Need to get off-island
Before morning light

17 | TEAM MARK

On the 20th Floor

I WOKE UP EACH MORNING in a bed that Susanne and I had picked out together. I returned to work for TWA—the same airline where she'd spent her final moments. Moving on from real-world disaster—TWA Flight 800, a Boeing 747 that claimed my fiancée as one of its 230 victims—is not so easily accomplished. If the human brain uses wrinkles to store information, mine had carved trenches to store seemingly endless accident and investigation updates about the aircraft wreckage that was delivered by gravity in so many pieces from the sky, through the ocean's surface, to its depths.

I looked at myself wearing my uniform in the mirror—three gold stripes on each shoulder, wings pinned to my chest, and the logoed necktie (a requirement since leaving the heat, humidity, and informality of the Caribbean). Who was I anymore, if not an airline pilot? Could I ever wear these ornaments again with pride?

TWA had me flying again, as a copilot on Boeing 767 aircraft from New York to prominent European cities. I avoided Paris as much as possible, although my dad insisted it was just another destination. My seniority allowed me to hold an equal mix of trips flying as the working copilot or as the designated relief pilot, but either way I was on perpetual autopilot, and my airline noticed.

While shaking off a six-hour trans-Atlantic time zone change and trying to make sense of the world without Susanne in it, TWA's Director of Special Health Services Johanna O'Flaherty greeted me with her traditional big hug when I returned to JFK from a trip one day. That was the warm-up for her true purpose. She's a woman with both grace and charm, but I could see a mission focus in her disarming eyes.

After pleasantries and small talk, she assigned me a mentor — or maybe Johanna used the word *counselor*—named Nancy. Upon deeper inquiry, it was revealed that Nancy was a company-sponsored psychologist. Nancy, and other trauma specialists, had volunteered or been recruited to work with TWA's many crushed souls after so many of our airline's coworkers and/or family had been lost on that single widebody flight. This is a side of an airline that most people never see — the human side behind the pressed uniforms and aviator sunglasses, where there is no printed emergency checklist to calm overwhelming emotions, no flight simulator to practice coping skills, and no technical manual on grief that could be studied and mastered. I was stranded in a land of despondency more foreign than any continent I'd ever visited. I had no maps in my flight kit to guide my feelings. Instead, I was offered a guide in the form of a petite woman with short dark hair, who worked at the United Nations and also had a private practice.

Johanna scheduled me to see Nancy every other week for a year. Did I resist? Of course I said no at first, but Johanna assured me — charmed me, actually, with her soft compassionate touch and lilting Irish accent — that this was entirely off the record, at the company's expense, and I could quit at any time. She emphasized that I didn't need permission from Nancy to continue flying like I did the company psychiatrist, Dr. Oshiro, who had cleared me to return to work. Stoic and stubborn as ever, I tried to resist, but Johanna's hypnotic gaze tethered me. Psychology was a perfect fit for her personae. I had to swallow my pride in order to allow her words to sink in, and then accept Nancy as my new counselor.

The bimonthly visits were promoted as a one-on-one discussion opportunity so that TWA could be sure I had someone who wasn't also grieving on my personal Team Mark — hence the outside consultant. For privacy, I was to see Nancy at her private practice instead of at the airline's Special Health Services facility.

Her office was in a Manhattan high rise. It wasn't actually hers; it was a temporary rental. Finding an unrelated name and apartment number on the lobby directory, and then waiting to be buzzed in after I dialed it up, made our midcity meetings feel clandestine.

> *On the 20th floor*
> *She's waiting for me*
> *She opens the door*
> *For my therapy*
> *On the 20th floor*
> *Office of psychology*
> *My counselor*
> *With a grief specialty*

Psychologists must all be huggers. That was Nancy's greeting, too. The twenty-story view was typical for New York City. I could see across the street into another building if we decided not to pull the curtains. I didn't know what to expect from meeting with a psychologist. There was no clinical feel to this setting. There were no medications on display, no diplomas on the wall; in fact the office was very clearly borrowed, devoid of all things personal. The office could have hosted a lawyer, a real estate agent, or just about anybody when Nancy wasn't using it.

> *The session begins*
> *With a big hug hello*
> *And she's never the first*
> *It's me that lets go*
> *She opens our session*
> *With how do I feel?*
> *My eyes are open*
> *But nothing feels real*

Session one was a meet and greet. It seemed I was supposed to guide our future discussions. It wasn't like you see in the movies; I didn't lie on a couch. We talked face-to-face and we didn't talk about childhood ad nauseam, although there is the death of my baby brother Daniel buried back there in my early years —abstract and distant unless deliberately recalled. In contrast, I wore Susanne's death as unabashedly as putting my underwear on over my uniform. And still it surprised me when psychology professionals noticed.

Nancy covered the basics: Why am I here? What did I expect to get out of our time together? Was I aware that everything I said was going to be kept confidential? I assumed correctly that she'd been briefed on my situation, which I imagined was boiled down to one line in her notes: Pilot's fiancée killed on his airline's jumbo jet.

This was "my time" that my airline and Nancy had set aside. Anything and everything was open season. Mostly I just wanted to ask, "What the fuck?" Not out of disrespect, but because the scope of what happened on July 17, 1996, seemed just too big to break down into manageable bites.

> *I get through my days*
> *From sun-up to sunset*
> *In a repetitive haze*

Through eyes that stay wet
So she offers to listen
And she nods once or twice
And only when time's up
She offers advice

There are no easy answers
There's no quick way to heal
There isn't a short cut
Through the pain that I feel
She walks me to the door
And she hugs me once more
Until the elevator opens
On the 20th floor

On the 20th floor
She sets me free
Until I need more
Of her therapy
On the 20th floor
Office of psychology
That's where I store
My broken side of me

18 – CUTTING MY WINTER TEETH

The Box the Twin Otter Came In

NO CLEAR-CUT PATH leads to a job with a major airline, but even while building turboprop flight time in the Caribbean I had my ideas about what else I needed to do. My internal Magic 8 Ball was pointing me in the direction of ice and snow. Building the right experience and connections are, of course, necessary, but each pilot also has to figure out his own way to stand out in a competitive market where military, corporate, and regional airline pilots are all fighting for the few new-hire slots offered by the big airlines.

I knew I was already lucky to be flying DHC-6 de Havilland Twin Otters in the Virgin Islands and Puerto Rico at my first regional airline while still so young, but the allure of perpetually sunny skies also had a down side. Fair-weather flying would earn me a patronizing pat on the head from the hiring departments I had my eyes on, not the hearty welcome-aboard handshake that I craved from an international air carrier. Island hopping around paradise was fun, but it seemed very minor league. In the 1980s, regional pilots were starting to gain the respect of the major airline hiring departments who traditionally preferred military-trained aviators. Revealing that I was based in the Caribbean was like having an asterisk next to my flying record. The footnote would then clarify me as less than worthy: no winter experience.

My best shot at cutting my aviation winter teeth was back in the northeast where I grew up. By 1987, independent regional airlines feeding major carriers were expanding. I needed to continue climbing the professional aviation ladder, and just like my previous marketing efforts, I sent out many a message-in-a-bottle. With a lucky tide and a persistent wind, my résumé found its way to the right person's desk. "Do you know any pilots at Command Airways?" asked Christine Morehead, the director of human resources, during my initial interview in Wappingers Falls, near Poughkeepsie, New York.

"I think so," I answered. "Maybe my old college roommate." This was before the age of cell phones and I'd become isolated down in the islands.

I'd brought with me an ATR-42 regional aircraft postcard that Howard had sent me. For job-hunting inspiration, I'd slipped it into the frame of my San Juan bedroom mirror when it first arrived. He'd written that he was flying them for Command Airways. Unfortunately, he'd stretched peer and fraternity-brother rivalry a little too far. "That name isn't familiar," Mrs. Morehead said. "Let's find him. Follow me."

I left my briefcase beside her desk, and she walked me down the hall to a small office where she showed me a wall-mounted seniority list of every pilot that was ever employed by Command—a thin line drawn through the few that had left. The low attrition rate was a positive sign that the pilot group was happy—an environment I looked forward to. We both looked for Howard's name, but it wasn't there. Clearly he had been pulling my chain with a little wishful thinking on his part. I felt that my interview was in immediate jeopardy, and right then I wanted to find him and deliver a bruising slug to his arm—the fraternal way to right internal wrongs.

I could feel the sweat building under my armpits and was glad that the jacket of my only suit concealed it. In desperation, I scanned the list for familiar names but came up blank. "This looks like a list of people I want to know," was the best I could come up with to say.

Mrs. Moorhead smiled politely. I could tell she found me amusing, but we both knew I wasn't acing this interview so far. "I grew up just over an hour from here," I said in an effort to recover from this seniority-list setback. "I'm anxious to learn how to operate in the heart of New York's airspace, which is the core of your route system."

"Well, Mark," she replied while nodding to the list, "we like to think we're famous for our pilot retention. If we did hire you, we'd want to be sure you'd feel at home here."

"Let me grab something from my bag." I wasn't stalling; I needed tangible proof that my name belonged on that exclusive pilot seniority list. I dashed to her office and returned with my National Airlines Official Junior Captain Certificate that I'd received on my first flight from JFK when I was three. Although I couldn't remember him, I could still read Captain Lowman's signature. I handed it to her and said, "The northeast is where I belong. I've been building my turbine time in the Caribbean to gain experience, but this is where I want to be."

She apparently liked my enthusiasm.

As it turned out, Howard was flight instructing across the field from Command's headquarters. He'd met a lot of the Command pilots socially and must have figured they would hire him before I resurfaced from down south in the islands. In the end, I was accepted. It was Howard's turn to be surprised when I later sent him a letter about my new employment, on Command's letterhead, borrowed from Mrs. Morehead specifically for the shock value. But I had to meet the VP of flight operations first.

J. Kevin LaWare made a point to scrutinize each pilot hired at Command. He invited me into his office with a firm handshake. When offered a seat, I sat up straight. He picked up my résumé and we reviewed where I was flying and went to school, and then the serious, double-edged questions began. "What would you do if the captain you were scheduled to fly with showed up drunk?"

I resisted the urge to avert his gaze while I pondered my reply. After all, the answer wasn't written on my shoes. "I'd refuse to fly with an intoxicated captain," I began, "and urge him or her to seek help from human resources or I'd be forced to report him." Somewhere there was a balance of doing the right thing for safety and being a team player as a crewmember. I hoped my answer acknowledged both. Captain LaWare kept a straight, unreadable face and looked at me unblinking. I met his silence with silence and waited for another question. If he wanted me to elaborate, he was going to have to request it.

"Under what conditions would you take the controls away from a captain?"

"First officers take the controls away from captains only in a life-threatening emergency such as if the captain were somehow incapacitated." I knew my place as a right-seat pilot—somewhere on the food chain below plankton.

"Would you report anyone operating one of my aircraft unsafely?" Now Captain LaWare's hands were folded across each other on his desk. I felt like this was the make-or-break point, the loaded question, and all the money was riding on my final answer. I wanted to use a lifeline and call a friend, but nobody could earn this job for me.

"I'd have a word with the infracting individual first," I said, while trying to gauge his reaction, "and go to management only if I believed the threatening behavior wasn't going to change."

He reached across his desk for a second handshake. His welcome-aboard speech was a combination of *we are a family* and *it's important to do things correctly and safely*. I was the 239th pilot ever hired in the airline's twenty-one-year existence. Pay was only $18,000 per year, but that was nearly double what I was making in the Caribbean. Captain LaWare emphasized that his door was always open. I hoped not to wear out his hallway carpet, but once in my new uniform, I'd find myself in that hot seat again answering uncomfortable questions.

I became a Shorts 330 first officer. That's second in command of a thirty-passenger seat airplane with a square, boxy fuselage. Instead of a single tail like most airliners, the unpressurized, twin-turbine 330 has two vertical stabilizers, each with a rudder. The main landing gear doesn't retract all the way, giving it a comical, nonstandard look in flight, but the airplane is safer than most to land with the gear up in an emergency that requires it. For an airliner, it may have been *fugly*, but at least it was slow. Whenever anyone laughed at how pokey it flew, I told them I wasn't paid by the hour; I was paid by the minute. On the bright side, at over six feet tall I could almost stand upright inside its cabin. In other turboprops (and even many modern regional jets) with their cramped, tube-like interiors, I have to nearly double over to crawl to the back.

One day, while my flight was taxiing out for takeoff behind another Command Shorts 330 at JFK international airport, the tower cleared the next aircraft to "follow the pair of Shorts." I snickered, but my captain had heard all the jokes before.

When our turn came, we took off and contacted departure on a preselected frequency. The controller asked, "Can you increase your rate of climb?" He wanted to make way for jet traffic behind us.

We were full of passengers and already doing the best climb rate we could manage. My captain replied, "Sorry, we have a load in our Shorts today."

I stroked my ship's sidewall like I was encouraging this square bird to give us all she had.

> *The tower asked us to climb a little faster*
> *Sorry, but with thirty passengers there's no way*
> *I told him, "We have a load in our Shorts"*
> *I could hear him laughing as he said, "OK"*
> *The Shorts was very slow*
> *Much slower than a jet*
> *But I got paid not by the hour*
> *But by the minute; that's better yet*

Approaching Philadelphia, a heavy Airbus was told to follow us visually to the runway. The widebody captain advised over the radio, "We just lost that Shorts in the trailer park," insinuating that our aircraft was ugly and it blended in with the background. I patted the top of the instrument panel as if comforting her hurt feelings.

> *As we neared our destination*
> *Approach told another plane to follow us*
> *"Negative sir, we can't see him against the trailer park"*
> *Said the snarky captain of the larger Airbus*
> *He can try to hurt my feelings*
> *But I still love to go out and fly*

The box the Twin Otter came in
Even if it's the biggest joke up in the sky

We lived with a reputation of flying Winnebagos with wings. Even as the object of comic relief for the jet jockeys, I was excited to be part of the greater game. Flying among the big birds was my drug of choice, and every trip into JFK or La Guardia was my own personal adrenaline rush. One day I received more than I bargained for.

My captain that day was Jerry Meader—one of my favorite people to fly with—but nobody called him by his given name or his airline position. He was affectionately known as the Colonel with respect to his U.S. Army rank. I've never met anyone who shook so many hands and wasn't running for office. Jumpseating pilots, ticket agents, sometimes even passengers would acknowledge him and ask how he's doing. Every time he'd reply, "Better than momma makes." He had a handful of colloquialisms that covered every occasion.

With a jovial smile and perpetually rosy cheeks, the Colonel never wore a long-sleeve shirt. He radiated warmth; I had to buy a surplus U.S. Army sweater, the kind with the shoulder flaps for my three-stripe first officer epaulets, to stay comfortable while flying with him in cold cockpits. The Colonel liked being able to see his own breath. I later learned during the harshest winter months to double my socks and occasionally wear fingerless wool gloves, also Army surplus, or I breathed on my hands. But this was a small price to pay in order to fly with such an enjoyable character. I was young and learning, and exactly where I wanted to be in time and space and personal experience. Already bundled up as fall started, I was working the radios as the Colonel lined up to land on runway two-two at La Guardia.

Passengers often told me they thought they were going to land in the water because the shiny charcoal-brownish reflection at the end of Long Island Sound was all they could see from their side windows as we descended until right before touchdown on runway two-two, which starts on a pier. From the cockpit, it's normally an impressive approach by the Throgs Neck and Whitestone Bridges toward painted pavement, which seems to reach out to meet us, with the Manhattan skyline ahead and just off to the right. The bone-white control tower protrudes from the terminal area, with sporadically spaced, hatch-like round windows, and it looks as if it belongs underwater in Captain Nemo's ocean world. This landmark would last until its taller modern replacement in 2011. When I recall this moment, the image my longing mind recalls feels captured in colored chalk. It's as if the airport's edges and the New York skyline were rasterized in dusty, straight, but imperfect lines. It's an artistry that my brain has given a nostalgic feel, in spite of my conscious wish to recall the moment cleanly and clearly as an event rather than a moment.

In every other way, this is the home of jets, and what I think of when I conjure an image of a real airport. La Guardia and JFK are where I visited as a kid, gazing in awe at the heavy metal finding its way up into the sky and eventually returning safely back home to drop off and pick up more people. To actually be a part of this process supercharged me. And if I was daydreaming at all, I was suddenly shaken back into the moment.

The Colonel and I were following a Boeing 757 that had just landed, and we were inside the final approach fix, less than 1,500 feet in the air, when the invisible force rocked us. Suddenly the Colonel was no longer beside me—the plane knife edged sideways and he was suddenly straight up above. Behind him, our left wing pointed skyward and the one on my side was aimed directly at the water. We'd hit the preceding Boeing 757's wake turbulence, and it rolled us instantly into a hard right bank. I'd felt my body spin but my stomach hadn't caught up yet. Small unsecured items like pens and charts rattled around the cockpit. My body absorbed the bite of my lap belt and the snap of my shoulder harness inertial reel as it locked. The number twenty-two painted on the runway was now on its side, along with my perception of everything else.

The Colonel pushed the left rudder pedal full forward and the interlinked returning right pedal drove my knee almost up into my lap. Simultaneously, he rolled the yoke full left deflection so our ailerons could help battle to level us. For a second all motion except our steady downward-sloping forward progress stopped as we popped out of the vortex and the flight controls bit into undisturbed air. Then our ship righted, which is to say we snap-rolled left until level and then rocked a bit as the Colonel settled the airplane exactly back on our intended flight path.

"Are you still going to land, or go around?" I asked, after I made the required 1,000-foot callout.

"Better than momma makes," the Colonel replied. His touchdown was smooth, and right at the fixed distance marker in the heart of the touchdown zone. He pulled the propellers through beta range and into reverse, then gently braked.

"That's the worst I've ever been waked," I said, as the Colonel cleaned up the cockpit—setting our transponder and radar on standby and re-tuning our navigation radios, while he was turning off the active runway as if nothing had happened. He was already readying our plane for our outbound flight, so I took his lead and brought up the flaps and zeroed the stabilizer trim—the first part of my after-landing duties.

"Hell of a way to run a railroad," he said. He was unshakable.

If he wasn't worried, I knew I shouldn't be. No doubt he had at least twenty thousand flying hours and had seen it all. I barely had ten percent of that number, but I was quickly building valuable experience. Next time I followed a 757 I'd insure we had additional spacing. That much I learned for sure.

I'd been bumped around by wake turbulence — the disturbed air that forms rotating vortices off the tips of other aircraft's wings — before. Flying across one, the downward jolt can make a pilot feel like he's been thumped on the head. The upward air follows with a swat in the butt. But drifting into one of those invisible air cones from behind causes Mr. Toad's Wild Ride to happen very quickly. Aircraft flying into rotating air rapidly become unhappy, and spacing rules have evolved to avoid this from happening.

The bigger the aircraft, the more distance we require behind it. Aircraft over 255,000 pounds add the word heavy to their call sign to alert pilots and controllers of their additional wake-turbulence risk. Out of respect for the rotational force they produce, we give them extra room. The Boeing 757 was certified under that arbitrary heavy weight, which means it didn't have the wake turbulence respect it deserved in the early days of its commercial service. Now it's well known that a 757 has almost as much punch as its heavier, widebody sister, the 767, and both require similar spacing requirements. I gained my respect for 757 wake turbulence the hard way. The rare design of those twin tails on the Shorts 330 offered a lot of available rudder, and right in the slipstream of each of its engines. That airframe anomaly helped save the Colonel and me.

A few weeks later, my boss, Captain LaWare, called me into his office. He made a point of clearing his time for me by putting aside the paperwork he was working on, folding his hands in front of him on his desk, and asking me, "Did you roll the airplane on your recent flight the other night?"

I thought back to my experience at La Guardia with the Colonel and started to tell him about the wake turbulence, even though that was a daytime flight, but he cut me off.

"Too long ago. That's not the trip I'm referring to." He clarified, "Actually, I meant last night — not last week or last month. Did you roll your airplane while flying back here to Poughkeepsie?" His voice and his eyebrows went up as he finished the sentence. He was wearing his uniform instead of a business suit. Of course he had the four worn stripes of a seasoned captain. My three stripes were still shiny and new. I knew he was qualified in both pilot seats and could replace me on a moment's notice if he felt the need.

"No, sir! The only airplane I've ever rolled was a Bellanca Decathlon back in college, and that plane was made for acrobatics." I instinctively opened my hands, palms forward as if I had nothing to hide.

"Did you do anything unusual with the aircraft?" He was looking me straight in the eyes with hypnotic concentration.

"We did have an empty plane on the final leg back into Poughkeepsie. Our flight attendant wanted to know what it was like to fly."

"So, you let a flight attendant sit at the controls in an aircraft entrusted to you?"

"Oh no, we didn't do that," I responded, sitting up tall and indignant. "She pushed all the seatbacks in the cabin down flat and spread out across them. Then we gently eased the airplane through a slow vertical arc. With her arms outstretched like a bird, we were able to float her around back there for about ten seconds at a time. We made her weightless. She told us she'd never had so much fun at work."

I waited through painful silence. Would he fire me? I loved my job, perhaps too much. This was my first aircraft type with a flight attendant onboard, and she was a knockout—and fun. I couldn't help wanting to impress her, and making her float was easy. It was simply a matter of unloading the lift like a carnival ride. Push forward on the control yoke and everything inside the plane wants to drift toward the ceiling. We usually do this gently enough that passengers barely feel it and don't complain. More aggressively, it's the same way astronauts obtain their weightless training, but their aircraft has a specially padded interior and is nicknamed the Vomit Comet. Nobody onboard our fun ride puked, so I thought we had gotten away with it clean. Without the landing gear and flaps extended, transport category aircraft are certified to withstand any load from two-and-a-half positive g-forces down to negative one g, and our brief zero-g weightless experience was well within that range.

"Well, Mark, I'm glad you didn't lie to me, because a mechanic in our hangar asked me who the numbskulls were that painted the bathroom blue. The lavatory water doesn't stay in the toilet when you put the aircraft through zero g-force maneuvers. Remember that you're flying an aircraft with a bathroom now."

"Oops!" I didn't mean to say that out loud, but I did.

"Yeah, oops. Now get out of here. And stay out of trouble."

I went straight into the hangar to ask the mechanic what brand of brew he liked to drink. I was sure my captain (not the Colonel) would split the cost for a case of beer to compensate for the cleanup we put this poor guy through. That's how we rolled. Everything was dealt with on a personal level. And more to the point, I learned the value of keeping it real with my boss.

Although the sacred times happened in the sky, Command Airways employees often hung out at the Woronock House at the edge of the Pough-keepsie airport—our local watering hole and restaurant. That pub is where I met up with a recently hired flight attendant named Nanette—a workout queen with a chiseled jaw and defined biceps and triceps. She could have appeared on the cover of *Shape* or any other fitness magazine. She immediately challenged me to a pushup contest in front of all of my peers. I was twenty-one and in shape, so I squeezed out fifty pushups—my friends counted them out loud together—before I rose to my knees. Nanette just smiled, dropped down and banged out fifty-one at a steady pace. She threw in some clapping pushups, and a few more one-handed at the end, just to rub it in. Of course she beat me, embarrassing me enough to enroll in her exercise boot camp to toughen up—a fine thank you for giving her a chance to float like a butterfly. She was impressive, with a hard body and a driven spirit—the kind of person who would do anything, if only to prove she could. Anytime any of us asked her how many pushups she could do, her answer was always, "One more than you," and she would prove it. We never did get an ultimate number from her.

It wasn't long before Nanette and I were scheduled to fly together after my embarrassment. Early one morning Captain Tony Fine and I met at our check-in desk. Neither of us had consumed our first cup of coffee yet, when in walked Nanette wearing a pressed, custom-tailored blouse over her formfitting skirt. The bowtie with the embroidered company logo rounded out her pristine outfit. Tony asked in front of our newly hired flight attendant, "Mark, is this the airplane that has the landing gear that sticks?" Then he turned his back to Nanette so she couldn't see him wink at me.

I realized this was my chance at payback for the public pushups. I said, as nonchalantly as I could, "Three different crews couldn't get the main gear down last week. But the mechanic swore to me that he finally found the problem and it's fixed now."

Nanette looked at me with a fierce stare. "It better be," she said quickly, flipping her hair as she turned on her heels and marched out. Tony and I had to bite our fists to keep her from hearing us laugh.

We had three separate flights into La Guardia that day. As you may know, that's a very busy New York City airport. Inevitably, we'd have to hold at some point as we were sequenced into the steady stream of arriving jet traffic. Holding is also known as circling. Command Airways had a waiver from the FAA that allowed us to fly visually down the Hudson River without an instrument flight plan, so we often made our holding pattern down low around the Alpine Tower and over the steep, picturesque cliffs of the Palisades, while waiting for a clearance from New York approach control to enter their airspace. This morning was no exception, and we were told it would be about fifteen minutes before we could be fit into the line-up of aircraft from all over the country that were landing at La Guardia.

Ding. Ding. Tony rang the flight attendant call bell, and Nanette answered, "Can I help you?"

"Well, maybe. We're having a little problem up here with that sticking landing gear. We hope that maybe you can get it to come down for us."

"The landing gear won't come down?!"

"Shhhh. Not so loud," Tony cautioned. "We need you to be discreet. We don't want to scare the passengers. The little green landing-gear light is flickering up here in the cockpit. We think the gear just needs a little nudge and it will drop into place. All we need you to do is casually go to about row five, and then jump up and down."

"Really?"

"Really. You *are* a flight crewmember, aren't you? This *is* part of your job. You're a safety specialist. We have to circle here until we can get that gear down, and then we'll be able to continue to La Guardia and land. We're counting on you. Now go do it ..." and here's where Tony played his trump card, "unless you think you can't handle it."

Soon we could feel her jumping back there. One of the effects of not having an autopilot is that we could sense all of the aircraft's changes in pitch. Often we could feel the flight attendant walking up and down the aisle, and we'd have to add the smallest amount of pressure on the control yoke to keep the plane level. Jumping? Well, that we definitely noticed.

After a couple minutes, Nanette was back on the interphone in the back of the plane. "Did it work?" Her voice was full of hope, pride, and a little fear. "Did I get it?"

"We're so close. You almost got it. Do it one more time," Tony replied. "A couple of big jumps and it's bound to come free. Give it all you've got. Jump really hard—as hard as you can."

This time I peeked into the cabin by cracking my cockpit door (the Shorts 330 has a separate door for each pilot). Nanette was jumping as if she were teaching one of her exercise classes. Her dark brown hair was flopping in her face, which was turning red with exertion. Her leg muscles flexed where they protruded from her skirt. It was an impressive display, and all of our thirty passengers were enthralled. I briefly worried that she'd ask some of them to help her. I'd have to call off this bluff before that happened. But this was her job, and she was damn well going to complete her mission. Failure wasn't an option. I watched her pull her hair back and bind it behind her head with a clip. Now she was serious about this task, and the stomping took on a new level of fury.

Finally, air traffic control cleared us to La Guardia and we stopped circling. Nanette called again on the interphone, "Did the gear come down?"

Tony responded, "Beautiful job. We're going in to land."

The air traffic controller probably heard me laughing while Tony acknowledged our landing instructions. I flew the expressway visual approach to runway three-one: one of the biggest aviation thrills I've had with my clothes on —almost forgetting about the stunt we'd just pulled. At 7,000 feet long, runway three-one is a short runway for a major U.S. airport, and runway two-two — the only other runway—crosses it like an X. Aircraft were using that runway to depart, so both arriving and departing traffic had to be carefully sequenced so they didn't meet — or collide — in the middle. La Guardia Airport pre-dates the modern parallel runway design.

There was an additional challenge that kept Tony and me occupied. Unlike the conventional straight-in approach over the water to runway two-two, I had to keep sight of runway three-one's pavement through the captain's side window across the cockpit to maintain position awareness as I made the long, descending left turn from 2,500 feet over the Maspeth Tanks in Queens. While still banking over the Van Wyck Expressway, Tony called out, "Tastee Bread Sign at 800 feet." That's a landmark now long gone, but this entire winding approach around Shea Stadium and Forest Hills made me feel like I was finally playing in the aviation major leagues. It's a universal pilot favorite, and it's always a thrill. I've since flown this same approach in a number of different types of jets, including Lockheed L-1011 widebodies that land weighing well over three hundred thousand pounds. A video of this approach would make an excellent commercial pilot recruitment tool, the way Top Gun spiked interest in the Navy's aviation program. I was grateful that Tony allowed me to have this landing. Pilots often trade off, but captains usually take the difficult legs.

Tony finally taxied us to our designated parking area after we cleared the runway. Command Airways' flight operations office was tucked away underneath the passenger terminal, where there were always three or four crews hanging around between flights. Tony and I watched from the cockpit as Nanette ran in to tell everyone how she'd saved the day. I completed the walk-around inspection while Nanette was inside, circling the outside of the aircraft almost at a dead run. Then Tony and I locked ourselves back inside the cockpit.

Our paperwork was delivered to the captain's side window. We didn't get to see Nanette's embarrassment as the other crews laughed and explained the joke to her inside our flight operations office, but she glared at us on the way back to the airplane, and she told us over the interphone all about how she was going to kick our butts when we eventually came out.

We were cowards for not facing her, but we kept our skin intact. At the end of the day, we knew it was safe to leave the cockpit when she finally began laughing, too. Infractions and misunderstandings were always settled at the airport perimeter pub. Tony and I offered to buy all of her drinks. When the waitress came by to take our order, I wanted Nanette to know our fun was payback, so I asked her, "What's your poison? Push-up Pilsner or Landing Gear Lager?"

The fun part of the job was offset by constantly preparing for emergencies or other unexpected bad things. In case of smoke or fire inside the aircraft, we cleaned our oxygen masks before our first flight of the day with Wet-Naps, little moist towelettes folded into a square packet, like the ones you get at a restaurant after eating lobster. "Hey Mark, why are these called Wet-Naps?" Captain Tony Fine asked me.

"They're napkins soaked in rubbing alcohol?"

"No, because they're smaller than wet dreams." It was a joke that gave him an inspiration.

That October, he put a lot of work into building a Halloween costume out of a flattened refrigerator box painted as a Wet-Nap packet on one side and a condom wrapper on the other. They shared a similar geometry in addition to their sexual references. Sadly, he never wore it at our company Halloween party. Even preparing for emergencies doesn't always guarantee a successful outcome.

Tony loved to fly, and in addition to his captain position at Command, he operated his own flight school. It was there that he became involved in a Cessna 150 accident while instructing. It was originally thought the two-seat airplane he was teaching in developed carburetor icing during initial climb-out after takeoff, and his only engine quit. He and his student crashed into the trees just off the airport. The student was OK, but Tony's head struck the instrument panel so hard that he lost his eyesight. They'd flown in an airplane certified before the FAA made shoulder harnesses mandatory, so it didn't have any.

Tony and I still keep in touch. He's done some experimental research with a company developing artificial sight through projecting sensory images on the skin. Also, his computer converts text to voice. Through Tony, I've developed a love for audio books, and we've mailed many back and forth. As far as I know, I'm the only one from Command Airways who ever saw his Halloween costume. I made a special excursion with friends to visit his storage locker where he stored it so we could see his secret masterpiece.

* * *

Without an autopilot, the Shorts 330 kept me busy at the controls through as many as eleven flights a day, although four or five was closer to average. I earned my winter experience through all these hand-flown trips. The Shorts 330 has de-iceable propellers that break up any frozen build-ups. I learned to make an announcement before activating the system, but only after panicked passengers screamed at our flight attendant one day. Chunks of ice flung off the props and crashed against the slab side of our fuselage. The noise resembled anything from a knock at the door to a gunshot, depending on the thickness of the ice accumulation. Passengers seated next to the engines jumped out of their seats if they weren't warned. The announcement soon became policy, and if I forgot it beforehand, I'd have to apologize. "Nothing to worry about folks," I would say. "That explosive sound is quite normal. It's just our aircraft shedding some ice. We do it all winter, and we do it on purpose, really."

The flight controls on the wings were balanced by low-hanging counterweights that were unofficial indicators of how bad the icing conditions were. Normally the size of fists, ice accumulation on these unprotected surfaces can grow to the size of bowling balls, which is very disconcerting, even though the wings, props, and tail were de-iced and clear of frozen contamination.

Because the Shorts was unpressurized, we couldn't climb over the weather and usually stayed below 10,000 feet. There were times when we remained in the clouds all day except for the takeoffs and landings, and even then the visibility was down near the regulated minimum. I've been onboard a flight that was number seventy-four for takeoff. Foul weather can really back things up. We'd be de-iced, and then it was up to the captain to decide how long the fluid would last before we'd need it again. Standardized de-icing tables that predict how long de-icing fluid will last in wet snow, dry snow, freezing rain, etc., are a relatively new development based on our experience as guinea pigs. This was why I'd come back to the Northeast. Passengers didn't want to fly low, slow, and through all kinds of weather, but I did for the professional challenge and on-the-job training. Sunny days were for vacation; overcast sky, snow, ice, and rain were for working—and cutting my winter teeth.

The Shorts isn't pressurized
And can't climb above the rain and snow
When ice begins to build up
There's just no place to go
I've got ice building up in places
Almost as big as bowling balls

But I have to make announcements
Before I shed ice against the cabin walls

In mid-1988, with a full season of flying through winter slop under my belt, two major airlines called me for interviews a fortnight apart. I hadn't yet become a captain, but I hoped to convince at least one of them that I had the requisite experience to move up to the heavy metal.

"Why should I hire you over a military pilot with over a thousand hours of jet time?" a Trans World Airlines senior captain asked me in front of the hiring panel.

"Sir, I'm sure the military has very good training," I replied. "But if you're hiring airline pilots, I'm already operating into and out of major U.S. airports. I'm flying up in the soup throughout the northeast corridor."

He smiled. I think the question was a trap to see if I'd take the bait and put down military pilots. Maybe he was one. Instead I trumpeted my own specific qualifications. "And when I break out, I'm shooting the river visual approach into runway one-nine at Washington National, winding in on the expressway visual approach into runway three-one at LaGuardia, or tracking the lights on the Canarsie approach into runway one-three-left at JFK International Airport. Sometimes I fly into all three airports on the same day."

Those must have been the right buzzwords, because he gave me a knowing look. "Kennedy tower gets all over you if you stray even slightly off the light track on the Canarsie approach, don't they?"

"It must be easier to fly it in my Shorts 330 than your Boeing 747, but I hope to find out."

"I hope you do, too," he said. His eyes radiated sincerity. The others subtly nodded in approval. I felt like I was going to explode. As long as I passed the simulator checkride and medical exam, I sensed I was becoming a major airline pilot right there in that room. And sure enough, within a couple months, I was wearing a TWA uniform.

The box the Twin Otter came in
It may not be that perty
You may be tempted to laugh and point
But I still love my Shorts 3-30

19 | OUTLOOK NOT SO GOOD

I THINK NANCY'S JOB was as much to get me looking ahead again after TWA Flight 800 as to help me make peace with the past. When she asked me where I saw myself in five years, it was the first time in my life that I didn't have an answer. My whole career I'd been forward thinking, planning, and making short-term sacrifices to achieve long-term goals. Now all I could feel was, *What's the point?* Susanne wanted to have children before she turned thirty-five. Nancy's five-year outlook put me right in the heart of all the dreams Susanne and I had made of building a family together. Now the view through my telescope into the future was dark, like the lens cap had been placed back on it. My internal Magic 8 Ball kept telling me to *Ask again later*, *Better not tell you now*, and then *Outlook not so good*—that matched my mood.

Nancy provided encouragement by explaining that recognizing my frustration and hopeless feelings was the first step in fixing them. I appreciated having a cheering section, but it didn't make me feel like my game was improving. She asked me to boil my feelings down into a single word. I didn't have to dig very deep to come up with dejected. I felt terrible, especially in her borrowed office with my guard down, but as she liked to point out: at least now I was talking about it.

Johanna, back at TWA, also kept tabs on me and asked me to stop by her JFK hangar office to talk when I had time before or after trips. Her favorite advice was, "Emotions we bury, we bury alive." The huggers both subscribed to the same schools of thought, and damn it if both of them didn't occasionally find ways to release the tears I was trying so hard to hold back.

Human Resources Director Christine Morehead had made sure I was part of the corporate family when she'd hired me back at Command Airways—a small, close-knit regional airline. As international and spread out as TWA was, I felt the same family bond here, and Johanna was the worldwide matriarch.

20 | PIGSHIP PROBATION

Long Live the Pigship

"YOU MADE IT, you made it," Rick shouted as he lifted me over his head—not an easy feat, as I was 6'4" tall and liked to eat and work out, even back in my early twenties. My Command Airways roommate was more excited for me than I could show while my head was pinned against the ceiling of our Wappingers Falls, New York (a suburb of Poughkeepsie) crash pad after TWA called to offer me a job, and I was ecstatic. No more turboprops for me—I was on my way to a new life in the world of jets. A seat was waiting for me in the next Boeing 727 flight engineer class. TWA operated DC-9, MD-80, and B-727 narrowbody jets, plus L-1011 and B-747 widebodies. B-757s and B-767s would be added during my tenure. All of these fantastic opportunities made me feel like I'd been accepted into an exclusive club and had to decide if I wanted to sail, water ski, swim at the beach, go golfing, or play tennis first, except in this club, I had to choose which planes I wanted to fly over the next forty years. Of course I dreamed about operating every one of these aircraft. This club, however, required an initiation.

The hardest part of any job is getting it in the first place — unless you're a brand new major airline pilot, which I became during the summer of 1988. It was then I learned that keeping my job required a full-time commitment for the first year. During this probation period, the company can fire any pilot without providing a reason. Donald Trump's *The Apprentice* and reality television hadn't yet been dreamed up, but the phrase, "Your fired!" wasn't far from every new airline pilot's mind. Even membership in the pilots' union didn't offer any protection until probation ended. We were on our own. It was a time to keep my eyes open and my mouth shut, which of course, has never been my strong suit.

> *The year of fire, one foot in the exit*
> *Ain't even got started and it's all on the line*
> *Do or die, in for all or nothing*
> *And everything's against you when you're doing your time*

A year didn't sound too long to keep my nose clean, but most airlines don't even start probation until after new hire training. Three months of basic indoctrination, systems classes with quizzes, and simulator sessions culminated by a four-hour checkride ripe with nonstop abnormalities and emergencies, all had to be successfully navigated before the probation clock began.

Simulators, as well as the actual aircraft, are capable of an assortment of noises to warn pilots of trouble. Picture sitting in a sweaty seat in a dark cockpit and hearing a combination of synthesized voices and various bells, whistles, and clackers. Their meanings must be interpreted and appropriate actions taken without hesitation. A successful outcome merely leads the sadistic check airman to happily push additional malfunction buttons just out of view: *Whoop whoop — pull up! Terrain — terrain! Windshear! Clack — clack — clack! Riiiiiing! Bth-bth-bth-bth! Stall!* And there are more.

After completing this rite of passage, twenty-five hours of actually doing the job of flight engineer on revenue flights began, with a check pilot looking over my shoulder. This is called line training and it too had to be successfully navigated; and only after that did my year of probation start. At any point, if I failed a test, if a personality conflict developed, or if I didn't live up to a superior's standards, I could be asked to turn in my airline ID for good. This point became extremely clear when one of my eleven classmates didn't make it through training.

> *'88 (aviate), desk job on a Pigship*
> *Everywhere's the same when you're sideways and blind*
> *Every flight could be the one to break you*
> *So brace for the worst while you pray to survive*

In most professions, losing a job isn't the end of the world, because you can step laterally into another one. But in the airline industry, it's Armageddon for a pilot's career. No other airline will look at a fired pilot's application. Imagine all the time, money, and effort required for a pilot to reach the necessary experience level to be considered by a major airline, only to become a pariah and unhirable because of a probationary termination. After years invested earning licenses and ratings and then putting up with piddly paying, flight-hour-logging jobs (flight instruction, night freight, or regional airline flying), failure during probation at a major airline tells all the others, *Here's someone who cannot play at the big-league level.* Game over. Time to take the aviation references off the résumé and start considering alternate vocations. With a Bachelor of

Aeronautical Science degree, my options outside of flying were very limited. *Would you like fries with that?*

Just how fragile my dream job remained in my tenuous grip was re-emphasized when another Mark, a pilot hired just ahead of me in 1988, was fired after he'd completed initial training but still within his probationary year. His crime? Torching an APU (auxiliary power unit). He merely tried to start the APU a second time after landing — something we all did in the simulator numerous times. The APU provides power and air conditioning on the ground so that the three main engines can be shut down reaching the gate. In the simulator, it often didn't start on the first try. But in the real world, extra fuel was introduced at the second start attempt, and when the APU finally did light off, it sent a fire plume out the exhaust pipe, which in the case of the 727 happens to be behind the top of the right wing and visible to the passengers sitting in the rear of the aircraft — especially at night. No real harm came to the airplane. However, the New York passengers started their own evacuation out over the wings — while the airplane was still turning off the runway at La Guardia. Mark touched a wrong switch at the wrong time and was fired as an example, filling us other new hires with fear and paranoia.

I began flipping switches in the cockpit even more carefully. Situated low and unprotected on my flight engineer panel was a switch labeled *Passenger Oxygen — On*. This was useful if the airplane suffered a rapid decompression at altitude. Any other time this switch was accidently triggered or bumped, we called it the résumé switch — while lamenting over the rubber jungle of masks and tubing that dropped throughout the cabin. The delay caused by such an error — mechanics repacking all the oxygen masks over every single seat — could send the responsible flight engineer packing for good.

One day onboard aircraft 4348, I was preflighting the cockpit for departure and reading the graffiti scrawled by previous flight deck occupants in various locations on the instrument panels. This particular 727 was nicknamed *My Hammy Vice*. One irreverent inscription, *No B-Scale*, was symbolically represented by a red circle with a line through it (the B-scale was a two-tier pay system that meant I earned quite a lot less than pilots hired before me). But the big winner was *Icahn Sucks*. What exactly he sucked was a matter of some opinion as numerous hand-scribbled messages tried to outwit each other — bathroom humor prominently displayed on cockpit walls.

I was deciding if I should try to erase the graffiti, write it up in the maintenance logbook, or add to it before the rest of the crew arrived, when a little boy ran into the cockpit and asked, "What does this do?" To my horror, out of the hundreds of switches, knobs, lights, and circuit breakers he could have chosen to try and play with, he was reaching for the résumé switch. I stopped his hand with less than an inch to spare. I let his hand go as he pulled it back and told him, "You can look, but please don't touch." I thought I was being polite while preventing a problem and was about to show him a few tricks that sometimes excited quizzical children: testing all the lights and making the cockpit radiate numerous colors at once, or testing any of the systems with synthesized voice commands. Sometimes I tell little boys that we have machine guns onboard while testing the stick shaker, part of the stall warning system, that rattles the pilots' control yokes and makes a rat-tat-tat-tat sound. Before I had a chance, he yelled, "Don't crash me!" and then ran all the way down the aisle to the back of the aircraft while screaming for his mother.

When I was finally signed off as a full-fledged flight engineer to work the panel on my own, the real job began. It was a seat once filled by mechanics. Now it was the entry-level position for a major airline pilot, a lot like sitting on the bench in the big leagues after performing as a starter in the minors. It was a necessary evil—a pilot position without an opportunity to actually fly the airplane.

Before every trip I was required to hand the captain a probationary report to complete. In case it wasn't obvious enough that I was a novice, I essentially had to say, "Look at me closely and decide if you want me to stay employed." Instead, I asked Captain Joe Burke while signing in for my trip, "Can I have your autograph and a bunch of high numbers?" while timidly offering him the dreaded form.

The focused intensity of the look he gave made me wonder if my humor was out of line. Some pilots took the responsibility of evaluating probationary pilots to heart and craved the power they had over our measly lives. Others used the opportunity for abuse, like asking for their bags to be carried to and from the aircraft. With exaggerated flair, Captain Burke pretended to write on my report while commenting, "RELIABILITY: He has all the qualities of a dog... except loyalty. LEADERSHIP: Even wielding a chainsaw, he couldn't get anyone's attention. ACCURACY: He has to take his shoes off to count higher than ten. JOB KNOWLEDGE: His coffee cup has a higher IQ. PERFORMANCE: The number of his mistakes is only eclipsed by their severity." Then he smiled at me and asked, "Shall I continue?" If I wasn't so mortified, I should have said yes just to see where this went. He was on a roll.

We walked out to the ramp and approached aircraft 7839, nicknamed Piggy Sue. Captain Burke stopped me before climbing the stairs leading up to the Jetway. He looked around as if admiring the cool, crisp morning before our first flight together. He breathed in deeply and dramatically while stretching his arms wide and said, "Great day to go engineering, eh Mark?" The emphasis was that I wasn't actually flying the aircraft, and it was the beginning of an endless stream of flight-engineer jokes:

"Q: What does a flight engineer have in common with a stagecoach driver? A: They both sit behind two assholes and catch crap all day."

Instead of controls to fly the airplane, flight engineers have a panel full of lights and knobs, and below that is a table used to fill out fuel logs and other required forms. It's literally a desk job. "Q: So what's the difference between a flight engineer and a dog? A: Dogs sleep *under* the table."

My ninety-day checkride, designed to see how a new pilot has transitioned from the constant training environment to the routine of flying with passengers, is an event with no built-in traps. A check pilot was assigned to simply watch me do my work. Sounds easy, doesn't it? It should've been another boring, routine flight. A pilot greeted me under the aircraft while I was doing my walk-around, or kicking the tires as it's commonly known. He wore a rubber pig nose strapped to his face. But first let me back up a little...

I was hired during June 1988; by September 1 was barely out of initial training and based in New York. After flying maybe four or five flights out of La Guardia and JFK, I was surprised with a transfer to Berlin, West Germany, where I was supposed to be based for at least a month, although I would stay longer. TWA had a small satellite base at Tegel Airport for thirty pilots. Stories from returning crews exaggerated that the beer was warm, the women were cold, nobody spoke English, Germans hated Americans, and everything was too expensive. Consequently, many chose not to fly there. The base was a well-guarded secret among select pilots, and I later had to swear an oath to maintain the propaganda smokescreen before returning to the USA. At the time of my first assignment, though, I still believed all the rumors. The wall that kept the Germans apart also concealed the secret life of our expatriate pilots.

Of course, the Berlin Wall had not come down yet, and there was no expectation that it ever would. I knew almost nothing about those two parallel retaining walls with a no-man's land between them that stretched around the entire city, covered with graffiti, on the West German side. Eventually, I became brave enough to make paper airplanes out of girlie centerfolds and float them from the tourist bleachers, past the binocular-staring guard towers, into where my fellow pilots and I were told was a landmine-filled certain death for those who attempted to cross. The olive-drab-clad East German guards picked up our pornographic paper airplanes without blowing up, or even smiling. But this familiarity and contempt for the wall would only come after months of living among the West Germans. Receiving the initial assignment and leaving New

York, I was awestruck by this opportunity, and I felt completely unprepared for what was ahead.

After the end of World War II, only flag carriers of the victorious Allied powers could provide internal German services to the western city inside the Soviet Bloc, effectively limiting it to Air France, British European Airways (later British Airways), and Pan American. Forty years after the war, TWA joined this mini Berlin Airlift, still moving people and products into and out of the former German capital that had been conquered, divided, and then isolated by the Soviets.

All of this international intrigue was news to me, a wet-behind-the-ears, just turned twenty-three-year-old new hire. My journey across the pond was also my introduction to deadheading, or riding to an assignment in the cabin instead of the cockpit. Peter von Halem, a very distinguished captain traveling in a three-piece suit, tried to explain what was ahead of me while we sat in first class heading toward our newly assigned European domicile. I had thought first class in a Boeing 747 was upstairs behind the cockpit, but I soon learned that business class had been up there ever since the piano bar was replaced in the era of the miniskirt and lunar landings. I'd obviously missed the memo back in grammar school.

Forward of the spiral staircase on the first floor was where the really big seats were located. Because this was my first time inside the whale—what pilots call the 747—I was assigned the solo middle seat in the nose cone, also known as the Captain Kirk Chair. This throne-like seat looked as if it ruled the first-class cabin. If I looked over my left shoulder at the seat across the aisle one row back and could see eight years into the future, and if we were going to France instead of Germany, I would have been smiling at Susanne, and Captain Gid Miller would be sitting behind me. I don't remember the registration number of the 747 I was riding in to my Berlin assignment, but it could have been the exact same aircraft that eventually became TWA's ill-fated Flight 800.

The flight attendants served my middle seat — or more correctly, they over-served it — from both aisles simultaneously. I enjoyed white wine with an assorted cheese and crackers plate complete with both purple and green grapes, and red wine while I watched chateaubriand cut and plated right in front of me, along with a medley of vegetables. I sampled sorbet with a cordial — Amaretto on the rocks — and followed it up with a hot fudge sundae complete with chopped nuts, whipped cream, and a topping cherry that I washed down with both Heineken and Amstel Light. When asked to choose, I just said yes and the crew kept replacing the beer bottles on my tray. I just knew I wasn't drunk, because I could still successfully tie the cherry stems with my tongue. My motor skills seemed to be functioning while I was still sitting down. When I arrived in Europe, and eventually in Berlin, I discovered I really was quite under the influence. I didn't over-drink; I was over-poured. Some guys can't handle Vegas; I couldn't handle first class.

Fortunately, TWA hadn't hired many pilots since early in the seventies, and the entire crew thought it was adorable to break in new blood. Drinking was allowed during pass travel as long as flight duty was at least twenty-four hours away. Accepting their first-class hospitality broke no rules. I was lucky that the crew also guided me to my connecting flight in Frankfurt, to the crew bus, and eventually all the way into my new home, the Schweizerhof Hotel in Berlin — the divided city.

My self-education began with learning the route structure that TWA flew within Europe using stubby Boeing 727s. From Berlin-Tegel, we flew daily to Stuttgart and onto Zürich, Switzerland, where passengers connected with a widebody Lockheed L-1011 TriStar to New York. The same thing happened to the northwest, where TWA connected Berlin with Hamburg and then on to Amsterdam, where another L-1011 was waiting. An additional flight left Berlin for Frankfurt to connect with a 747, and that was the route that brought me into this European mini hub.

We sometimes flew south to Istanbul, Cairo, or Tel Aviv. Occasionally we had flights over to Brussels or north to Copenhagen, Oslo, or Stockholm. I'd been trained on how to keep the aircraft systems functioning — but offered nothing on the airline's European operations. I'd officially receive that after I upgraded to first officer, if I could ever hold European flights again once qualified up front. For now I was flying sideways at the panel and blind to where we were, but soaking it up as fast as I could.

As a flight engineer, I wasn't provided with any maps or even a window to look out of. My job was to bring the cabin pressure up and down; change power over from various sources like the engines, the APU, and external power cords; and to interface with the flight attendants. Mostly what I did was read checklists to the other pilots.

I had to memorize all the responses to the blue normal-procedures checklist for every phase of flight. I'd also spent many hours in the simulator learning the yellow checklists for abnormal situations and the red checklists for true emergencies. Color-coding was part of the KISS (keep it simple stupid) system.

When I boldly asked the guys up front to see a map, I was usually talking to the back of their heads. My forward-facing fellow pilots always answered, "This is pilot stuff; get back to your engineering."

The closest I came to actually flying the plane was to trim the throttles on the center pedestal so they were in sync and didn't create an annoying hum throughout the aircraft. If air traffic control said, "You have opposite direction traffic at twelve o'clock," I'd have to look over my left shoulder instead of straight ahead to help visually spot it out in front of us.

To add to the mystique, we were always flying through one of the three narrow corridors that cut across East Germany into and out of Berlin. Soviet-built Tupolev Tu-16 Badger bombers and an occasional MiG fighter sometimes pulled up next to us as unofficial escorts. I had no frame of reference that prepared me to see a communist military jet alongside my airliner. It was exciting, surreal, and very cold war. I kept the emergency deviation procedures taped to my clipboard in case these foreign fighter jocks, the weather, or a system malfunction forced us outside the protected corridor, even though I wasn't actually flying the plane.

The mature flight attendants called constantly. They bragged openly that they were having their own personal summertime and they had about a quarter of a degree of comfort zone for the cabin temperature. In the three-pilot, everything-manually-operated 727, the heating and air conditioning systems were difficult to control accurately, especially for a rookie. For the cabin attendants, this was the most senior and coveted flying for them as they came over the ocean once and stayed in Europe for ten days, completing their entire month of flying in one shot. On one trip I had four flight attendants whose seniority numbers were two, three, four, and six out of the entire eight thousand cabin crewmembers employed by the airline. They were all hired in the 1950s, well before I was born (in 1965). One tried to set me up with her granddaughter. Really? Yes, really.

Almost daily, one of these ladies brought meals up for the captain and first officer and then told me, "I'll be back to breastfeed you later, Sonny." Each thought she was completely original with that tired line. One flashed me for added effect, to which the copilot said after she left, "Thirty-six Cs are great, but not thirty-six longs. She should have quit doing that a long time ago." Sexual harassment wasn't tolerated—it was graded.

We didn't always keep the cockpit door locked back then, well before 9/11. I learned to lock it when one of my captains announced over the PA, "Ladies and gentlemen, TWA has put together the finest group of flight attendants for your traveling pleasure today. Unfortunately, due to the weather in Paris, they couldn't make it here, so instead we have Ingrid, Igan, Beth, and Mary to serve you." The pounding on the door began almost immediately, and the captain advised me not to accept a crew meal that day. On my skimpy probationary pay, that was a big sacrifice.

I once offered to carry the bags of a hunched-over flight attendant—who was well into her sixties—up the Jetway stairs. She looked fragile and could hardly have been ninety pounds soaking wet. Her reaction startled me. She punched me in the chest and declared, "Junior, when I can't carry my own damn bags, I'll retire. Now get out of my way!" To add insult to injury, she accidentally knocked my ID off of my uniform shirt, but I didn't realize it right away. At my flight engineer table in the cockpit, I had a moment of panic. I couldn't fly the trip. I told the captain, and he began conferring with the first officer. They questioned whether they could smuggle me out of, and back into, the country if I never left the cockpit. It wasn't until pushback time that a ramp agent found and returned my ID. It had been run over by the pushback tug and the clip was totally flattened, but I was excited to have it back and hoped the few minutes' delay wouldn't get me into trouble.

All this was just finally starting to seem routine, although I didn't know where I was most of the time, when my ninety-day checkride sneaked up on me. As luck would have it, Captain Kenneth Cook was in charge of my flight that day. He wasn't just a captain and a check pilot, but also the regional director of the entire Berlin operation and all of the European 727s flying for TWA. Like the famed British explorer James Cook, this Captain Cook was very much in command. Picture a rosy-cheeked cop with lots of uniform stripes and TWA's twin-globe logo on his hat. He wasn't directly evaluating my performance. He ruled the aircraft while a check flight engineer — the fourth pilot in our stubby aircraft—shipped over to fill this square in my file. Cockpits in general don't conjure up images of vast amounts of space. This check flight engineer rode in a jumpseat and literally looked over my shoulder. I was about to meet him on the ramp in the shadow of the 727 before my flight. Recall the pig-nosed pilot under the plane ...

Another job of the flight engineer is to make sure the aircraft is in a satisfactory condition to fly. I walked around it before every flight to verify the tires weren't flat, fluids weren't leaking, damage wasn't apparent, the lights worked, and I checked a long list of other potential problems. I exited down the aft airstairs, and by the time I reached the nose gear, there was Bill, in full uniform and staring at me from behind his rubber pig snout mask. My checkride had begun.

Bill followed me through the rest of my walk-around. Captain Cook was not as amused as I was by Bill's humor as we stepped into the cockpit, and I immediately felt tension build between these two pilots, either of whom could end my career. It felt like double jeopardy. I stared at my panel and tried not to take sides. Even the first officer looked out his side window to avoid unnecessary communication. There I was, riding sidesaddle around Europe with two management pilots in the same small cockpit where I was just trying to do my job so I could keep it.

At TWA, the 727's nickname was Pigship, and to fly her was to love her. They came in two sizes: stubby (series 100) and stretch (dash 200). Although fast and well-built, it took them forever to climb, and they came down like a pound of bacon. The joke was that if pigs could fly, they would be 727s. But for those of us who climbed into a 727's cockpit, Pigship was a term of endearment, and each of the old birds had a different porcine nickname. The one we were flying that day, nose registration number 7831, was Boeing Oink. I hoped somehow the crew's mutual admiration for the aircraft and the excitement of flying within Europe would unite them, but I kept my mouth zipped just in case.

I wouldn't use routine to describe this flight. The captain became irritable right away. It turned out he had good reason. During the climb-out from Berlin, while heading toward Stuttgart, his electrically heated side window started overheating. In fact, the treated glass started growing air bubbles inside of it, which I took as a bad sign as I'd never seen anything like it before. Aside from the captain getting roasted, I wondered if we were going to get a shower of shattered glass followed by a rapid decompression and a few-hundred-miles-an-hour cockpit windstorm. That would ruin our scenic bird's-eye view of Europe.

There are two switches for windshield heat in the stubby 727 cockpits (four in the more common stretch 727s), and Captain Cook turned off the one on his side, which seemed logical. But the window grew hotter as I simultaneously pulled out the yellow abnormal-procedures checklist and reached up to turn the other window heat switch off. Bill grabbed my forward-reaching arm and stopped me from his jumpseat.

"We have company procedures," he said, "in place from generations of experience. So, no freelancing your own solutions. Leave the switches alone until you've read the checklist. At least let's leave the heat on the good side instead of turning it all off. It's cold out there."

I said, "No. This is a Series 100 stubby. I need to turn the other one off for control of the captain's side window." I couldn't name a single city we flew over, but I thought I remembered what I'd just learned in training about the aircraft's systems and how they worked.

"I already got the switch off," the captain said. "Get hold of Paris dispatch and tell them we're diverting into Frankfurt."

I made the mistake of asking, "Paris, sir? Aren't we over Germany? Can't I just call Frankfurt directly?"

He yelled, "Paris coordinates all of our European operations; just let them know what we're doing."

I tried to read the yellow checklist, but the captain said, "Forget the checklist, make the radio call. We're getting this bird on the ground right away."

"Yes, sir," I replied, reaching up to turn off the other window heat switch once more with one hand, flipping though my clipboard for the Paris and Frankfurt radio frequencies with the other. Bill reached up and turned the first officer's window heat switch back on and said, "I told you to leave that alone."

Somehow, I reached Paris and then Frankfurt operations to warn them of our imminent arrival and ran all my descent and diversion checklists while the captain and first officer flew the plane to our new destination, which was nearby. I was in the weeds trying to accomplish everything for this unscheduled landing, and the captain's windshield glass now had a lot more air bubbles and was very hot. I had no idea if it was going to stay intact or pepper us with pieces. At last I picked up the yellow abnormal-procedures checklist again and read it to myself. It merely said to turn off the affected window heat switch, which I vaguely remembered was different from the stretch 727-200. TWA had very few of the stubby 727s left and it was rare to fly them.

"Captain, ready for landing," I said. "I suggest you turn off the other window heat switch, too."

He ignored me, and we landed. During the taxi in to the ramp, I shut off the remaining windshield heat switch as part of the after-landing cleanup. The left side window looked like clear Swiss cheese and some of the air bubbles were the size of golf balls, but it had held together.

In Frankfurt the crew was quiet and the air full of tension. The windshield slowly cooled as we shut down the entire airplane, and Captain Cook wrote the malfunction up in the maintenance logbook, red circling it, which graphically told the mechanics that the plane couldn't be flown until the problem was fixed.

Our Stuttgart passengers were rebooked on another airline, and we ended up deadheading to our base in Berlin in the cabin of another TWA 727. I sat way back in coach and avoided my crew, feeling like it was just a matter of time before I'd be sent all the way home.

Back in Berlin, a flight engineer buddy of mine, Chris Terry, took me out to the Europa Center for a big mug of Warsteiner beer. At the local tavern we called The Office, beer was served in full-liter, vase-shaped, gold-rimmed glasses. Its real name was George's Restaurant und Bierkonter. It was decorated with intricately carved wooden panels and hosted a piano in the back where Pan Am and British Airways pilots often crowded. If you go there today, there's still a plaque in the bar honoring the TWA pilots—we gave the owner that much business.

Before Chris ordered a second round, I told him I didn't want to run into my crew. "They might show up here," I said. He told me about Charlie, another pilot whose wife, Cathy, had just arrived from the States, who was throwing a welcoming party for her in his hotel room. We agreed to go and paid our bill—two beers, probably the cheapest tab of my career.

German beer is strong, and the effects from that first liter of beer were already kicking in. We decided it would be great culture shock for Cathy if we changed into our traditional Turkish outfits that we'd bought on a recent trip to Istanbul. I thought it would be funny, and I needed a laugh. With a bottle of duty-free Bell's Scotch in my hand, we headed for Charlie's room and knocked. To my horror, Captain Cook answered the door. I stood frozen in my headdress and purple outfit that resembled pajamas.

"What the hell are you supposed to be?" Captain Cook asked before I could turn away. His ten-year-old son and twelve-year-old daughter came running to the door. "Is this the guy you've been complaining about?" his daughter asked. "He's cool!" My job was saved by a preteen.

It turns out that Captain Cook had done some research after venting to his family about having his ear nearly melted off. He realized that on the stubby 727-100, the first officer's forward windshield switch also controls the captain's side windshield across the cockpit and vice-versa. This is what I had unsuccessfully tried to tell him in flight. As a total greenhorn, I might have been lost in Europe, but I did know the inner workings of the 727 systems after all. Captain Cook put his arm around me and said, "Next time some prick tries to tell you not to do your job, you tell him to shove it—even if it's me."

From that night forward, Ken Cook became a mentor to me. He later became a great friend as well. He told stories of his early days with the airline— stories of building a still in Saudi Arabia and hiding it from the authorities. Large sugar purchases were explained away with, "The ladies are baking again. They love to cook." There were more stories about princes and burning cars, but I can't remember them well enough to do them justice. Ken held court at Charlie and Cathy's party and kept us entertained until the bottle of Scotch ran out.

Not all of his stories were of the exotic overseas variety. My favorite was when crew scheduling called him at home in the middle of the night for a trip he didn't want on his day off. "Captain Cook," the scheduler said, "we have a 6:00 a.m. departure for you out of La Guardia." Still half asleep, but without hesitating, Ken handed the receiver to his wife and said loud enough to be heard over the phone, "Honey, I think this call is for your husband."

I'm still friends with his family. Unfortunately, he died young—at fifty-five—in 1995, but not before going out with a bang. Ken played hard but he knew his job inside and out. One thing that really rubbed him the wrong way was incompetence. For most of his career he competed for management positions with a pilot he loathed. At fifty-two, he walked into the New York chief pilot's office after his nemesis had been promoted to that position and announced, "I can work with incompetence, but not for it,"—and then turned in his resignation.

Ken's decision was famously justified within the inner circles of TWA pilots when this chief pilot later called a 747 captain into his office to chew him out. He berated this captain for numerous noise violations while departing from Tel Aviv, and continued to belittle him with threats that our right to fly into Israel could be suspended. This was all documented in a letter the chief pilot planned to put in this pilot's permanent file. The captain took the letter, wrote something on it, and asked if he could use the office copy machine. He made numerous copies and then handed the original back to the chief pilot and left with a sly smile. On the note, which he posted in flight operations crew-staging areas around the country, he wrote, "This is the flight that the chief pilot pay-assigned me for so he could build his own 747 experience." In other words, the chief pilot flew it, and the scheduled pilot was paid to stay home. Hence, the chief pilot had been the one to improperly fly the airplane that day. The last laugh was enjoyed by the entire airline.

After his career with TWA, Captain Ken Cook went to Africa to fly volunteer relief missions. While there, he was diagnosed with jaundice and pancreatic cancer. He was airlifted home and lived eighteen months after a six-month prognosis. I traveled to Connecticut to see him whenever I could. The treatment aged him rapidly and he lost weight. He loved to shoot handguns, so we went to the range together.

I was a 767 first officer by then, and I wore my uniform for the first time as a pallbearer when his time finally came. The night after his memorial service, I crossed paths with the gal who later became my fiancée. Death and love were colliding. I think Ken would want me to believe that he had something to do with guiding me to the latter.

My major airline career started while TWA was celebrating fifty years of crossing the Atlantic Ocean. I feel I was trained by the best, the ones who did what it took to get the job done and knew the incidents and accidents of their peers that created the procedures we now follow. But the greatest training came on the job rather than in the classroom. There's a lot to learn beyond the environment of the schoolhouse, and surviving it has very little to do with book smarts. Airline life is a culture and not just a job. That's why there's a yearlong probation. When I remember my early TWA days, I always smile, though I might not always have been so amused at the time.

O, the days when pigs could fly
(Pigship roll call)
°Porky's Pride, Thunder Pig
Queen of the Sty, Swine Flew
Lard Limo, Ham Tram
Piggy Sue, Pork Chopr
Warped Hog, Sky Pig
Picnic Ham, Spring Chitlin
Pickled Pigs Feet, Makin' Bacon
Bacon Bomber, Aurora Boarialis
Petulant Porker, Heavenly Hog
Porker Forker, Porky's Petunia
Pigmalion, Kermit's Desire
Hammy Fay Bacon, Truffle Hunter
Strato Swine, Short Lardage
Pigadilly, Old Lang Swine
Lark Sakes, Kitty Hog
Pig O- My Heart, Pork Du Jour

21 | THERAPY

"IF SUSANNE WERE HERE NOW, what would you say to her?" Nancy was acting straightforward in her approach to therapy, but it felt like a curveball to me. I didn't want to talk to her as if she was Susanne. Patrick Swayze, Demi Moore, and Whoopi Goldberg played out that three-way channeling into the other world in *Ghost*, but I wasn't buying it.

Nancy pushed on. "Would you want Susanne to find someone else if it had been you on that flight instead?"

"That's the hard part. I'm the pilot, and she died on my airline's proudest jet — our flagship. This whole fucked-up situation should be reversed, but it's not. I know I have survivor's guilt, but knowing it doesn't make it go away. And I'm not ignoring your question. Susanne really wanted a family. I only wanted that with her. She'd have made one with someone else eventually, but without her, I don't want that anymore. Your backwards logic doesn't work with me. I'm not Susanne."

"Well then, you'll just have to believe that she'd want for you whatever you eventually decide you do want. It sounds like she understood the ways that you two were different and she made you happy. Now you're going to have to make that your own job again, whatever direction that takes you, and I feel safe to say you have her blessing."

I sat with my face scrunched up — hostility brewing toward Nancy for attempting to speak for Susanne, a gal she'd never even met except through our conversations. Whatever body language I was exuding translated into the low, dark growl of a dog about to bite. As a trained counselor, Nancy easily read my hostility.

"Maybe you have some unresolved issues with Susanne. She was taken suddenly, with no chance for goodbyes or reconciliation, even for simple disagreements or misunderstandings. Maybe I can't speak for her, but I can give you permission to let them go."

I still wasn't buying into this role-playing. I know Nancy meant well, but I just wasn't feeling it. I explained my core beliefs to Nancy: I'm not religious, and I don't feel there's any more interaction I can have with Susanne, ever, no matter how badly I want it.

She was persistent. "Still, maybe you want to ask or tell her something. If you don't want to talk about it, maybe you can write her a letter. I don't have to read it. Sometimes just putting your thoughts down will help you sort through them."

"She's gone. Forever gone. What does it matter what I think? I can't do anything about it now."

"But you're still here, Mark. Your feelings do matter. Maybe you can't tell them to Susanne, and you're having trouble feeling comfortable enough to tell them to me, but you don't have to keep them locked up inside. Holding on to all your anger isn't going to help you in any constructive way. Let's try this. If the situation were reversed, what would you want to tell Susanne to do if she had to live on without you?"

This hypothesizing was wearing me out, but I think it was supposed to, just like a physical workout should make me feel exhausted but also build a sense of accomplishment. I did admit one thing to Nancy that I hadn't told anyone else: since TWA Flight 800, the streetlights often go out as I walk past them and then relight after I pass by. It's the strangest thing, and it happens to me all over the world. My heart keeps trying to convince me that it's Susanne's way of showing that she's watching over me, but I'm a stone-cold realist, and I refuse to believe it. I think electricity isn't as stable as we are led to believe by its abundant availability, and the same intermittent lighting happens to everyone, but most people never notice. Nevertheless, if I was the guardian angel believer type, that would be my sign from above.

22 | BEFORE CRM – THE FIVE P STORY

City in the Sky

I STAYED IN EUROPE during my first few TWA years as often as I could successfully bid and hold the Berlin base. So much about that operation was worth guarding as a well-kept secret. Even so, occasionally a gremlin slipped through.

Captain All-About-Me was five-foot-five any way you measured him. Handsome was not a word often used to describe him, except maybe when he evaluated himself in the mirror. His self-image — viewed through fisheye spectacles — and what I'd seen and experienced of him so far as our month together developed, were two barely intersecting worlds. His mostly thinning gray hair didn't cover the scars from his personal aircraft accident that he bragged about surviving. Even from his own version of the story, the accident should never have happened. That was the subject he was currently monologuing for the third or fourth time, and our group of seven TWA crewmembers was a captive audience in a crew van on an early spring morning in 1989, on our way to the Berlin-Tegel airport.

Our captain sat in the front seat next to the young driver and had already changed the radio station to find appropriate background music for his soliloquy. Techno was the driver's choice. The captain tried all the presets in frustration. Finally he dialed the radio with the seek button until he found soft rock. I was surprised he accepted Nena's "99 Luftballons" in German. He also rearranged all the heating vents to blow on himself, leaving the rest of us to breathe on our fingers. Before we'd even left sight of the Schweizerhof Hotel, he'd criticized just about everything — from the driver's appearance, to his handling of the vehicle, to the route he planned to take to the airport. Now the story of where our leader earned the head scars — that he self-consciously rubbed — was in full force, along with some of his favorite witticisms, that seemed to work their way into every one of his stories.

"You know, we never really lose our hair — it just migrates to places we don't want it, like our nose and our ears." I felt sure he was going to emphasize this point by sticking his finger into those orifices, but thankfully he didn't.

Nothing about this man's behavior would have surprised me. This wasn't our first trip together, but it had been a long week and the month was still young. Unless I could trade trips, a doubtful proposition at the small inter-European satellite base we had in the late 1980s, I would be stuck with this captain for the entire month.

I was still a flight engineer. My first officer whispered as we held our own conversation behind the captain's back. Ken had many years with TWA, about twenty, and I was still in my first year, although I was rapidly becoming a regular in the Berlin base by successfully bidding to stay month after month. This was a different Ken from my mentor Captain Ken Cook, the flight manager in charge of all of TWA's satellite European domiciles. I loved Germany and was trying not to let my newest captain ruin the intrigue of living among the Europeans and flying for the major international airline of my dreams. My first officer was my co-conspirator. Together we were going to have to make the best of our month with Captain All-About-Me. The other four in the van were flight attendants sent over from New York on a ten-day rotation and they were also whispering among themselves. The captain didn't seem to notice the side conversations as he droned on. Just to play it safe, I looked forward, feigning my attention to our half-turned-toward-us captain, while I instead concentrated on what Ken was saying.

"Mark, he's a notorious pain in the ass," Ken said, "but you have to put up with him and keep your nose clean while you ride out the remainder of your probationary year. Just do your job and you'll be fine. Be glad you missed the really dark years."

I thought about how this month was already going — not well — and wondered out loud, "The dark years?" My face scrunched up at just the right time, by pure luck, and our captain took it as a raptured acknowledgement for his hair-migration joke. He continued his story with renewed vigor. Hand waving was added, and I saw that he was now in the zone for his speech delivery. So much the better, for his internally focused energy meant that he paid us even less attention.

Ken continued with his low-volume, backseat explanation, "Captains used to have absolute autonomy. Yearning for the days of wooden ships and iron men, they longed for the return of flogging."

Just then our captain inserted another of his favorite clichéd quotations. "The beatings will continue until morale improves." I stifled a giggle, but mostly because Ken and our captain seemed to be on the same page of completely different books.

"While most of our pilots will make you laugh," Ken said, "there were a few historical tyrants who would make our current captain look like only a baby bully with training wheels."

Ken was sharing some TWA folklore, which I later heard in bits and pieces from other sources. I felt honored to be receiving the oral history of my proud airline, which went back all the way to the pre-World War II original airmail routes. In the meantime, our captain had gotten to the part about his private, light-twin airplane losing an engine and then letting it flip upside down at low altitude. A good part of multi-engine aircraft training is dedicated to not letting that happen. But the drama of that anecdote was long gone by now, since I already knew the ending—I'd heard it before ad nauseam.

Ken didn't even pretend to listen, but he gave me a nod toward the captain. "On the way back, whatever time he tells us to meet him for dinner, I'll meet you in the lobby half an hour before. We can slip out unnoticed."

I nodded in agreement. It was bad enough spending time listening to that self-absorbed narcissist while on duty. I wasn't about to give him any of my recreational time. Throughout the month, Ken and I slowly moved our meet time further up as our captain became suspicious that we were dodging him. By the end of the month, we were out the hotel door by four. Our month went by, and I never shared a meal with Captain All-About-Me unless a flight attendant served it.

Over schweinshaxe und bier, Ken introduced stories of other notorious captains who flew for TWA well before Ken's or my time. I picked up more bits and pieces of TWA's infamous aviators throughout my career. Cockpit yarns have lives of their own and grow with age and retelling, although I'm reasonably sure that truth is still among the ingredients listed somewhere on the label. Welcome to the rumored gossip of the once great airline, TWA, which I still love.

People make this job easy, or people make this job hard. Most of the time, the act of moving airplanes is pretty straightforward. It's the coping skills we learn as flight engineers and first officers in that tiny classroom called the cockpit that make the job of airline pilot especially challenging.

No newbie flies very long without learning the oral history of his airline. Sure, Howard Hughes was a big part of the foundation of mine, and accounts of his escapades and idiosyncrasies abound, but you can watch the movie *The Aviator* for most of them. What vexes new TWA pilot recruits—already on edge from probation pressure — is the folklore of the notorious Five Ps. We hear rumors and references to them on long flights, in crew buses, and on layovers in bars and restaurants. These captains took no guff. Their dubious antics galvanize us like campfire stories. I remember tales of the One-Armed Brakeman and the Boogieman keeping me awake at my first sleep-away experience back when I was ten at Camp Pemigewassett, the same camp my dad attended in his youth. The Five P fables are my airline's version of ghost stories. For example, there's one about the captain who allowed a flight attendant to serve him and his first officer dinner at the same time while an FAA inspector was riding in the cockpit jumpseat. Procedure was for each pilot to dine separately while the other monitored the airplane. The inspector asked this captain what he would do if an engine failed while they were both eating. Without hesitation, the captain lifted his entire tray, including his drink, and dumped it over his head and into the inspector's lap.

These captains kept their crews on the verge of mutiny. Early in my career, the legends about them instilled the fear of insubordination in me, a flight deck crime punishable by job termination.

I know their real names, but since they belong to a generation of pilots before me back in the Boeing 707 days and I've never met them, I'm going to rename them more appropriately: Captains Pride, Personality, Primero, Pompous, and (P)Loner. That's right, the fifth P didn't really start with that letter, but since Captain Loner (also a pseudonym) was an equally or even more a virile member of the group than the other four, he was affectionately renamed to fit as Captain Ploner. That habit stuck, and any captain could be labeled irascible in conversation merely by adding a P to his last name, and the reference would be clear.

A single episode about another notorious captain, who exceeded even the Five-P status, captures the essence of captain's authority taken too far. As far as I know, none of the original Five Ps were ever fired. This honorary sixth P was forced into retirement, even before he could return from Europe.

Captain Pretentious commanded his Boeing 707 from 35,000 feet over the North Atlantic. He piloted the airline's most versatile aircraft, received top pay, and enjoyed senior routes from JFK to Europe, in this case probably Paris — maybe even called TWA Flight 800 back then. It's very likely this trip continued all the way around the world with the same crew, because TWA circled the globe in both directions in this era. Twin globes depicting the whole world are part of our official logo. When the crew arrived at Charles de Gaulle and eventually the Celtic Hotel, the layover location the airline used before the Concorde Lafayette where Susanne and I stayed generations later — and where she was headed on July 17, 1996 — they could expect to take a short nap and then enjoy a nice glass of Merlot with a thick and tender filet cooked to order. Captain Pretentious could even send it back to the chef three or four times to make himself happy, which according to legend he often did. He didn't yet know that this would be his last trip.

Captain Pretentious rang the first-class galley with two short chimes, the one right outside the cockpit door. Joseph, the purser, picked up the handset and extinguished the call light. "Hello?"

"Always identify yourself when you answer." He recognized Joseph's voice but loved telling people what to do.

"Yes, Captain, this is Joseph in the forward galley. You called?"

"Of course I did. I need a cup of coffee. Hot and black."

"I'll put on a fresh pot and be right up after I help Marge finish her first-class dinner service. The passenger meals are ready and we're serving them hot. I put yours in to cook, and it will be about twenty minutes for them."

"I called because I want the coffee now. Go to the back and get a cup if yours isn't fresh."

"Captain, it'll just be a few minutes to make some here and finish serving the meals."

"Now. Go back and get me a cup now. Don't make me tell you again." He hung up the interphone.

I want a coffee at 40 West
Is that so hard to do?
When I give an order
I expect it carried through

The knock at the cockpit door didn't come fast enough for Captain Pretentious, but it was only the time it took for Joseph to make the trip to the aft galley for coffee and not enough to have completed the meal service. Joseph entered the cockpit when the flight engineer opened the door for him. Moonlight came indirectly through the cockpit windows. The cockpit lights were down low and it was difficult for Joseph to see, as he was accustomed to the brightly lit cabin where the lucky half of his passengers were dining. He was irritated, but he held his tongue and tried to remain professional. The captain hadn't asked for anything for his fellow pilots, and they'd been wise enough not to add any requests to the captain's demand. They preferred clean food and drinks, not stuff that had been tampered with by angry crewmembers, not that that kind of thing ever happened.

"Here you go, Captain."

"What took you so long?"

"I had to go to the aft galley to get this. The coach flight hostesses have their serving cart in the aisle. We maneuvered as best as we could."

He took a sip. "This isn't fresh, either."

"It's the best I could do. I did put a fresh pot on up here so I'll bring you a new cup with your meal when it's ready."

"Listen, when I give an order, I mean it. Do you know what captain means?"

"Of course I do. It means you're the captain of this ship."

"It means I'm in charge. You can't define a word with itself. Captain means I'm the boss. There's no appeal over my word. I have final authority over everything that happens on this aircraft. When I sign the logbook, I sign for it from nose to tail and for everyone on it. Is that clear?"

"Crystal, sir, but I can't deliver what I don't have."

"I don't think it is. I don't think you get it. When I give an order, it's to be carried out right away without question."

> When I sign the logbook
> That means from nose to tail
> The captain is the man in charge
> On jets and boats that sail

"Captain, with all due respect, my passengers are my responsibility, and I was in the middle of a meal service."

"Don't second guess me. When I tell you something, you do it. End of story."

"Right now the meals I pulled out for the remaining passengers are getting cold. I now have to heat them back up before serving them. And the passengers who are already eating are going to want to get rid of their trays while I'm still serving."

"You're questioning me again. When I say to do something, you do it. If I have to show you who's boss, I will."

> Don't you dare talk back to me
> Or I'll fire you on the spot
> You see me wearing four gold stripes
> And when I look at you you're not

The captain turned to the first officer and said with his full authoritative voice, "Gear down."

"What?" The first officer looked at him incredulously.

"I said, *Gear down!*"

"Sir, we're over the North Atlantic at 35,000 feet. There's nowhere to land within hours of here."

"I said gear down. If you don't do it, you won't have a job, effective immediately. If I could throw you all the way off this pressurized airplane in flight, I would. Put the gear down or get out of my cockpit."

The first officer looked back at the flight engineer for support for an instant, but was met with an uncomfortable stare. Tentatively he reached over to grab the gear handle but stopped. He still hoped for the order to be rescinded, but it wasn't. He must have considered pulling it out of its mechanical detent and then lowering it, but the consequences outweighed the order. With the purser, first officer, and flight engineer all staring at him, the captain reached over and slammed the gear handle down himself. "If I have to continue doing everything myself, I'll have you all fired."

The plane shook as several thousand pounds of hydraulic pressure opened gear doors, lowered the giant wheels into the slipstream, and reclosed the doors in the normal sequence. The noise and vibration rivaled flying into the heart of a thunderstorm. The flight engineer, after shaking off the initial shock, eased the throttles up to maximum continuous power to compensate for the extra drag as much as possible. Still the captain had to lower the nose immediately in order to maintain airspeed.

Pilots are trained for hierarchal submission. Flight attendants are trained for service. Joseph was the one to point out the obvious. To be heard over the wind noise he had to shout, "You're crazy; you've just put our lives in danger. You're not fit for service."

"And you're fired," the captain yelled back. "I want you in a seat in the far back of this aircraft, and I don't want to see or hear from you again. I'll have your job before we reach the pavement in Paris."

The first officer interjected, "Sir, can I put the gear back up now? It's driving up our fuel consumption rate, and we've left our assigned altitude. We need a descent clearance, and there's no way we can fly like this and hope to make Paris without burning up our reserves."

"You'll put the gear up when I tell you to." After a three-second pause, while all three pilots watched the plane shake and the altimeter unwind, he ordered, "Gear up."

It wasn't the first officer or the purser who went home in a passenger seat. As we all would hope, Captain Pretentious's termination happened as fast as the story could reach the New York chief pilot by phone.

On wooden ships with iron men
Many miles away from shore
The captain's word was law back then
But we don't need tyrants anymore

And on that flight
He ruled through the night
But planes don't fly forever
As he flew
The crew all knew
His rule ended with the gear lever
It's a city in the sky
It's a city with a king
In charge of his last endeavor
It's a city in the sky
It's a city with a king
And time for a new ruler

Although such an extreme is a rare exception, perhaps a fault of the seniority system that rewards time of service over individual competency, this episode marked a need for something that was endemic in our training by my arrival in the late 1980s — *cockpit* (and later crew) *resource management.* CRM emphasizes the value of crewmember input while not eroding the captain's ultimate authority. While no system is perfect, CRM has helped aviation evolve from the keep-your-mouth-shut-while-I-crash-the-airplane single-pilot mentality to a true crew concept.

Still, not everyone always embraces teamwork. On my next trip with Captain All-About-Me, he said to the flight attendants, "No need to feed us today. I brought leftovers from dinner last night for *my* lunch." That was how he punished us for dodging him now that he'd figured out we weren't going to meet up with him after hours. We didn't starve, though. The flight attendants left our meals hidden in the oven and served them to us quickly in first class when our overlord went inside to pull up the paperwork between flights.

It's a city in the sky
It's a city with a king
Those who make a living
Must kneel and kiss his wings

23 | OUR PARENTS' CHILDREN

NANCY ASKED ME if Susanne and I had written our wedding vows, and if somewhere in them we'd promised to stay together *until death do us part*. We hadn't planned our big day as far as the vows, and their ultimate meaning came as a shock, to say the least.

Nancy tossed around clichés like *Nobody gets out alive*, and *Carpe diem — Seize the day*. I developed the feeling that this session wasn't supposed to be very productive. Maybe it was intended to be light and airy so I wouldn't become apprehensive about attending therapy. The whole idea of counseling is alien to most airline pilots. We are the decision makers — autonomous and self-assured. I certainly felt like I was, until my world exploded.

Nancy was also interested in another death in my family — the loss of the other important woman in my life — and we discussed our roles as our parents' children and the expectation that we'd outlive them. More than once she made me reflect on that earlier difficult time and what I did and didn't learn from it. I thought I was here to talk about Susanne, but during this visit our time together revolved around my mom.

24 | SUCCESS AND SILENCE
Anaphylactic Shock Reaction

AFTER SITTING SIDEWAYS in the cockpit all over Europe with Captains von Halem, Cook, All-About-Me, and a variety of others, while Captain Cook was throwing his TWA resignation letter on his chief pilot's desk and heading over to Africa to fly relief missions for Caritas because he couldn't work for incompetence, I was upgrading to first officer in 1989 and actually flying my first jet — the Boeing 727. This three-engine workhorse represented a lot of firsts for me: it was my entry position as flight engineer at a major airline; it was the first jet I flew as a first officer; it was the plane on which I'd eventually upgrade to captain; and I would also become a 727 check-airman and train other pilots in the simulator. Consequently I have a strong attachment to that airplane, but the really big thrill was when I first handled the flight controls and felt the power and performance of the mighty Pigship.

After FE/FO-transition ground school (transition training is the technical term for moving from one seat to another, and in this case from flight engineer to first officer) and a dozen nights in the simulator, including a checkride, I met Captain Skip Eberts in Tulsa for my inaugural flight in the 727. For fun I called him Captain Skipper. He was heavyset, his skin was red with mild sunburn, and he smiled under a salt and pepper mustache. Blue-framed reading glasses dangled on a retaining strap over a bright red lanyard that contained his airline ID. We waited, along with my first officer training partner and our flight engineer, for the last flight that was going to stay overnight while Captain Skipper briefed us on what he wanted us to accomplish.

You may be surprised to know that many times when a pilot flies an airliner for the first time, it's with passengers onboard. We learn in the classroom and in a simulator, and then we fly with specially anointed pilots called check-airmen on actual revenue flights until we're signed off as a fully qualified crewmember. I've done this many times. In subsequent years, the first time I flew a B-767, B-757, L-1011, or an MD-80 was with passengers onboard. The exception is when a pilot flies his first airplane for an airline. So before I could fly a 727 with passengers, I had to do it in an actual, empty aircraft in the middle of the night.

Captain Skipper loaded up the 727 with fuel. Since we weren't carrying anyone in the cabin—no passengers or even flight attendants—we had lots of available weight to spare. I looked back at all those empty seats and longed to float around the cabin through a few zero g-force maneuvers, but had learned my lesson about that. Skip wanted to give us as much practice as the night would allow before the plane was needed for the early morning revenue flight to St. Louis. He took the left seat while the flight engineer that we borrowed from the training center took his seat at the panel. My training partner, Dave, and I took turns flying touch and goes from the right seat or watching from the forward jumpseat until the sun came up. This is better than the ultimate amusement park ride. We made figure eights around the airport to save time. After we took off on runway three-six right, we looped around 270 degrees to the right to land on runway two-six, and then took off again without stopping, looping back around another 270-degree left turn back to runway three-six-right. Up and down, round and round. Gear up, retract the flaps—turn, turn, turn—extend the flaps, gear back down. I made eighteen landings, and my partner did the same.

Sometimes I bounced the big bird on, and Captain Skipper would critique my technique, or lack of it, before my next attempt. He and the aircraft were highly tolerant of my initial rookie landings in a way I'm sure passengers wouldn't be. There's no feeling like learning by doing. Actually having my hands and feet on the controls of a 144-seat jet can't be described without using sex as an analogy. I'd dreamed about it, read about it, watched it, and was now finally doing it.

After thirty-six times around the pattern, we finally taxied in and put the plane to bed, although the morning flight crew was probably already on their way out to the airport from their layover hotel. In the distance, jagged cloud-to-cloud and cloud-to-ground lightning danced in the unimpeded frontal system that was marching toward us across the flat Oklahoma horizon. The way it lit up the twilight sky looked like celebratory fireworks specially ordered by Mother Nature to honor my first jet landings. I was as happy as a professional pilot could be. When I look back at my life, that moment is a top ten snapshot of my success. It belongs in my emotional highlight reel with my first solo, receiving the job offer phone call from TWA, and proposing to Susanne.

Perhaps what happened next is the root of my psychological predisposition for not letting myself ever become too happy. Emotionally and professionally, I'd reached the top of my mountain, only to be pushed off. Years of therapy might convince me what I already intellectually know—that the world is not out to deliberately chop me down—but I still feel that way sometimes. As soon as I started flying regular trips as a first officer and enjoying flights into what I grew up believing were real airports—La Guardia, JFK, and Washington National—in 172,000-pound, three-engine jets, my mom died.

Mom didn't have the aggressive, almost rival relationship with me that Dad and I shared; she was all-the-way supportive. Raised with three sisters, she subsequently mothered only sons. Nevertheless, she'd adapted to a masculine household and was always there for my younger brother and me. Once Tim and I were both enrolled in elementary school, she'd returned to teaching as a substitute, but her full-time job was making sure my brother and I turned out all right. She drove me on my paper route if it was raining, made sure we always arrived on time at all our sports activities (where she cheered like hell), and was an amazing cook. She was the security blanket of my youth. She forced me to try new things: shish kebab, meatloaf, cooking my own meals, traveling to Peru as a high school exchange student, and even learning how to drive. Dad would let me fly his single-engine airplane, but his metallic blue-gray 200,000-mile Mercedes was off limits. I primarily learned to drive with Mom, or occasionally with Dad in Mom's car. If she'd known how to fly, she would have been the one to teach me that as well.

My brother and I called Mom's Ford Fairmont *the green shoebox*. Its defining feature was a radio that cut out during right-hand turns, which forced the backseat passengers to sing the missing lyrics for the privilege of riding along. Learning to drive meant no more backseat off-key singing. Mom didn't just shuttle me to baseball and football practice before I earned my license; she conferred with the coaches and lost her voice while hollering during the games.

After I went to college, a young cop stopped my mother on her way home from the grocery store. "Mrs. Berry, I can't give you a ticket for speeding," he said. "You cheered through all my junior Babe Ruth baseball games. Please drive slower and have a great day." Mom's community involvement seemingly helped raise my entire local generation. As the female in our household, she was the cement that held us rockheads—Dad, my brother, and me—together.

Dad tells the story of my mother's passing with more detail than I do since he was there, so I asked him to write the upcoming guest passage. Don't worry; you're in good hands. He's a pilot, too—and I'll still be here at the other set of controls. But before Dad and I take you back to that day, I need to add a little background I learned way too late to avoid the estrangement that her passing amplified with my brother. My mother's death catalyzed a total family meltdown.

I knew I wanted to fly for a living, so my ambition drove me with a passion uncommon in teenagers who often take the time to explore their options first. I left for college six days after high school and graduated in two and a half years, staying straight through the summers to get ahead. I didn't realize the pressure this put on my younger brother. After high school, he didn't know what he wanted to do, so college was a short, unproductive experience as he lacked the determination to see where it could lead him. Instead of throwing more money into school, he returned home to live with our parents. It wasn't a triumphant return, and I think he felt bad about it, but he needed to conserve cash and come up with new goals.

I was renting a room in a crash pad on Long Island, close to JFK, and the drive to my childhood home in Connecticut was just over an hour. When I visited, my brother resented me. "Hey bro, how's it going?" I asked. I wasn't even met with a silent stare. He looked through me as if I didn't even exist. He was nineteen and trying to find himself. As a twenty-three-year-old first officer, I didn't have the judgment to know he needed to do things in his own time. I watched him live in my parents' house and ignore them completely, too. "Tim, what would you like to eat?" our Mom pleaded in an effort to make conversation and dinner. She stood directly between him and the TV, and still he slouched on the couch with his arms crossed while he scowled with a hostile, unfocused glare. He couldn't even be bothered to tell her to move out of the way. Perhaps it was just his way of dealing with not yet establishing his independence, but it made me angry to watch her frustration. I should have realized it was my parents' responsibility to finish raising him, not mine.

I believe death is final. The upside to this philosophy is that I don't waste any time accomplishing what I want to do and say in this lifetime. It's a strong motivational force to feel there are no second chances—no next life. The downside is that I'm less patient and understanding than many of my religious friends. At twenty-three, I was even more so. I wanted my brother to make things right with my parents for supporting him and giving him the time, space, and money to accomplish whatever he eventually decided he wanted to do with his own life. Time ran out before that happened.

Based in New York and flying domestically, I still craved Europe. My buddy Chris Terry and I often hopped over on our days off and explored new locations. We were regular riders on TWA's trans-Atlantic flights, making full use of our pass benefits. I think I slept in first class more often than my crash pad. We'd budget our expeditions by freeloading hotel rooms with friends still based overseas.

On a significant excursion to Frankfurt in the summer of 1989, we rented a car and four of us drove up and down the Rhine River looking at castles. We took another pilot, Steve, and a crew scheduler, Tracy, with us. We sampled local

Riesling wine and mostly drank Bitberger Pils. Every few kilometers, we'd see another towering stone fortress and shout, "Look, it's the Rheinstein, the most famous castle in all of Germany." We were fools on a wandering self-guided tour, but you couldn't slap the smiles from our faces. I took lots of pictures and promised to share extra prints with everyone when the film was developed. This was well before digital instant gratification.

Tracy went back to New York early as Chris and I had more time off. Chris met his future wife working at the hotel, so our trip became more than just an adventure for him. I eventually returned to JFK on a 747 jumpseat — a cockpit seat available to traveling pilots even when every cabin seat has been sold and the flight is full. While looking out at the world from this second-story perch, I wondered how the captain ever learned to taxi such a massive machine on which the wheels of the landing gear are some large distance behind the steering tiller and brake pedals. I fell in love with the Boeing 747 and craved to fly the majestic whale someday. I had no way of knowing that a devastating blow would eventually crush this dream, along with many others.

After we landed in New York at JFK, I found a message waiting for me in the crew computer advising me to contact Tracy, who was back working in crew scheduling. Since that busy office was at the far end of Hangar 12's central hallway near where I parked my car, I decided to drop by in person.

The fact that crew schedulers aren't allowed to put personal messages in a pilot's computer mailbox was the first clue I missed. That the entire crew-scheduling office — more like a small stadium entrusted to manage the chaos of an entire worldwide airline — went silent when I walked in on them was another clue that sailed over my head. Detective work was clearly not in my future. I strolled past many staring faces and sat my butt right on Tracy's desk. I faced her, but she turned away. "What's the matter?" I asked. "Did your dog die?" I was staring at the back of her head and the long, straight black hair that hung down to her shoulders. Slowly she turned.

Tracy had tears just forming. Mostly her eyes looked wet as she handed me a piece of paper. "Your dad wants you to call him at this number," she said.

This was before cell phones were common. I didn't have one, neither did my father, and I think the few people who did had to carry around a shoulder satchel for the lunchbox-sized battery. I looked at the Connecticut area code and the Riverside exchange and immediately surmised it must be the house of my parents' best friends, the Vances. "Did my dog die?" I asked.

Mr. Vance is a guy with a huge heart, but his delivery was always gruff. I knew he liked me, but conversations with him always seemed stoic and soldiery, like a drill sergeant trying to use his inside voice. When he answered the phone, crying and at a loss for words, all the alarms in my system finally tripped at once. Here, as promised, I'm turning this part of the journey over to my father.

SILENCE | BY W. LEONARD BERRY, JR.

It was Saturday morning, and I prepared pumpkin pancakes for Trish and me. I ate three, and she had two. Within minutes she said she was having trouble breathing and wanted to go to the hospital. I knew of her allergies but thought the flare-shaped EpiPen, always in the ready, would at least buy time. It didn't effectively kick in, and the mad dash to Greenwich Hospital began. Normally a fifteen-minute ride, I accomplished it in about half that time by racing down the wrong side of the street at full speed—horn blowing.

> *It was just a Saturday morning*
> *But her heart was racing*
> *And she was having trouble breathing*
> *Dad raced full speed with his horn blowing*
> *His mad dash*
> *Running lights*
> *And driving down*
> *The wrong side of the street*

After pulling up to the emergency room entrance and yelling for help, a couple of nurses appeared. "Shall I call for a code?" one asked the other. The answer was, "Yes!"

> *They all did their best*
> *Even cracked her chest*
> *But by now you know the rest*

The doctors began a desperate attempt at revival, and periodically one would come out to the waiting room to let me know the results of their efforts. A Franciscan brother on duty at the hospital came out of the emergency operating area, looked at me, and silently passed. His eyes said all I needed to know. He was probably thinking: *You are not one of the people I look after, and your loved one is no longer living.* The doctors finally came out and confirmed Patricia's death.

We had been married twenty-seven years, and ten minutes after a normal breakfast conversation she was gone. I found out the cause of death was an anaphylactic shock reaction to the pancake spices. Her windpipe swelled shut. There was nothing that could have been done about it, short of a tracheotomy.

Anaphylactic shock reaction
That's what the doctors said
After their desperate attempt at revival
And they pronounced my mother dead

What to do next? After seeing a local priest I knew well, calls to the family began. The first, to Las Vegas, began with the words, "This is the hardest call a son-in-law can make—Trish is dead." I don't think anything said after that registered.

Next my two sons, Mark and Tim, were notified. Mark was piloting for TWA and using days off to travel in Europe, and crew scheduling said he'd be back in the States in a couple days for his next trip. With both brothers attending, a very moving funeral memorial service took place shortly after their return to Connecticut.

Then the other shoe dropped: Tim and Mark were not talking to each other, and I wasn't sure why. It took me awhile to find out. It boiled down to Mark's accusation that Tim didn't treat his mother right, and by her suddenly dying, there was no way to correct the situation. No words would pass between brothers. Their attitudes were locked.

I knew of her allergies
To flowers, pollen, and honey bees
With Mom gone, angry feelings
With Mom gone, total loss
With Mom gone, angry feelings
Angry feelings and total loss

Looking back, I can understand the hurt. While growing up, teenagers often talk back to their parents if they think they can get away with it. But Tim used a different tactic; silence. He wouldn't even answer to a friendly good morning. I thought this more than a little odd to have a son eating and sleeping in our house but not speaking to his mother. I let it go, assuming it was just a teenager phase, and would soon pass. Sudden death prevented any return to normalcy. For what seemed like forever, I walked on eggshells, trying not to upset the good lines of communication I had with both young men. Mark blamed Tim for his actions, and not talking to each other was the cure. Tim's reasons for not talking to Mark were a little less clear. Who said silence is golden? It's not; it hurts.

Four plus years went by. It's easy to say the words *four years*, but it's a very long time. I'd hoped for a prodigal-son-type experience to end this standoff, but it didn't happen. Both brothers were in a no-talk mode, and nothing was going to change. Then one day, totally unexpected, it did. Mark returned from a scheduled flight in Europe via Boston and made a point to see Tim. Instantly a retro switch was thrown between them, and silence came to an abrupt end. They are once again best buddies. They talk to each other, snowboard together, and have taken an eraser to the silent years. It's like it never happened.

– W. LEONARD BERRY, JR.

I've got it — control of the story again — although it took a long time for me to get control of my family life after the loss of my mom.

> *Anaphylactic shock reaction*
> *That's what the doctors said*
> *After their desperate attempt at revival*
> *And they pronounced my mother dead*

I still feel awful looking back at my contribution to our complete meltdown. As upset as I was, I failed to recognize the additional pain I caused my father, and I wish I could have a do-over. My brother also needed my help and emotional support, and my neglect was inexcusable. To both of you, I'm sorry.

Death is the ultimate loss of control for a pilot who is used to studying, training, and mastering difficult tasks. After my mom died, I buried myself in my work for two big reasons. First, the airline was my other family. With Mom gone, and with my toxic, angry feelings toward my brother, I turned to the people who understood me best — my airline family. Second, I craved for a sense of control to return to my life. There's nothing like moving heavy metal in three dimensions, peering down on the earth from the Godlike perspective of the tropopause, and repeating the familiar mantras of checklists and procedures.

The reunification with my brother is one of the greatest gifts Susanne gave me during our time together. She arrived in my life during the silent years with Tim. I know she loved me and tried to understand my angry perspective, but I could tell she was hurt by my callous attitude toward Tim. She loved her brothers, and as my relationship with Susanne grew, she asked, "If we ever get married, would you invite your brother?" My *no* was automatic, but I could see in her expression that she was trying to hide her disapproval. It wasn't an overnight revelation, but as the idea of proposing to her grew, so did my interest in resolving my differences with Tim. Falling in love allowed me to do some long-overdue growing up. As my dad said, one day, with my life changing in amazing ways with Susanne, I cold-called my brother and told him I was going to be in Boston and wanted to see him.

Tim's and my actual conversation over dinner mattered less than the olive-branch effort I'd finally extended. I bid more trips out of Boston to catch up on lost time. Tim, Susanne, and I all attended my dad and Faith's wedding together, five years after my mom's passing. When Susanne died on TWA Flight 800, my brother became one of my closest friends. There's no longer silence between us, but I still have issues with success. My darkest times always seem to immediately follow my greatest happiness.

25 | REFUGE

NANCY HELPED ME build the puzzle of how I ended up in her office. She couldn't do the healing for me, but she strived to point me toward some sort of understanding.

Formerly, my airline life was my refuge after my mom died and my family life dissolved. I had lots of aircraft switches to flip, buttons to push, and dials to read while I reprogrammed my life without her. It's also what made losing Susanne years later even more difficult. Along with the loss of my present and future family with Susanne when she died, I also lost my place to hide in my work. When TWA wouldn't let me bury my feelings in the comfort of the cockpit, my internal pinball machine tilted. When Susanne died on my airline, I had nowhere to turn. Every crewmember knew somebody on TWA Flight 800, and I was a catalyst that magnified all of their grief. If our plane was our church, and they were the mourners on either side of the aisle, I was the widower in the pew with a view.

Nancy tried to adjust my internal switches and dials, but it was the buzzer to Nancy's makeshift office that became my reset button outside the entryway to what became my bimonthly man-cave, long before that term was made popular. Inside her office, I had a place for a time out, and I began to appreciate it, but old habits die hard. An object in motion remains in motion.

After Nancy prodded me through recalling the death of one brother, my estrangement and rebonding with my other brother, outliving my mother, and unraveling the competitive relationship with my father, she next turned her focus toward the other people I chose to surround myself with. She asked about my airline family, and I recalled a trip before my time with Susanne.

26 | MY AIRLINE FAMILY —
WHERE DREAMS ARE FREE
Dirty Double-Crosser

When I wander, I do so with uncommon resources. I have always relished the unlimited access I have to the world during my time off and the constant exposure to people who feel the same way, whether they're running from themselves, too, or just seeing the sights. Forget the Knights Templar or any other secret society you've heard of; the best and most expansive inner circle is the airline family. Without secret handshakes or hidden temples, we wear prominently displayed ID cards, meet at a loose collection of favorite worldwide watering holes, and bond over our shared lifestyle of relentless training and perpetually new horizons. Or maybe it's the shared knowledge of endlessly recycling an outfit not too dirty to wear — something out of our Rollaboard suitcase that passes the sniff test without braising our nose hairs — that joins us.

In 1992, during the silent years after my mother's death and before encountering Susanne at the cove party, with only carry-on baggage, I ventured over to Africa by way of Oktoberfest in Munich. Singing drinking songs while swinging rain barrel-sized *Biersteins* inside Germany's major brewery tents seemed like a great way to unwind. But the real adventure lay waiting in the form of a pre-arranged photo safari in Zimbabwe. So I left the seven million-person beer-fueled bacchanalian orgy behind and pass-rode on Egypt Air down to Cairo. Pass riding is the cousin of jumpseating, and they're both forms of aircraft surfing. I'd sit at the airport and try to catch a ride on an aluminum wave that's flying in the general direction of my preferred destination. This airline benefit could also be confused with aerial hitchhiking. Non-revenue travel is the perk of airline life — after the camaraderie of the people who share it, of course.

My realization of how small the aviation world really is began when another pass-riding pilot sat next to me on Egypt Air. He was heading to his new job at Transmed Airlines, an Egyptian-based Boeing 737 outfit. I asked him if he knew my friend Chip Sherden, a furloughed America West pilot working there. He did. So on a whim I followed him to the hotel where most of that airline's pilots were living and beat on Chip's door. "Open up," I yelled, "it's the police!"

I could tell Chip was only mildly surprised by my unscheduled visit when he replied, "You sounded exactly like a cop does not." The world isn't so big that Cairo is a safe refuge from pilot buddies showing up unexpectedly and initiating an impromptu trip to see the Pyramids.

Chip and I hired a cab for the day and we set off for Giza with a couple of road brews. The cab driver's eyes glared disapprovingly, but he maintained a smile with his tight lips. I considered whether it was wise to drink openly in a Muslim country, but Chip said, "Don't worry about it"—and he lived here.

Cairo is dusty. It's like looking at the world though a dirty beer bottle, and we were doing that, too. The taste that the abrasive air left in my mouth was more like chalk. It also carried the grit of sand but without the hint of salt I'd experienced at beaches around the world. I couldn't even wash it down with my Stella Export—the local lager that's not to be confused with Belgium's Stella Artois— but I tried. For a local beer, Export was the way to go. It had less formaldehyde than the domestic concoctions (at least that's the rumor), which tasted like they were made with Nile water—river swill with a kick.

The road was bumpy, and we had become used to the shaking and jostling as we passed through a village on a two-lane street when the buildings emptied their people all around us. Panic materialized from nowhere. People were screaming and looking blankly in all directions.

"What's happening?" I asked the cab driver, but his English was only as good as my Arabic—which is to say we were on a strictly hand-signal relationship. He turned around with his fists in the air, knuckles up, and shook them maniacally. Chip and I ducked down in the back seat. "Does he mean someone is shooting at us?" I asked. "Is that the international signal for machine gun?"

"I don't know, but keep down," Chip said. "Two Americans would be a big prize for extremists." I knew the beers en route were a bad idea.

Our driver kept the cab moving, albeit slowly, while weaving around a lot of people in the street. Eventually we cleared the village and looked up. He kept trying to tell us something in Arabic, but we couldn't understand.

Finally we reached the Pyramids. We were shaken, but the other tourists seemed calm. We thanked our driver with a good tip and our one Arabic word: shukron. Egyptian pound notes feel like they were just dug up—my cats' tongues feel less gritty. I was more than happy to spend them all before I left the country. Then the cabby surprised us with, "Welcome."

As we stretched our legs and walked towards Cheops, the Great Pyramid, we encountered a group of German gals. I recognized their language, but unless they were comparing the ancient wonders to Bavarian beer tents, I didn't have a prayer of understanding them. "*Spechen Sie Englisch?*" I asked.

"*Ja,*" one replied.

I told them of our shake-up on the ride. Chip helped by mimicking the driver's machine gun choreography with his hands. Then I asked if they knew what had happened.

"There was earthquake. It stop now."

That explained what the cab driver was trying to tell us with his shaking fists. Even his hand signals were lost in translation.

"Do you think it's safe to go into the pyramids after an earthquake?" Chip asked me.

The German gal answered, "*Ja,* they here for more six thousand years. I think they here a few more." Chip and I admired her world view.

One of my all-time favorite quotes was delivered in the shadow of Cheops. As we approached the edifice, there was a pile of rocks along the side of the path that caught my eye. I passed my camera to Chip while I held a square stone over the top of the pile like I was stacking. It's all in the camera angle, so I instructed Chip to get on the ground to line up the shot. Just a little amateur trick photography—I wanted it to look like we were building our own pyramid.

The young German women stared at us incredulously. At the base of a world wonder, we'd become their entertainment. I thought we were going to get chastised for our foolishness. Instead, their English speaker said, "Dreams are free." I still carry that quote with me and refer to it when friends say I'm attempting the impossible, like trying to train my cats not to shed on my bed.

Giza was only a one-day photo op, a cultural diversion, and another wonderful detour en route to my real destination—Zimbabwe. I needed to leave that night for Harare, the capital, where my buddy Katherine was waiting, but first I needed a visa for Ethiopia to connect through Addis Ababa, where maybe I'd take a look around while I was there (nonstop flights to Harare were non-existent). Many flights leave Egypt in the middle of the night because daytime is often too hot for takeoffs, at least while carrying a significant load of passengers, cargo, and fuel. So Chip and I grabbed another cab and set off for the Ethiopian embassy.

I carried two extra passport pictures, but the woman behind the counter demanded, "You need three." Her expression and tone of voice were far from cordial—scowling and curt.

"Will a photocopy be all right?" Chip asked.

"Yes, but we don't have one. You must come back."

We didn't have time to return before they closed, and I detest being stifled by functionaries. Chip felt the same way, so he responded, "Do you have a bathroom I can use?"

She nodded vaguely, and that was enough to set Chip in motion, opening doors and peering inside every room in the building. I didn't realize he'd grabbed my passport, but he came back with three pages, each having my picture on it.

"Where did you make these copies?" the officious female demanded.

"Not here, obviously," Chip replied. "Because you don't have a copy machine. Remember?"

She gave me a murderous stare, then rooted around in her desk drawers. After fumbling with a lot of office supply clutter, she stamped my passport with something she'd found, and then Chip and I left. Only when I checked in at the airport did the ticket agent point out that I had a *transit visa*. That bitter bureaucrat had the last laugh. I could leave Egypt, but I couldn't step foot on Ethiopian soil. Maybe I was supposed to bribe her for the photocopies? Perhaps she didn't like Americans? Possibly she'd lost her house in the earthquake? I'll never know.

I boarded Ethiopian Airlines for the connection via Addis. Before landing, the flight attendant conveyed an invitation from the captain to join him in the cockpit. As I sat in the jumpseat of the 757, looking out over Ethiopia for the first time, the captain explained that Trans World Airlines instructors had trained his airline in the 1950s. He wanted me to know I was an honored guest onboard his aircraft. I hadn't yet been born, and even if the captain had, he would have certainly been only a child at the time. Yet we shared a collective camaraderie passed down from a previous generation of pilots working together for airlines based on different continents.

I watched him land—a perfect grease job that I knew he was proud of demonstrating for his TWA guest—and it was the first time I saw a runway with turn buttons at the end—a little extra pavement on the side of the runway to make it wider for about the length of an aircraft. The captain made a tight 180-degree U-turn in this remarkably limited space. It reminded me of the small but scary Monster Mouse rollercoaster at New York's Playland amusement park, which hung its riders out over the edge of the track before making each turn. I swore our nose wheel was going off the pavement, but he knew his ship down to the last square inch like a New York City cab driver, and we backtracked along the runway to the terminal.

Ethiopia looked like what I expected of Africa — amazingly green in some spots and barren in others, but the air was a lot cleaner than the dustbowl of

Cairo. Modern buildings mixed with tin roof huts, and the land spread out over rolling hills with distant mountains. I was glad for the view from the cockpit because I wasn't allowed to leave the airport on my transit visa. For a nation that reached out for hunger relief funds with starving, pot-bellied, nearly naked poster children, I was surprised they didn't want me, or my tourist dollars, in their country. God forbid I prime their economy with foreign currency. I was confined between glass walls in the transit area until my connecting flight to Harare departed.

Eventually I made it to Zimbabwe. Katherine had spent a couple days at the hotel pool unwinding and had made friends with a traveling oompah band from Germany while waiting for me to arrive. Oktoberfest was everywhere. I bought matching leather pith helmets to put us in the adventure spirit and we started our photo safari in Hwange National Park (formerly known as Wankie). Katherine has a thing for leather. I still remember the provocative outfit she was wearing when we first met years before. I was in Albuquerque, New Mexico, working my way west, trying to catch a ride on Southwest Airlines. That's where I saw the tall, strong, French-braided brunette standing off to the side of the check-in counter. Notable was her short, hot-pink leather miniskirt, showing off two tanned, athletic legs to best effect.

I don't recall the clue that first tagged her as a fellow non-revenue traveler, but I could feel it. Maybe I saw a Southwest luggage tag or pass-riding paperwork in her hand instead of a passenger ticket, but I think it was more intuitive. I believe non-revs give off a pheromone that can be detected only by other airline employees. Most likely it was her body language — that combined look of hope and apprehension we all have as the number of remaining seats dwindles with each called-out name from the standby list that isn't our own. We both wanted to belt our butts into one before our selected aircraft pulled away.

"Do you think we'll both get on?" I asked, risking a conversation-opening gambit.

She sized me up formally, although I'd caught her peeking at me while I was checking out her attention-grabbing skirt. "It looks pretty tight. Who are you?"

I knew she meant the passenger load, not her outfit, but I couldn't help smirking. I think she really wanted to know if I fit before or after her in travel priority. She smiled as I replied, "TWA." She probably heard it as *other airline*, and that definitely put me behind her for a chance at a seat.

Both our last names were finally called, and we exchanged first names on the Jetway. Normally only middle seats would be left, but Katherine finagled two together at the back of the plane where the working flight attendants usually save a resting spot for themselves.

"Do you want to see my mouse tattoo?" Katherine asked over complimentary cocktails — something else she was able to finagle.

"Um, excuse me?"

"My mouse tattoo," she repeated, this time grabbing the inside of her pink leather skirt and just barely starting to slide it up.

"Let me think about ... Yes," I said, trying to be funny but definitely not pulling it off.

She inched up her skirt a little more. "Do you see it now?"

"No, not yet."

She got her skirt to the edge of revealing more than those smooth, enticing legs. I took the bait and leaned in, trying to see where they met in the middle and if this mouse tattoo was hiding somewhere on her inner thigh. "See it yet?"

I took my time and finally whispered, "No." There was just enough pink leather shelter left to keep the question of whether or not she was wearing a thong a mystery. Definitely no tattoo.

Suddenly she yanked her skirt back down. "Oh well, I guess my pussy ate it!" I knew then that I was going to get along great with this gal.

She had a protective outer shell that didn't melt in my hands or my mouth. We both agreed not to go too deep — emotionally. Mostly we had a solid friendship — two independent people who wanted to see the world, anywhere, anytime. She understood that the travel monster had to be fed. Sometimes I wouldn't hear from her for weeks or months, and then the phone would ring.

"Zimbabwe," was all she said. It was all she had to say.

"I'm so in." She somehow knew I had vacation coming up. My guess is she had other friends at TWA who looked up my schedule for her — early cyber stalking, but I wasn't complaining.

"After you finish playing drinking games at Oktoberfest, find your way there. Meet me in Harare. I'm taking British Airways through Heathrow."

"Let me do some research and call you back."

So I'd looked into it, and then we were both here on the Dark Continent. We rode in an uncovered Jeep three times a day through the game park. Giraffes, unafraid of humans, nearly stepped over us to cross the dirt road. The night ride led us face-to-face with a water buffalo, almost on cue after our driver told us they're the most dangerous animals on the range. They snort and look just plain mean, so I had no problem believing their reputation.

We slept in a tree house built on stilts at the Sikumi Tree Lodge and watched game graze underneath us from the perch of our elevated wooden deck while admiring the beauty of the plains. Mosquito netting around the beds added to the feel of the continent that was very much alive. A steady stream of vodka tonics was supposed to make our sweat less appealing to airborne pests, or maybe it just made us notice them less. This was no zoo experience. I kept expecting a giraffe to peek its head in our window and wondered what I might offer to feed it. Well, none did, but we saw lots of them up close. The kneeling warthogs were among my favorite. Every sunset, I watched them rooting for food with their snouts while Katherine worked the knots out of my neck and shoulders and kept our wine glasses full. I was young enough to mix liquors and not suffer the two-day hangover that would haunt me today.

From furry new friends to one of the natural wonders of the world, we wanted to see it all, so we set out for Victoria Falls on Air Zimbabwe. The flight was almost sold out, so we bought full-fare tickets to guarantee ourselves seats. Pass benefits are great, but if an airline employee tells you he never pays for flying, he's lying. Sometimes the peace of mind of becoming a normal ticketed traveler is worth the extra money. We still received the sincere welcome of the crew who could sense we were air staff—just as easily as I'd sniffed out Katherine's non-rev status in Albuquerque when I'd first met her—and they gave us tips on the best place to stay.

I woke up in the Makasa Sun Casino Hotel—advertised as *the closest hotel to Victoria Falls*—to the sound of crashing water and a family of monkeys in our room. They ran across our bed, leaped off the dresser by the window, and swung like Tarzan from the hanging branches that they caught. It was a startling wake-up call, but a lot of fun to watch once I realized they were just playing. I kept thinking they must have a collection of shiny watches and jewelry in a tree somewhere, but all of ours were accounted for.

By pure luck, we saw *the smoke that thunders* during the dry season—the best time. Excessive mist hides most of the falls' beauty during the wet season. After some contemplation, we crossed footbridges stretched across the Zambezi River into Zambia that would cause Indiana Jones to pause. The sheer cliffs on either side dropped off the equivalent distance of a football field from end zone to end zone. In the movies, the middle slat would always break, and the camera would zoom in on the broken pieces falling for an eternity. I worried I'd become the unsuspecting tourist whose foot would cause this, and I'd be left dangling and clinging for dear life. It was just as well we didn't have enough time to do the bungee jump from these suspension walkways into a river raft, but we were excited enough already about this trip.

I thought TWA's route structure was expansive, but this experience made me feel at home well beyond the reach of my airline's printed city timetable—the adventurer's sacred worldwide pocket companion that was once available for free at every ticket counter and has long since become a relic replaced by online travel information. From fellow airline traveling accomplices to cockpit views of countries beyond my passport documentation's reach to local lodging tips, aviation is a passion that's in my blood, and I'm happily surrounded by people who feel the same way. The crews who make airplanes move worldwide are more than a network—they're my extended airline family.

We're dirty double-crossers
While the world goes out to play
We show up to work
Over every holiday
We're dirty double-crossers
We're always in the air
If you want to go somewhere
We're the ones who'll get you there

27 | WANDERLUST

NANCY FIGURED OUT that my primary way of dealing with stress was by escaping. I may be a fighter at heart, but when there was no clear enemy, when it was grief I was dealing with that couldn't be physically punched, then I'd hit the road. To effectively run away, I couldn't just tie some old clothes inside a handkerchief at the end of a stick and shove off down a river Huckleberry Finn-style. My kind of escape often required vaccinations and visas.

Faced with this accusation, I asked, "Can't we just call it wanderlust? If it's an affliction, I'd rather have a more poetic name for my need to disappear over the horizon."

"I didn't say it was a bad thing," she told me. "And perhaps it's therapeutic. Living for the moment, day by day, does have a way of unlocking your mind when it's stuck on negative thoughts."

I was glad she wasn't headed down the direction of taking my travel benefits away. After my experience with the company psychiatrist, I harbored a secret feeling that these sessions could have consequences, even though they were set up purely to help me. I told Nancy this, and she again assured me our meetings were strictly confidential. I could share them, but she could not.

It's a sad fact — one that Nancy helped me acknowledge — that we can never recapture our innocence. I wondered if I could ever be as happy traveling alone or with buddies as I was before I'd fallen in love. I disclosed another of my previous adventures so Nancy would understand their importance to me — this time it was a visit to the Greek islands. I was still vehemently defending what was never at stake to begin with, but I wasn't always rational while rebuilding my life without Susanne.

28 | ARE YOU A CARDINAL?

Cardinal Puff

I WAS SITTING ON the matted floor of the gym when that first shot of pain startled me. I had my feet together with my knees spread out wide, my hands around my feet, and my elbows were gently pushing against the inside of my legs to stretch my hamstrings and groin. It was my left knee that snapped, crackled, and popped.

Working out usually has a magical escapist quality and a way of making my mind feel better, as well as my body. *Never stretch, just start out slow.* I'd be a lot healthier if I'd followed my own advice. As a man of the world, young and independent, it pissed me off that I was brought to my knees for doing something as cautious as stretching.

I toughed it out. Instead of legwork, I exercised my upper body that day with some bench pressing and pull-ups on the Gravitron machine—a workout tool I both love and hate. I would address it formally as an adversary when approaching. "Good morning, mean old Mr. Gravitron." I didn't take it lightly— I already knew gravity is a law.

As a kid, I hated doing standing leg-over stretches. My football and baseball coaches would make our entire team bend at the waist and stretch one leg at a time, reaching with our fingertips and bouncing for our toes. I just knew this was a bad idea. Now experts agree the bouncing part was a mistake—like secondhand smoke, lead paint, and asbestos turned out to be. I think the whole stretching thing is the problem. It's a painful fact that I tore my knee while stretching before a workout.

In a few days, the pain in my knee subsided. I'm not a doctor, but I don't think we have a lot of nerve endings in our knees. The subsequent amount of tearing and grinding damage I did to my meniscus while running and hiking without any additional suffering seems to indicate this.

Running was all the rage, and additionally I was training myself for a marathon. I didn't have a schedule or a trainer or anything fancy. I just wanted to run 26.2 miles for the satisfaction of accomplishing it. I started with a 2.2-mile loop in my neighborhood, worked up to 3.3, 4.4, and then 5.5-mile jaunts. The further I pushed myself before connecting between two extremely winding and hilly — yet somewhat parallel — roads seemed to magically add 1.1 miles to my path. Then I started adding the loops together to make longer runs. I never ran two days in a row, and I followed the general rule that muscles need forty-eight hours to recover. I felt I was doing everything right — what could go wrong?

I felt runner's high for the first time when I reached half my goal, and I believed what I'd read somewhere: if I could run half a marathon, I could run the whole thing. I ran 13.2 miles in a single day just before leaving for Greece on holiday, as the Europeans put it. The Aegean Sea was beckoning.

A little hilly island has held a special appeal ever since I first discovered it, where whitewashed walls meet golden sand and I can wade half a kilometer out into turquoise water before I'm in over my head. This was my dream retirement location where I can start to taste the feta cheese and olive oil whenever I fantasize about it too long.

My buddy Cary and I set off for the Greek island of Ios, the place I'd scouted the year before as the best place for beaches, nightlife, beautiful women, and excessive drinking. Finding an actual relationship had yet to congeal as a desirable objective, although everybody told me that would change when I met the right one. Susanne was still a few years over my horizon. Perhaps I wasn't completely over the death of my mom. I didn't have Nancy to talk through these kinds of things yet. Travel and adventure still ruled my decision making, although looking back, this excursion did reveal my preference for Scandinavian women.

My liver was in shape along with the rest of me. Calories couldn't stick to the half-marathon man. Cary's and my alcohol infusion began on the beach with topless Swedes who took off what remained of their bikinis to go swimming so they wouldn't have to sit in wet fabric when they returned from the water. Cary and I admired more than just their logic. Along with what nature gave them, they also shared their vodka-soaked watermelon with us while everyone passed around an acoustic guitar. Scandinavian goddesses are hard to say no to, and free food and drink — all in one oversized ripe gourd — is a pleasure best experienced in their company, on the sand, and overlooking our favorite new windsurfing cabana at the edge of postcard-quality, denim blue water. We spit the seeds into cups to keep the beach pristine. I learned the basic open guitar chords, how to strum along, and lyrics to a few universal songs. *What do you say to a drunken sailor? Way, hey, an' up she rises.* For that entire sea shanty, all I needed to finger on the fretboard was an A-minor and a G. Paradise can also be educational.

For dinner we all gathered in the high village, tucked away from marauding pirates of old, and fed our euphoria with Domestica white wine, Greek salad (heavy on the feta), and fried calamari. Conversation revolved around retiring to this perfect world—idle banter that I still entertain in my daydreams. Those famous whitewashed buildings were kept spotless with continual coats of paint, rumored to contain asbestos, possibly accounting for the cough we all acquired more than a week into our vacation. Of course, it couldn't be our abusive level of alcohol consumption—combined with the intensity of the summer sun and a total disregard for adequate sleep—that drove away our health. Denial is a beautiful thing.

Nevertheless, we were young and seemingly indestructible, and we continued with our nightlife migration ritual. Following dinner, we spread out among the many local bars. The Swedes favored the Blue Note, owned by Francesco, who also owned our hotel. We took turns slamming shots while lying on the bar, and the first round of Amstel beers always came from the Swedes. They would shout, "Because we are Swedish!" as a toast with every round they bought. Cary and I would protest, but the Viking descendants had a war-like quality about them in their insistence. They even carried around a giant flag from their home city of Goteborg to mark their new territory, which they claimed they *captured* from their city square. I think they mistranslated stole. Nevertheless, it made them easy to find anywhere on the island. They were like a marauding wave of blond hair, except they never put on their beer muscles. Not a single fight broke out during my entire stay on Ios. They were fun Vikings, raising many a glass or a mildly protesting woman over their heads—but never a fist.

It was after everyone was really good and liquored up that we all met at one of the two Irish pubs for dancing. The Dubliner Pub usually had live music, but the Sweet Irish Dream allowed dancing on their stone tables. That's where I was, long past midnight, shaking, bouncing, and singing to the music with a couple dozen of my new closest friends, when my knee gave out.

In slow motion, I recall twisting to share my attention with three sweaty, T-shirt-and-shorts-wearing, barefoot ladies at once—all of us up on the elevated stone slab table together—when the ripcord was pulled inside my brain, and every signal was lost except my internal emergency override alarm. Pain penetrated my alcohol-infused fog, and I collapsed in order to instantly take all of my weight off of my mutinous left leg. On my way down, I reached out with both hands to maintain some stability, and I ended up grabbing handfuls of T-shirts and what was inside them. Nobody took offense. The severity of my injury was reflected in the suddenly concerned faces of these three gals. My expression of pain must have startled them more than my inappropriate body contact.

When I tell people I was dancing on a table in Greece, they always assume I was drunk (I was) and that I fell off (I didn't). It wasn't climbing up on a table, as irresponsible as that sounds, that did me in. It was the twisting moment I put on my knee. If I'd tried that drunken spin maneuver on the floor, the same thing would have happened. My body spun, but my knee stayed in place. Even with alcohol washing my brain and flowing steadily through my veins, I knew I was in big trouble.

I crawled down from my perch and tried to sit in a chair. Cary and Nikolas, one of our new Viking friends, intercepted and carried me out of the bar to sit on a rock and deep breathe some fresh air. What a beautiful world it would be if that's all I had needed. The clean Aegean breeze is void of interfering smells except the gentle hint of salt infused by the sea, unless a whiff of calamari frying up in some olive oil happens to drift by from a nearby open window, unusual this late at night. The sea's breath whispered a healing quality through my racing mind but sadly had no effect on my injured knee. Cary asked me how much it hurt, and I said, "We'll know in the morning." The idea of leaving the party hurt almost as much as the swelling.

Although my celebratory resilience earned a collective laugh from my concerned friends, I couldn't straighten my knee past a thirty-degree angle. Putting any weight on it was completely out of the question. Just then, Pernilla, one of the living, breathing, and smiling Nordic goddesses that Cary had a special crush on, passed by and saw I was injured. She gave me a huge hug, kissed my cheek, and wished me, "You to feel better."

"I helped him," Cary said in hopes of a similar embrace.

"You're a good man," she said, this time in perfect English while smiling even bigger, and then she left into the night, leaving behind a faint scent of peach—either from her perfume or body lotion. Whatever it was, it seemed to invisibly pull us along, but I was going nowhere without help. I was grounded with a damaged left main landing gear.

"You lucky dog," Cary said, with the spell that Pernilla had cast during her brief appearance only now slowly draining from his far-off eyes. "That was my hug and kiss you just received. Where's the nearest table so that I can twist my knee?"

Cary and Nikolas had to carry me back to my hotel; I had no hope of walking. I slept off the intoxication and truly felt the damage I had done in the morning. If you've ever crawled to consciousness through throbbing pain and the dread of fully awakening, then you know. Before this injury, I'd woken each morning to the feeling of great anticipation for the day ahead. Several times whole hoards of Swedes were already in my room turning on lights and opening curtains, and one would invariably say, "Take morning piss. The day has long begun." But this morning my mind kept telling me to keep my eyes shut and stay in my dream world. My knee overshadowed any hangover signals and dominated my thinking. It was Francesco, our Greek host, who knocked on the door and then told me in broken English, "Doctor come. Doctor here come. You stay." As if I had a choice.

"You will live. 5,000 drachma please." That was the official prognosis. The doctor had knocked, entered the room I was sharing with Cary to conserve funds, looked at my knee without touching it, and delivered his short speech—as well as his bill—all in one breath. The only thing to admire about him was his efficiency at lining his pockets.

I had Cary pay him from my wallet. On an island ruled by locals, with ships only arriving once or twice a day, what else could I do? The doctor had performed my exam, the entire transaction was completed in less than two minutes, and he was gone. Cary looked at my knee, mimicking the doctor's useless gestures like he was communing with Athena for guidance, and then said, "I would have told you that for 2,000 drachma."

It was Francesco who found the only crutch on the island. Not two, just one. I used it to hobble around the village. I wasn't going to let a little thing like being lame ruin my fun. Francesco has a full mop of dark hair complete with a bushy mustache and a curly salt and pepper beard. He looked fifty from the perpetual summer celebrations, but he was only thirty. He offered me free Kamikaze shots to kill the pain if I could hobble to the Blue Note Bar that night. I looked at Cary in my pathetic one-crutch state and said, "So I got that goin' for me, which is nice."[3] I tried putting my crutch to Cary's neck like Bill Murray did with a pitchfork in *Caddyshack*, but Cary easily brushed it away.

That night Cary and I went to the village for dinner and met two English girls we'd met the day before. Ios attracted a fully international clientele, even though we'd mostly been adopted or conquered by the Scandinavians. We bonded with these lasses over a drinking game — surprise, surprise. "Are you a Cardinal?" Cary asked as an icebreaker.

"Sure as shit I am," they both responded in unison.

Cary's mouth opened and a barely audible, unintelligible sound came out. I think he tried to say, "Holy crap."

I just laughed. Cary hadn't traveled very much—I'd teased him that his passport cherry had been broken when we passed through immigration in Athens

---

3 *Caddyshack*. Dir. Harold Ramis. Perf. Bill Murray. 1980. Film. Billy Murray's character Carl Spackler's dialog.

and he received his first international entry stamp. His job was selling wireless microphones to musicians, and aside from the occasional Austin or Los Angeles convention, he was usually chained to a desk on Long Island. Cary's sudden realization that his favorite New York drinking game was also known in this far corner of the world cheered me up. These lasses knew how to play Cardinal Puff.

What can we do
With a full can of beer
A bunch of our friends
And some time on our hands?

I'll tell you my story
About the Great Cardinal Puff
Do my finger tapping
And other sacred stuff

So here's to the Cardinal Puff
For the first time tonight
Watch the choreography
And be sure to get it right

They key to the game is that once you've solved all the intricate rituals associated with consuming a beer — specific hand and body movements, finger tapping, bouncing in your chair, and carefully chosen words — you then have to immediately answer the magic question the correct way every time it's asked or lose your status. "Are you a Cardinal?"

"You bet your sweet ass I am," was the line we'd learned on Long Island, but our new friends' reply was just as good, if not better.

Once disordained for failure to reply correctly, it took two current Cardinals to witness your successful repeat performance of the game to reclaim the title. Errors required finishing the object beer and then starting over with a fresh one. If you didn't get it right early on, the inebriation would make the task nearly impossible. Playing this on Long Island, I witnessed one of my buddies puke over the railing of my apartment and directly into my roommate's open Jeep that was parked in the driveway below. So far, everyone in Greece was keeping their liquor in their stomach.

To pass or fail the challenge
We each drink a full beer
Becoming a Cardinal looks easy
But it's harder than it appears

Are you a Cardinal?
Any time that question's asked
"You bet your sweet ass I am"
You'd better answer fast

So here's to the Cardinal Puff
For the second time tonight
My finger tapping looks the same
It's close, but not quite

To pass or fail the challenge
Put the can to your lips
Everything matters
Even how many sips

Cary couldn't stop commenting that the game was making it around the world. Maybe it had long ago, and we were just learning about it. I think it's drinking that will eventually bring about world peace. So far we were getting along great with Greeks, Swedes, and English lasses. I bought the next round of Amstels.

Are you a Cardinal?
Any time that question's asked
"You bet your sweet ass I am"
You'd better answer fast

So here's to the Cardinal Puff
For the third time tonight
Have you paid attention
Think you can get it right?

Once a Cardinal, always a Cardinal
The table is dry

Now you've seen me do it
I dare you to try

Conversation turned to the physician's visit, and one of the girls asked, "Was the doctor a man or a woman?"

"Can't women become doctors in England?" I asked. It seemed like an odd, sexist question coming from a seemingly educated female.

"Oh, good," said the other gal. "You saw the real doctor then, if it was a woman who came to visit you."

"No," Cary corrected, "the doctor was a male." He explained the 5,000-drachma prognosis of my probable survival. He tried to sound Greek as he mimicked, "You will live," while once again pretending to touch all around my knee without actually making contact, just like the doctor.

"It's a good thing he said that," the first girl said with excited, dramatic emphasis. "The only male doctor on this island is a veterinarian. If he didn't think you'd live, it's his habit of shooting his patients."

I looked at Cary and punched him on the bicep. Then I said, "See, 5,000 drachma wasn't such a bad deal after all."

I felt bad eventually taking the only crutch off the island. I had no choice. Three days after the Sweet Irish Dream table-dancing debacle, the swelling had gone down a little, but my knee was still locked at a thirty-degree bend. Cary moaned about having to carry my pack down the hundred and ten giant steps to Ios Harbor in order to catch our ship to Piraeus — the Athens Harbor. I told him that if he did a good job as my Sherpa, I'd put in a word with Pernilla for a hug. He didn't find my comment as funny as I did. I was trying not to focus on the surgery I expected in my near future. I further aggravated him by making the obvious connection between his name and his new task. "Are there two r's in Cary?"

Back in the States, I consulted an orthopedic specialist. I received an MRI and then asked Dr. Rodda if I needed surgery. "Do you mind not being able to walk?" he asked in return.

"OK, good point." Surgery was scheduled without further questions. He offered some friendly advice and told me that people over two hundred pounds or over six feet tall aren't made to be runners, and I was both. "It's too hard on the joints."

Awesome advice, except a little late. It turns out I'd torn my meniscus in that stretching accident, and then I was grinding it up with my marathon training.

The lack of nerves inside my knee allowed me to do some serious damage without feeling it. Shredded was the word Doc used after surgery, once he'd spent a good part of his day repairing it. I was still groggy from the anesthesia when he visited my hospital bed and explained that in his twenty-five hundred arthroscopies, mine was the longest of his career — three hours and twenty minutes. Any longer and he would have had to open me up for conventional surgery, which takes much longer to heal. I guess I won the prize for the most damage that was still manageable with tools guided through fancy straws into tiny incisions. He'd carved away two-thirds of my meniscus, leaving me with as large of a sliver of protection between my bones as possible, which still wasn't much.

The nurses — really fun and personable ladies in their fifties — and I developed a steady banter during my hospital stay. Post-op, they came to help me out of bed to use the bathroom.

"Ladies, I don't mind if you watch, but I can handle this, even though it's a two-handed procedure," I said for grins.

No sooner did I sit up, than projectile vomit spewed from my mouth. The world's fastest bedpan came from behind the closest nurse's back, and she caught every drop. She had the dexterity of a center fielder, and the Yankees could have used her. My mother would have cheered until she was hoarse.

After I spit one last gooey chunk into the bedpan, I commented that they seemed entirely too prepared for that. "Is there something you weren't telling me?"

"Most patients expel their anesthesia that way when they awaken," the center fielder said with a straight face. "It's the body's way of cleansing itself." I kept looking for a smile, but it was only in her eyes.

"Thanks for the lack of warning. Is there anything else I should know?"

"Well, most male patients also produce an erection under anesthesia," she explained. I could tell it was killing her not to laugh. "But yours should be back to a manageable size to urinate with by now, in case you have any more fluid left in you. Do you still want to try and reach the bathroom by yourself?"

"I guess I'll let you help me. Did I get a blue ribbon?"

Now her face finally lit up. This was the tail end of a joke I'd told them about a guy and his dog that both snored and how his wife solved the problem by tying ribbons around their erections. You've probably heard it. Just in case you haven't, the guy wakes up the next morning after a long night out drinking, looks at his dog, looks under the covers, sees both of the ribbons, and says to his faithful four-legged friend, "I don't know where we've been, Spot, but it looks like we won first and second place."

I'd told the long version of that joke to the nurses pre-op in order to make sure I bonded with them. People naturally try harder to save someone they relate to—at least that's what I figured. Rolling into surgery is scary, and I wanted my apricot-colored-scrubs-and-mask-wearing team to do their absolute best. It pays to be nice to the people who have my life in their hands. I guess my pre-op pep talks had made us a little closer. But hell, if fifty-year-old nurses can catch every drop of my puke and keep me comfortable during a record-breaking surgery, I'm glad they also have a sense of humor. At least they were smiling and not laughing at my erection. Where's Pernilla and my honorary Viking clan? I think I need another hug.

When Cary called to check up on me, he didn't ask how my surgery went; he asked, "Are you a Cardinal?"

> *Are you a Cardinal?*
> *Any time that question's asked*
> *"You bet your sweet ass I am"*
> *You'd better answer fast*

"Sure as shit I am." European living was rubbing off on me, and it would be a Scandinavian who eventually found her way all the way into my heart — but I had more emotional growth to do before I was ready to meet Susanne and start our intense relationship that would end with "until death do us part" even before we could utter those words in a ceremony.

29 | BREAKTHROUGH SESSION

NANCY WAS INTERESTED in my other relationships — the ones that didn't grow to Susanne's level. Perhaps she wanted me to see that I could build one with someone new someday, based on having had meaningful relationships in the past that didn't end in untimely death. The one that came to mind was quite the other extreme. It's one I really didn't want to talk about. It's the one that could have ruined my ability to have any kind of relationship at all before I ever attempted one with Susanne.

"That's perfect. That's what I want you to talk about today, Mark." I could see her eyes glow with anticipation of a breakthrough session brewing. This emotional scar that she suddenly wanted to pick and rub raw had caused me to do some heavy thinking on my own, while struggling not to hold all women accountable for the actions of a single malicious one. But that lesson hadn't come easily.

I told her a quote from a Jethro Tull song: "He who made kittens put snakes in the grass." [4] And then I had to explain, "Everyone is different. In my wander-lust days before Susanne smiled at me through her defensive posture, and we began our brief but intense odyssey together, I wasn't careful."

---

4 Anderson, Ian. "Bungle in the Jungle." *War Child*. Jethro Tull. Ian Anderson, 1974. Vinyl recording.

The Secret the Darkness Completely Concealed

"I'M PREGNANT."

Her eyes stared at me for my reaction and my reply. I still wasn't used to looking at her with hair she had deliberately cropped short, vindictively because I'd told her I loved her long, full locks I could run my fingers through and that also made a curtain around us when she kissed me from above. Her hair color varied with her mood, but I'd found the thickness, texture, and feel appealing. Anything I said recently seemed to be used as a way to punish me. I was giving my globetrotting a rest and attempting a real relationship with a Long Island gal, but I was starting to guess that she wanted me to break up with her so she wouldn't have to be the one to do it — and now this happens.

What other statement puts a man in such a strong spotlight? This is the single moment when a woman evaluates a man for the rest of his life: Will he support the family she's making? Many men pass this parental inspection with their partner of many years. They welcome the family plan they'd discussed and made together. But this game-changer was just dropped on me by a girlfriend of six months who'd become stubborn and difficult, and those were only the beginning of problems that were starting to show.

Our relationship was short and intense, only half a year between introduction and signs of procreation, and it began with her entrance into my close circle of friends that wasn't just another day at the beach.

The day a New York State judge ruled in the early 1990s that a woman can go topless anywhere it's appropriate for a man to take off his shirt was the best day imaginable on Long Beach, Long Island. That is if you're a red-blooded American male in his late twenties as I was. Bare breasts bloomed everywhere along the sandy shore. Unlike my experience in Europe where upper body tan lines didn't exist, bright white skin reflected the midday sun, exposed in open daylight for the first time. Sun worshippers kept generously massaging SPF-50 lotion where bikini tops used to be in order to prevent sunburn. This only added to the natural beauty of the ocean shoreline. *Natural* being the key word. Our little beach community suddenly felt as exotic as the Greek island of Ios. But the new topless phenomenon wasn't limited to the sand and the water. I took a walk to my lunch spot where the smell of baking bread lured in everyone downwind for many blocks.

At my local deli the owners even took down their sign
"No Shirt" and "No Shoes" was suddenly fine
And they gave free cream-cheese bagels to topless girls standing in line
I was sandwiched between them and gladly paid for mine

I ran with a tight group in my Long Beach days, and our core was made of pilots and flight attendants living in crash pads: houses holding more people than they were made for, except that we were rarely all in town at the same time. Whoever wasn't out flying gathered together on the beach at the end of Michigan Avenue in the section known as the state streets. That's where I took my testosterone-driven intensity out on our homemade volleyball court. Several crafty flight attendant friends constructed support poles out of PVC, complete with tension ropes attached to scoops that we buried in the sand to keep the net taught. We even stretched and secured a perimeter rope. I wore my jet-black, hard plastic CTi2 leg brace — doctor's orders for sports — to prevent twisting my knee and further damaging my meniscus, but my buddies thought it was secretly spring-loaded to increase my vertical leap, and friendly accusations of cheating abounded.

Those of us on reserve, which was most of us back then, clipped our beepers to the net. The game paused with a concert of groans whenever one of them sounded its chirping wail. We knew that meant crew scheduling was looking for one of us to work a short-staffed flight to some faraway city. But as we counted the widebodies climbing out over the Atlantic Ocean from JFK, full of our fellow employees that had thankfully not called in sick for work, we killed endless summer days in the sand underneath the New York air traffic departure corridor. TWA Flight 800 was among them, launching daily without incident, usually while we were breaking down the net for the evening. But while the sun was still high in the sky, our volleyball court attracted the locals and was the primary catalyst for making new friends outside of the airline industry. Nothing was riding on our games except pride and bragging rights, but we played with the intensity of the AVP — albeit without the requisite skills of those pros.

I remember when *The Body* first appeared — she didn't just walk up to our court, she circled all the way around the rope perimeter. Then, when she didn't successfully divert us from our game, she circled again—stopping occasionally to make exaggerated poses. She put on a one-woman bikini fashion show to compete for our attention.

Between fighting for points, I noticed her hair was dark copper—not the shiny orange of a new penny, now mostly made of zinc with only a trace of copper—or a natural redhead who'd been out in the sun, but more the hue of a copper pipe you might find in your unfinished basement if you rubbed it raw with a towel. It was a color that came from a box to make her look as she'd chosen to appear, or maybe so the people of her past wouldn't recognize her. It was long, flowing, and fell loosely over her shoulders and partway down her back. She shook it with a wide bending roll of her head for dramatic effect or to brush it out of the way of her eyes without using her hands. "Do you mind if I play in the next game?" she finally asked.

We were asked that question a lot, and sometimes we'd welcome a stranger to fill out a team that was missing a player. Beeper attrition was a common condition. The Body was one of those newcomers who we did work into our rotation. She had a pair of the most perfect breasts that bounced as she bumped or set the ball for our spikes. I mean, seriously, what mortal would deny her the opportunity to play when she asked? As attractive as what Mother Nature gave her in the front, it was the muscle bands that stretched over her rear and accented her bikini bottom that drove us all wild. This gorgeous creature became the worst dating experience of my life.

This is a story about a gal not worth mentioning by name
But it's a lesson in life worth remembering all the same

Somehow we drifted together. I don't even remember our first date as it's been overshadowed by later events. Moments of margaritas, matinees at the movies, and midnight marauding missions all blended together without cranial chronology. Marauding missions deserve some explanation, however.

My airline circle of friends all cooked in or dined out together. We walked into each other's houses without knocking, and we nearly worshiped a pair of often-stolen artifacts that continually changed hands. It was the highest honor to possess Wimpy, a 250-pound lawn jockey, and paint him in your own theme colors. The all-girls house decorated him in panties and garters and displayed him from their roof. There's no telling how they put him up there. Kevin, a former Marine honor guard, painted him in the style of his full military dress uniform, and for a while, Wimpy guarded Kevin's front door.

Stealing and painting Wimpy was our version of a fraternity prank, like redecorating the rival school's mascot statue in our own school's colors. The tradition lasted until the day Wimpy was smuggled out of bounds and apparently just disappeared. Perhaps Wimpy was painted as a spy and sent out into the field. Whoever had kidnapped him was keeping him deep undercover, and nobody would admit to the feat.

A substitute was soon found — a flight attendant's porcelain replica of the RCA dog. Petey (not Nipper — the name of the real RCA dog) became the new object of interest. Petey's initial abduction included a ransom note — cut from magazines and newspapers — demanding a case of Corona for his safe return. *P.S. Don't forget the lime.*

Like Wimpy, Petey stood almost three feet tall but was much lighter. Once officially in play, Petey was taken on boat trips, posed with passed-out comrades (who thought they would be left unbothered while tucked into their beds) as pseudo incriminating evidence, and even sent to Paris on overnights. Imagine working a trip across the pond and receiving word from a fellow crewmember that Petey is in your cargo compartment and now you have to bring him home — after carrying him around the city of romance and taking pictures with him, of course.

Our local bar, The Saloon, sometimes displayed travel pictures on its wall of shame. That was where Polaroids of Wimpy and Petey occasionally appeared — featured in all of their various colors and exotic backdrops as they were paraded around the world. This was the camaraderie of our group.

At some point after her volleyball appearance, The Body was indoctrinated into our clan, and then she and I just slid together. The first time I offered her a buddy pass to travel with me, someone called her my girlfriend, and from then on she was.

Life was carefree, easy, and fun. One of my long-lost friends from high school caught wind of the good life and came to visit just when The Body needed a new roommate in her beach house. I didn't know it then, but the only two chronic fabricators I've ever really met in person had just begun sharing a common roof.

> *She's a girl that I've tried very hard to forget*
> *One of two true deceivers that I've ever met*

I'm changing my old school buddy's name here because, underneath his aversion to the truth, I know he really does have a good heart and an honest interest in being a good friend. But the rest of his title is real. My Long Beach friends called him Gary-If-That-Really-Is-His-Name, and they used that full title with every reference to him—never shortened.

The first little fib that tripped him up was after Missy—a gate agent and one of the only twins in our airline circle—confided that she liked him. He told her he was a year older than me, and that raised a little red flag, but I held my tongue while in front of her. Privately, I asked him, "Why? She already likes you. You don't need to bullshit her about your age to impress her."

He swore to me he really was a year my senior.

"You must really be dumb then," I said, "because when I met you I was a senior in high school and you were still a sophomore. I had to haul your ass all around town because you were too young for a driver's license. It's bad enough you want to bullshit my friend, but now you're going to lie to me, too?"

"I swear on my mother's life. I'll bet you twenty dollars."

"Sucker bet. I like your mom, so I'll just take your money." I shook his hand and then asked to see an official government ID—his driver's license would do. It seemed like an easy way to teach him a lesson and to make enough money for the first round of margaritas that evening. I vaguely remembered he'd had a habit of stretching the truth back in high school, but I figured an additional ten years of growing up should have helped him grow out of it.

He refused to open his wallet. "The date on it is wrong," he said. Clearly he was going to try and blow more smoke up my butt.

"Dude, back in high school you might have fooled the DMV to become older so you could drink underage, but then you'd at least have the license to show me. So let's see it."

He started to shake his head no, then he lowered his eyes and looked down at my feet, so I asked, "How about if we call your mother? I won't tell her you've staked her life on your proclaimed age, and it'll be good to talk to her again. I'm sure she remembers when she pushed you out into this world."

"She's not at home," he replied immediately, as if he could know. The poker face he tried to wear looked more like a joker face, but he wasn't kidding around.

"I think I still remember your parents' home number in Connecticut. Before cell phones, I had to memorize phone numbers like everyone else." I started pushing imaginary buttons in the air because visualizing a keypad helped me remember. "Two-zero-three, six-six-one, nine ..."

He threw a twenty-dollar bill at me and walked away. That's when I realized some rare people don't outgrow their lying—they practice perfecting it.

The Body was no better. When I asked her what color the sky was, she said green, her favorite color. She believed in Santa Claus and UFOs, and not in a cute way for entertaining children. Merely mentioning either didn't exist caused her to tighten up her fists and clench her entire face, growl, and then stop talking to me for days. All that was missing was foot stomping for a complete tantrum, and she was capable of those too. I should have taken this as a warning sign, but it was cute at first, plus youth and a steady state of arousal clouded my judgment. I was learning this lesson about compulsive equivocators both barrels at a time, and my education had just begun.

Gary-If-That-Really-Is-His-Name told The Body that he ordered furniture for their apartment, but it never arrived. Still, he insisted it was coming. *I called them, and it's back-ordered. The store lost our address. Their driver called in sick this week.* His excuses weren't even consistent, and this added to his credibility issues.

He took a job hand tossing dough at a new pizza joint and told everyone he had been given part ownership for his start-up venture expertise. Hmmm, it should be no big surprise that this didn't turn out to be the case. I was used to an honest group, full of camaraderie and without ulterior motives or complicated social issues, so I gave him the benefit of the doubt.

Meanwhile, The Body quit or was fired from her job in Manhattan — I was never quite sure which. After a brief period of unemployment, her next position was an easier commute, but to an entry-level position on Long Island. As a newly hired assistant, this was less than a lateral move, but my issue with her wasn't about what she did for a living — we all have our own course to set. The problem was her insistent claim to my friends that she was now an art director, when in actuality the closest she ever came to that title was while shining her boss's nameplate on the outside of the door in front of which she was stationed. We were an easygoing, friendly beach crowd that appreciated a laid-back lifestyle over wealth and power. There was no need to try to impress us, and this job title fabrication didn't sit well with me. It was as if The Body and Gary-If-That-Really-Is-His-Name were competing to tell the biggest whopper.

One day, Gary-If-That-Really-Is-His-Name confided in me, "Mark, I don't know how to say this, but The Body is cheating on you."

I knew I couldn't confront her directly because the source of my information would be obvious. As it turned out, I didn't have to interrogate her — she denied it without even being asked. "I feel like I'm living with a spy," she said, "even though I'm doing nothing wrong." She must have suspected that his loyalty to our friendship would trump his ability to keep internal roommate activities confidential. But whom should I believe? What should I do when forced to choose between two friends — both of whose honesty and integrity were becoming increasingly questionable?

After agonizing over this dilemma, I went with the American legal standard — innocent until proven guilty. So far I had an unreliable witness telling me I was being cuckolded, but he offered no hard evidence. Plus, I didn't want to disrupt the fringe benefits I was receiving from The Body. It's true: sometimes my little head did the thinking for me. There's a joke that God gave man two brains, but only enough blood to operate one at a time.

One night during tickling and horseplay on the couch, The Body's knee slipped between the pillows and she twisted it. There was no tear, but it swelled for a while. Her workouts and sports participation were put on indefinite hold. Her doctor prescribed more movies and less volleyball — none actually. It was surprising how quickly she started putting on weight, but I didn't want to upset her or appear insensitive by saying anything.

She became moody, too, so I figured she was depressed from being sidelined from the outdoor fun. I rationalized that once her knee healed, we'd be back on the beach regularly, burning up the extra calories on the volleyball court, and that would cheer her up. In the meantime, she covered up more, and her interest in sex stopped. My buddies counseled me that women want it less when they're feeling self-conscious about themselves, but I'm sure you can see what's coming. I didn't.

> *She had a six-month rule, I only learned later*
> *That was how long she'd let someone date her*
> *Before she moved on, because her stories would unravel*
> *She hated to be dumped, so she'd pack up and travel*
>
> *But this time was different; she had another plan*
> *Only later I learned, that she'd slept with another man*
> *Without protection of course, and nature kicked in*
> *She insisted it was mine and stop living in sin*

And now we're back where this dark chapter of my life started — her finally telling me what she'd known for some time. She played it off as a new revelation though: "Oh, by the way, *I just found out* I'm pregnant."

It was amazing how religious she became when it suited her. The gal who never went to church in nearly the full year I'd known her, while dating her more than half of that time, suddenly became a devout Catholic with a prominent pro-life platform. What sounded more like the truth came out later in a hospital bed conversation as she claimed she'd had an abortion at seventeen and had promised herself never to repeat it. This little secretive proclamation hadn't come up prior to our becoming sexually active or even during the discussion time immediately following the post-pregnancy announcement. Instead, she claimed newfound religious principles and declared she was taking this full term with or without me. My opinion didn't matter at all. She only wanted to know if I'd be involved with raising her child. Notice she didn't say our child.

> *And suddenly she found God; suddenly she's pro-life*
> *She didn't ask, she demanded, to become my wife*
> *I attempted to discuss the options remaining*
> *But her mind was made up, she ignored my campaigning*

This required some serious soul-searching on my part. I was still in my twenties and I wasn't sure yet if I wanted to bring any children into this world — especially with a gal whose integrity was in question. But she wasn't offering me a choice. We had practiced safe sex, but was this one of those *only ninety-eight-percent-effective* situations? I didn't have the luxury of pondering that for long, because a baby I wasn't ready for was already on its way.

I recognized that I needed some external guidance, and I went to visit my dad — who I could always count on to see things objectively. He was blunt and pointed out, "There's no way to fight this situation. You've made your appeal to abort, and it's been flatly rejected. Adoption is no option, because she plans to keep it."

Dad helped me focus on the remaining choices. He also confided that although he didn't think I was planning on procreating, he was still happy he was becoming a grandfather. Under his guidance, I made the decision to try to become the best father I could. That meant growing up quickly, as I felt totally unprepared. "Nobody's ever really ready," Dad said with a wink, "even those of us who think we are."

The fact that I now planned to be involved with the baby partially appeased The Body, but our relationship still had a long, long way to go.

> *I refused to get married on account of the baby*
> *But I didn't rule it out — after it's born, well just maybe*
> *We'll see how we're doing, and if our relationship grows*
> *We're not ready now, but in the future, who knows?*

"Without a wedding," she said, "the baby will get my last name instead of yours."

I think she hoped I'd propose for that reason alone, but I didn't. After an uncomfortable pause, I asked, "Should we start thinking about first names?"

"I have. I'll let you know what I choose."

Again, she didn't want my opinion. I think she had some relatives' names in mind, and she planned to dictate everything. I'd agreed to participate, but she didn't treat me as a partner. This wasn't an arrangement that made me feel our relationship was improving. The more demanding she became, the less interest I had in making our relationship official. I'd accepted the expected baby, but the baby maker was still doing everything to drive me away. I think she finally realized this, and that's when we started having sex again.

Growing up, I once overheard my parents' conversation with a neighbor from down the street. It was no secret that she and her husband weren't getting along, and my dad asked if they were trying to work things out. I still remember her reply, "Well, we still fit together."

I told The Body this story and said that maybe we needed to start over. I asked her on a date and then took her out to dinner. In spite of the obvious, we tried to keep the conversation light over a large Greek salad and a shared chicken Parmesan hero—one of our staple meal selections. The evening should have ended with a simple goodnight kiss, but it ignited something. She still had a way of looking up at me with wide-open eyes and a subtle tilt of her head, and we both realized we'd have to find a way to make this work. She invited me in, and my smile was immediate.

She put on some water for tea and then undressed for bed. When she pulled the aqua silk teddy over her head and shoulders, it caught above her breasts for a second and then stuck again above her belly until she pulled it all the way down. It was at this moment I realized I hadn't been informed as early as she'd known, because her bump was now clearly beginning to show. It finally hit me that the weight gain was not because of her knee injury. Our fighting had kept us apart, and nature hadn't waited for us to work things out. She saw me looking and explained, "The doctor said it's OK through my eighth month, and towards the end you'll have to position yourself from behind."

This was the kind of cooperation I'd been looking for.

She loved tea with honey, so I made some. When the kettle whistled, we shared an oversized, forest green, full mug. That evening had an effortless intimacy, almost like our first time together. When the mug was empty, I slid out of my clothes and climbed under the covers.

Mending our relationship was back on the table
We weren't getting along, but somehow we were able
To be civil at night, after we turned out the light
And do something together, instead of fight

We kissed for a long time, and I caressed her belly. Finally, she'd had enough attention for the baby and moved my hands to her breasts. Her nipples greeted me at attention. She was giving me the green light and the heavy foreplay began. I traced almost every part of her with my tongue before rolling on top.

This was one of life's special moments — sprinkled with intimacy and reconciliation. Stress, squabbles, and serious decisions slipped away as I slipped inside of her. I thought about making this last rather than racing for the explosive finish. She rose up to meet each thrust as our fingers locked together on either side of the pillow—my arms holding me up as well as pinning hers to the bed. I kissed her forehead as she buried her lips in my neck. Against my best effort at restraint, our energy grew and our pace began racing.

> We worked our way up to the rhythm we'd known
> My abs rocked her belly that barely had grown
> And she received every thrust with a passionate moan
> Until suddenly they stopped, like she'd hung up the phone

> And wet, I felt wet, more than any orgasm yet
> But something was wrong, that I couldn't interpret
> So I asked her to tell me if she was all right
> But all that I heard was the silence of the night

While my engine roared, hers suddenly seized. Her grip relaxed, and she melted into the mattress. We were suddenly soaked in more fluid than I'm capable of producing in a year, but this wasn't a mutual climax. Subliminal sirens rang in the back of my head, and they were trying to alert me that something was wrong.

"Honey, are you OK?" My question was met with unbroken silence. I asked her again with the same lack of reply.

> I asked her again and still got no reply
> So, I gently got up and set out to try
> To turn on a light and see what was wrong
> It was then that I wished that my stomach was strong

As I rolled off of her, I felt our bodies separate with the reluctant resistance that equaled pulling a peanut butter and jelly sandwich apart. In no way was this normal, so I slid off the bed and shuffled cautiously across the floor with my arms outstretched. As I switched on the light by the door, the darkness blew away, and I was totally unprepared for what was revealed.

I'll never forget what was revealed
The secret the darkness had completely concealed
There was blood, blood, and more blood, literally everywhere
Her body was covered from her toes to her hair

It pooled on the mattress and dripped onto the floor
And bloody red footprints had followed me to the door
I too was naked and covered in red
And her eyes froze in shock as I returned to the bed

She'd miscarried her baby at the worst possible time
And the scene of our lovemaking now looked like a crime
The bed was a red puddle and the walls were all splattered
But she was still breathing and that's all that really mattered

Holy bloody hell. *The Exorcist*, *The Texas Chainsaw Massacre*, and a host of other popular horror movies had not prepared me for the unexpected carnage that had inexplicably replaced the tranquility of our lovemaking lair. My initial reaction was shock, but then I kicked into action. I had to. I'd always been a little squeamish, and if I didn't get moving my stomach was going to empty. She looked at me with empty eyes and I told her, "Everything is going to be OK."

My first thought was to lift her out of bed. I had to remove her from the scene of so much of her own blood if I hoped to help her frozen panic wear off. Then I had to rush her to some immediate medical help.

Lift, carry, rinse, press, dress, transport, and rush. My mind broke down my mission into single-word commands — about all I could comprehend in the moment. I recall Dad racing Mom down the wrong side of the winding streets with his horn blaring. This night I ran more than a few red lights.

I scooped her in my arms and took her to the shower
And rinsed us both off at this ungodly hour
I rolled up a towel and squeezed it between her thighs
She still wasn't talking but there was a response in her eyes

It took every ounce of my strength and remaining willpower
To distract her from shock as I cleaned her in the shower
I made her close her eyes while I scrubbed us both clean
I washed away more blood than I'd ever seen

I said, "Stay in the bathroom" and handed her a receiver
Get an ambulance coming, we have to leave here
I cleaned up the room as fast as I could
Losing this much blood couldn't be good

Sitting in the tub she hadn't dialed 9-1-1
She said, "It's a boy. I don't wonna lose my son."
"We have to go to the hospital right away."
"No." She said, "No. They'll take him away."

"You're hemorrhaging inside; you'll die if you stay.
Your life is at stake, you need to do as I say."
I got her out of the shower and into her car
Even running red lights, the hospital seemed far

There was no heartbeat. The Body took the news at the hospital really hard. I'd be lying if I told you I wasn't relieved.

I felt like I'd just saved her life, but she hated me for not grieving the death of her pregnancy. That's where our political views about life disagreed. She felt that her baby had died, and I viewed this event with a more clinical perspective as a miscarriage — albeit at the worst possible time. My logic was that nobody celebrates *conception day* — we count every year on our *birthday*. This didn't offer her any comfort; in fact, she glared at me. Counselors later told us that women feel attached to the new life as soon as there's a heartbeat inside the mother's belly. Men, as visual learners and lacking the umbilical connection, don't always bond to the baby until after it's born. Great discussion for the classroom, but it didn't help things between us. Even before we left the hospital, she grew cold toward me. Soon I would discover that she'd made it her personal mission to make me suffer.

She survived the experience but her pregnancy died
And soon after that night I found out that she'd lied
There were lots of indiscretions, and the identity of the father
Will always be a mystery, but why even bother?

It's hard to imagine she would want sex while she healed, but she quickly circulated. The worst thing she did was to sleep with one of my roommates. I know — it's inexcusable. He'd watched this whole dating, pregnancy, miscarriage, and subsequent parental counseling situation occur, and then he did it anyway. It took me years before I'd even talk to him again. His excuse? "A stiff dick has no conscience."

> *She blamed me for all this because six months had gone by*
> *And I hadn't proposed and she'd continued to lie*
> *And she knew that I'd leave her when the truth came to light*
> *And it's my fault that her God took her baby that night*

My roommate's indiscretion had a bright side. It opened the door that revealed many other episodes. Apparently the odds that I would have been the actual father were of the order of any one particular horse winning the Belmont Stakes — Long Island's contribution to the U.S. Triple Crown. Gary-If-That-Really-Is-His-Name had been telling the truth for a change. It was time to sever my ties with The Body.

> *We parted ways, severed clean, never more to be seen*
> *If you've ever been lied to then you know what I mean*
> *But as we move forward we bring with us our past*
> *To make better futures and look back in contrast*

It's still difficult to look back at this encounter. It put me in a really dark place and forced me into a quagmire of introspection. A couple years later, I met the true love of my life — but was I ready to build a family with the right woman? I struggled at first not to let one gal's deceit affect another lady's love — easy to say, but hard to do. If my time with The Body had any meaning, it was a test of how deep inside myself I could dig for strength and compassion. Years of independence had given me self-confidence, but could I function as a life partner and potential parent? Eventually I decided that during a crisis, I had — but this life lesson was learned from the worst possible instructor. I buried myself in my work again while chewing on everything that had happened. Flying is, after all, both fun and therapeutic.

> *It's a time I now remember only as a life-lesson learned*
> *Some sort of emergency merit badge I earned*
> *I was tested that night to deal with severe trauma*
> *And with that lesson learned, I'd had enough of her drama*

> *One aversion to children that I'd always had*
> *I didn't think that I'd be a very good dad*

I was squeamish and knew it and felt a dad should be
Strong in the stomach and never get queasy

When his child gets hurt, a dad needs to be there
He needs to be able to provide urgent care
That I might not be able to handle this chore
Was my biggest fear that I felt to the core

But as bad as this experience has weighed on my soul
I know that it's pulled me out of a very dark hole
Now I know I can handle what life throws my way
I can ignore all the blood and still do OK

Captain Ken Cook and I flew together on Boeing 767s out of JFK and revisited some of our favorite haunts in Berlin during our layovers after ocean crossings. Eventually I was awarded training as a first officer on the Lockheed L-1011, still the largest aircraft I've ever flown. At 430,000 pounds, it can almost hold the weight of three fully loaded Boeing 727s inside of it—almost. But then Captain Cook—my friend, my mentor, and someone I could always talk to—became sick. He was diagnosed with pancreatic cancer, and his doctor told him his life expectancy was six months. A true fighter, it took eighteen months for his body to quit, but all too soon he passed away. Life was peppering me with all the hardest lessons.

31 | LOSING THE LOTTERY

Susanne (lyrics by Mick James)

NANCY GAVE ME PERMISSION to talk openly about all of my losses — my mom, the miscarriage trauma, Captain Cook, and especially Susanne. For some of my friends, it became a painful reflection every time I brought her up. Others were more tolerant, but I began to feel like an old empty-nest mother whose every conversation begins with, *Remember when...?* I knew I couldn't live in the past, even if it was a daily struggle to remind myself. In Nancy's office I could talk about anything and she would actively listen. I told her about the magic moment Susanne entered my life and how I'd made her a promise for a lifetime.

And now we come to the bitter bit. I lost the lottery, but you might ask, "Who hasn't?" Everyone knows the odds are millions to one of picking six out of six numbers, especially when each number can pop up anywhere from one to fifty-nine. Every ticket loses, with the rare exception.

Statistically speaking, flying on an airliner is the safest form of transport; the odds are far greater of dying on the highway. Want real risk? Ride a motorcycle or, better yet, mount a horse. In commercial aviation we have redundancy (at least two of everything): checklists, certified pilots and mechanics, federal oversight, and a long list of other rules and procedures to maintain safety. The odds of dying in an aviation disaster mirror the odds of winning the lottery — only the consequences are life-ending instead of life-changing. Here are some of my losing tickets, leading up to TWA Flight 800.

First, Joe Heuchert died flying single-pilot night freight at Midnight Express when his trim tab jammed and his elevator cable snapped. We went to Embry-Riddle Aeronautical University together and were also bouncers at Big Daddy's Lounge on Daytona Beach. He was one of my few friends who smoked. He told me cigarettes weren't going to kill him. I wish he'd been wrong — lung cancer would have given him a lot more time than uncontrolled flight into the terrain. His plane had just been returned to service after an overhaul. No matter how well maintenance does its job, it's always hard on an aircraft to be taken apart and put back together. Like surgery on humans, there's always a necessary healing time while everything settles. A trim tab on the tail of an aircraft allows the force of air flowing over the flight controls to be neutralized as the plane changes speed. Joe's jammed, so he had to push and pull harder on the control yoke to make the airplane go where he wanted. That's when his elevator cable snapped under the extra force. It's like losing the steering cable in a car, except in this case, Joe could no longer control up or down. His plane drove him straight into the ground.

Then Kathy Digan died in an Air Virginia takeoff accident. One of the two engines on her Swearingen Metroliner aircraft failed during takeoff during low outside visibility. The aircraft crashed not very far from the runway. I also knew Kathy from our aviation university, where only one in twenty student pilots was female. I once watched her balance a full food tray while climbing over chairs and our table to reach the only empty place to sit in the crowded university cafeteria. She was engaged to my good buddy Roc. In all the years since, Roc and I have talked about her accident exactly once. He's chosen to live with her loss in nearly total stoic silence.

My former roommate Rick Duney from Command Airways—who picked me up over his head when TWA called to hire me and used to dig clams with his feet—later died in a Ryan Air DC-9 icing crash in Cleveland. He's also the only pilot I ever met who wore a gold tie clasp across his throat—a remnant from his Wall Street days. He gave up a superior paycheck and bonuses from the financial world for the excitement of aviation, and he once told me, "Flying is more fun than cold calling." Back then nobody knew how critical a completely frost- and ice-free pair of wings was to the 10-series DC-9. It's the prototype and the only model without leading edge slats. Those moveable extensions on the front of the wings have helped all later models of DC-9s produce low-speed lift and prevent stalls. This was a lesson learned with Rick's blood.

We members of the aviation community who have earned our wings and move airplanes for a living, although measured in the tens of thousands, is a small and overlapping group. We know each other in degrees of separation much smaller than the traditional six. The airline world is an extended family, as thick as blood when some is spilled.

I was thirty years old and felt I'd lived through the rough years—the training years, the multiple-leg days always approaching duty-time limits, and the low-wage, dues-paying jobs. TWA was an international flag carrier and met every requirement of my dream job. I was healthy, and I loved going to work. My days off were spent riding for free on airplanes all over the world to see new places. Even during that time while riding on Ethiopian Airlines from Cairo, Egypt, through Addis Ababa to Harare, Zimbabwe for a photo safari, their crewmembers were overtly welcoming because TWA had trained their flight department back in the 1950s. The world was wide open when my path crossed with Susanne's.

She was born in Denmark
Destined for the world
Raised in New England
A simple down-home girl
So full of life
So full of hope
When the hand of fate closed

After I proposed in 1996, we house hunted together, began plans for our wedding, and discussed when to start a family. Nine days before closing on our new home in Westport, Connecticut, she went on a business trip on TWA while I stayed behind — a reversal of our usual routine.

At last we caught certainty
She had become so happy
A newborn rising sun
Faded without warning
Who stole her life
Who stole her hope
Damn the hand of fate that closed

In the predawn darkness she kissed me goodbye. I was still half asleep in bed, and she was already showered and prepped for her long day ahead. Her teeth were brushed and they shined in the light of the single bedside lamp. Her Blistex lip gloss rubbed off on me as I barely responded — conscious of my morning breath. She didn't seem to mind. For the tenth or twelfth time, I pointed out that her blue blazer and green pants didn't go together. It was a running joke, and she admonished my sense of fashion — or lack of it — with her standard quip, "I won't be here to dress you today. Maybe when I return we can find Garanimals in your size. Just remember not to mix the predators with the prey and you should be able to learn to dress yourself without my help."

"Have fun in Europe," I said, "and say hello to Captain Gid Miller for me." Susanne had seen my pictures with him in exotic ports of call such as the bazaars of Cairo and Istanbul where we'd fended off venders promising bargains: *Look, almost free! Finest quality, my friend. Come to see my shop. No charge for just look.* Gid was a true humanitarian and handed out Egyptian pounds or Turkish lira to beggars pulling on our pant legs. Gid had also watched me attach *Now the Bear Flies TWA* bumper stickers to the Euro Berlin sales office main window — risky espionage that was a right of passage when I was a new hire, although Gid was too much of a gentleman to encourage such behavior. Susanne turned the bedside light off so I could drift back to sleep, and headed out for a full day of work before driving straight to JFK International Airport. She never came back.

> *I knew so briefly*
> *Two years, give or take*
> *I grew to love her*
> *Something in her way*
> *So full of life*
> *So full of hope*
> *When the hand of fate closed*

The last I ever heard from her was a call I missed, recorded on our answering machine. Her final words were mostly a reminder about radon tests that we were conducting to complete our housing inspections. It's a mini cassette tape I play once every year just to hear her voice again. She's in the first-class lounge TWA called the Galaxy Club, enjoying a glass of wine, eating shrimp, and waiting for her flight to board — TWA Flight 800 — and she sounds happy. That flight took off but didn't land. The plane blew up on July 17, 1996, at 8:31 p.m. Eastern Daylight Time.

> *Where's the justice for the innocent?*
> *Where's the truth that bears her name?*
> *Where's the justice for the innocent?*
> *Life will never be the same*

The National Transportation Safety Board put together an 876-piece three-dimensional jigsaw puzzle from the wreckage. My own reconstruction has been an even bigger challenge.

On that Wednesday summer night in 1996, I sat at my computer in Greenwich, Connecticut, drafting my will. The irony is not lost on me. I'd just purchased the software to help me do it. I was about to have a wife — what the program called a *life event*. Susanne and I were living with her mom and youngest brother until we closed on our first house. "I'll be home in a few days," Susanne said, "just like one of your trips, Honey-Bunny." She'd picked up that term of endearment from her new favorite movie, *Pulp Fiction*, which surprised me because she hated guns and violence, and that film was rife with both.

Twice during the spring, I'd been able to trade into the flights Susanne took to Europe for business so I could be her personal pilot. TWA was now flying the heavy summer schedule, and Susanne's flight this time was on a Boeing 747, not the 767 that I flew, and so it didn't work out for me to be her Rain Man—her excellent driver.

We wondered if she'd make VP before I upgraded to captain. Not only did Susanne speak Danish, French, and English, she could balance her checkbook down to the penny without the aid of a statement. She was going to become the chief financial officer in our relationship. We'd worked that out.

When her boss scheduled this trip, Susanne and I decided I needed to save my days off in the weeks ahead to close on and then move into our new home. So instead of traveling to Europe with her, I sat in shorts and a T-shirt in the room I used as an office—sweating without air conditioning through an evening slowly cooling down from ninety degrees—when the phone rang.

"Turn on the TV! Turn on the TV!" my lifelong buddy Glenn shrieked, bordering on hysterical.

"What channel? Why?"

"Any channel. It's on all of them."

"What's on all of them?" I asked.

"Just turn one on, quick! A TWA plane went down."

"Went down? Where?"

"Off Long Island. Just turn on a TV!"

At first I thought, *Damn. It's almost guaranteed that I know someone on that flight. They're going to have quite a ditching story to tell. I hope nobody has been hurt.*

In 1996 I'd been an airline pilot for ten years with eight of those at TWA. Plus, I'd spent several previous years as an aviation student and then a flight instructor. I always knew someone whenever a plane went down, probably because I know so many people in the business. The odds were different for me, like buying thousands of lottery tickets changes the odds of winning. On those rare occasions when I don't know someone onboard—I know someone who knows someone. This is what was going through my mind as I stared at the TV.

Every channel aired the breaking news, and I'm not sure what I actually saw on the screen. At first glance it looked like giant yellow rafts were in the water, probably because that's what I was expecting from a downed aircraft. Either I just saw the aircraft wreckage under yellow night lighting, or I observed rescue rafts supplied by arriving boats—either way I didn't remain a spectator for long enough to analyze the scene. I didn't have time to watch; I needed to do something.

Smith Point, Long Island was only a couple hours' drive from Greenwich—less if I once again drove like my dad while racing my mom to the hospital. I didn't know yet that the outcome would be the same. I was thinking I could help and was trying to figure out how I could best be of assistance. I've been trained to evacuate everyone out of a completely full aircraft in ninety seconds, even with half of the emergency exits blocked. We even practice ditching exercises in a pool—donning life vests, deploying the sea anchor, erecting the canopy, and activating the emergency locator transmitter.

I could picture trained coworkers coping with a difficult situation. Then the TV announcer said, "TWA Flight 800, a flight bound for Paris…" I froze in my tracks.

"Damn! That's Susanne's flight!"

In my head I was suddenly onboard with Susanne, and I visualized crew-member friends of mine assessing emergency exits, opening doors above the water line, and ordering passengers outside and into life rafts with strong commands: "Open seatbelts! Come this way!"

I knew Susanne was in good hands, but none of this was happening on TV the way I was expecting. Instead, I continued imagining Susanne taking the whole emergency in stride but expressing her frustration about the sudden change in the outcome of her flight. She was a strong swimmer and loved the water but very much a clothes horse, so having her business outfit dunked in salTWAter would tick her off big time.

I was puzzled that I didn't see the evacuation procedures unfolding on the news the way they were playing out in my head. If only I could have seen Susanne's blue and green outfit from the angle of a news helicopter, or her dazzling blonde hair amid passengers and crew scrambling to safety, the image would have settled the tiniest doubt that I was keeping hostage in the deepest dungeon of my mind.

I slipped out of my shorts and hopped into a pair of jeans. In a split second, I grabbed my airline ID and clipped it onto my shirt to look official. I reasoned that I'd need it to reach the scene of the accident—no doubt some sort of protective perimeter and triage would be established by the time I arrived. Stuffing my passport into my back pocket, I dialed the one person I knew would have some answers.

Captain Greg Arikian was a friend, mentor, and the head of the Critical Incident Response Team for TWA. I needed him to point me in the right direction and grant me access through the emergency responders to reach Susanne, wherever she was. He took my call.

"Greg, I'm heading out the door. Tell me where to pick up Susanne. She's going to be pissed that she's missing her meeting in Paris and stuck in wet clothes."

"Mark, stay right where you are," Greg responded. "Don't go anywhere."

"No, Greg. Susanne's on that flight. You won't find her on the crew list; she's a full-fare, first-class passenger."

"Mark, listen to me. Don't leave wherever you are. Don't go down to Long Island."

"Are you crazy? Susanne's plane just ditched! I'm going down there to get her. Are you going to tell me where to go, or do I have to figure it out on my own?"

"I need to know if there's anyone there with you. I'll come if I need to. Where are you?"

"I'm halfway out the door, waiting for you to give me some damn directions."

"Mark, sit down. Listen to me. I don't want to have to be the one to tell you this on the phone, but there are no survivors."

"What do you mean? Seven-forty-sevens can fly with both engines out on the same wing. What happened? Did they lose three? What can fail so many engines—a fuel problem?"

"Mark, *listen to me*. They didn't ditch. We don't know why, but it blew up. There's nowhere to go. There's no one to pick up."

I put down the phone and took a seat. I think Glenn was the first to arrive at the house. The rest of the night was a blur except the worst part—Susanne's mom came home. She wanted me to tell her Susanne wasn't on the flight. There had been talk of her going a day later. The extra car she'd hung onto since college and used for airport and New York City trips notoriously broke down. Susanne used to start it with a screwdriver, and even then it started only for her and nobody else. Susanne's mother's last hope was that I would have news that her daughter somehow wasn't onboard. Once I told her mother otherwise, it would be official. I had to tell Susanne's mom that her worst fear was true.

It was an unbearable night. Friends of mine took turns watching over me. One of them eventually turned off the TV. I don't recall going to bed, but at 3:58 a.m. on the morning after TWA Flight 800 exploded, my cell phone rang and I answered it. "First Officer Berry, we need you to take Concorde over to Paris and work right back."

Hearing the word Paris, my heart skipped a few beats and then re-engaged with a grinding clutch, causing my stomach to send an unpleasant bile taste into my throat. The voice was Eddie's, a crew-scheduling buddy of mine who probably thought he was offering me a rare opportunity to ride Concorde on the company's dime, despite the awful disaster our entire airline was struggling with. Swallowing hard, I grimaced in the dark as I replied, "Eddie, Susanne was on eight hundred." I sensed I couldn't have hurt Eddie more if I had punched him in the gut.

"I'm so sorry, Mark," was all he could say. It was the beginning of a feeling I later named *the plague*. Just by existing, I drove darkness into the hearts of my friends through the simplest interactions. Grief and loss were like sores and lesions that caused involuntary discomfort in all who encountered the unfortunate one.

Finally I told Eddie, "I called the chief pilot to get taken off the schedule. Doesn't it show in the computer?"

"It probably does, but I'm only working from the monthly volunteer-extra-flying list. I'll take you off of it, too. I'm so sorry again, Mark."

I'd forgotten that I'd put myself on the volunteer-extra-flying list because Susanne and I were financially committed to buying a house. I'd recently purchased her engagement ring, so any extra money was very welcome. My airline always scheduled peak flying during the busy summer travel season, so our schedules were already full. TWA also tried not to train any pilots during the summer months, because everyone was needed just to cover the schedule. Even with all hands on deck, extra flights were occasionally offered.

Everyone assumed incorrectly that Susanne was a flight attendant because I was a TWA pilot. She wasn't a crewmember, but she was traveling for work. GE Capital bought her that first-class seat—diagonally behind my favorite Captain Kirk chair. She died on my airline in the safest hands of my TWA mentors and peers. I woke up the next morning to the special kind of hell where my fiancée was dead in the real world, and I could feel her slipping away in my fading dreams where she was very much still alive.

My nights became my refuge. Close friends tried to console me, but what is there that can be said in such a situation? Only much, much later did the fact that they tried mean a lot to me. Two months earlier I'd promised Susanne that we could handle anything life threw at us, as long as we did it together. She had lost her stepfather to disease, and my mother had died after breakfast—having succumbed to an allergy attack. I'd hoped to go a long time before another person close to Susanne or me passed away, and I took comfort in the knowledge that I had her to help cope with it. Never did I imagine I'd have to face her death as the next one in my life.

To say I felt it should have been me onboard that flight instead of her is a gross understatement. I go away on so many trips with such regularity that it's hard not to imagine Susanne as the one having to listen to my final words, either on an answering machine or the way of so many unfortunate aviators — captured on a cockpit voice recorder.

Occasionally, someone less trained than a mental health professional wants to dig inside my head — a new acquaintance, another pilot, or a fellow writer — so they ask, "What's the hardest thing you've ever had to do?" Without hesitation it was the day I had to speak in front of seven hundred people — most of whom I knew — at an overcrowded church that was only designed to hold about four hundred, to deliver my final words for Susanne at her memorial service. Difficult as it was, I managed — with my buddy Warren standing nearby, ready to take over. Knowing he would have to stand in for me if I broke down somehow helped me through my reading.

The pews were squished full, the perimeter was filled with standers, and from the podium I could see an ocean of heads stretching out the door and into the street where the police had placed saw horses for crowd control. I stopped looking up and read from my prepared sheet of paper.

In Memory of Susanne

I really wish I had the rest of my life to share with her
I really wish that I could make things just the way they were

No one feels her loss any deeper than I do
But that is mine to carry and not what she'd want from you

Let me tell you about the time we shared and how she lived her life
Let me tell you why I loved her and asked her to become my wife

We grew up together, she was practically the girl next door
But I was just her paperboy, had no idea that there'd be more

Twelve years after high school our paths met yet again
I looked into her eyes and knew I loved her starting then

We're in the '90s now and computers are the rage
We kept in touch by email mostly at this stage

I met her mother and her brothers and we started off as friends
And now the bonds she built between us I hope never ends

I moved out to St. Louis for training that was unplanned
She just smiled and said, "Honey-Bunny, of course I understand"

My airline filed chapter eleven and I worried if we'd make it through
She said, "If the worst happens, then I'll support you"

She earned the Circle of Excellence trip at GE Capital
That gave us one wild adventure in Aspen just last fall

We had a serious side to us but it was always fun
As we tried to pull our lives together into one

We lived together all this year and I miss those little things she did
I couldn't stick my hand in my own pocket without finding Blistex that
she'd hid

And now the time has come much too soon to say goodbye
Nobody has the answers, no one can tell us why

You knew how much I love you, even more than I love to fly
Susanne, you were nothing less than perfect in my eye
I will carry you in my heart until the very end
Peace, love, and happiness ... to my dearest friend

It would be a long time before I accepted how much my life had changed. I was the moron trying to grab his baggage before moving to the emergency exit. It was I who was unable to leave my personal items behind. In fact, I read every book left in her room as a way to try and hold onto her after she was gone. I imagined her reading *Corelli's Mandolin* with me, then I returned it to the library for her. I read *A Year in Provence* from her nightstand. I cried when I passed her bookmark. To this day, I want to tell her how it ends.

Now when I fill up my gas tank, I buy a single quick-pick lottery ticket. Some call it *the loser's tax*. Everyone knows the odds are millions to one of picking six out of six numbers. Odds and statistics make great theoretical discussions — but in real life, I've lost the lottery before.

32 | INVESTIGATION AND SPECULATION

One Day

THE COVER OF *Time* magazine on July 29, 1996, depicts a piece of debris—what appears to me to be a rear section of a wing with a fuel dump nozzle—floating and reflecting in the ocean water that's more blue than I remember. The cover story: "TERROR ON FLIGHT 800."

> "The Destination was Paris, but instead a TWA Boeing 747 burst into flames at dusk, falling into the sea off the coast of New York and setting its waters ablaze. Now, even as America mourns the 230 victims, the country must discover whether this catastrophe is the latest angry assault on its soul." – J Conrad Williams, *Newsday*

TWA Flight 800 ended up filling the headlines for the entire summer, remained in the news for years, and still receives extensive coverage every anniversary as one of our nation's worst aviation disasters—the second worst in history at the time. Only the Tenerife Airport disaster in 1977 between two 747 aircraft (KLM and Pan Am) had a greater loss of life with 583 fatalities. While so many friends, coworkers, and I were still in shock, my local paper barely left room for the movie listings—most of the headlines were quite proximal:

"TRAGEDY IS PERSONAL FOR A NUMBER IN GREENWICH"
– Susanne Youmans and Jonathan Lucas, *Greenwich Time*, July 20, 1996

> While investigators look for reasons why TWA Flight 800 crashed into the Atlantic Ocean on Wednesday night, the human tragedy of the disaster is being felt poignantly in Greenwich by family and friends of Susanne Jensen.

"SCHOLARSHIP FUND TO HONOR VICTIM"
– Maureen Kennedy, *Greenwich Time*, July 23, 1996

"TRAGEDY TEACHES US TO CHERISH LIFE, FAMILIES"
– Ellen Warren, *Greenwich Time*, July 23, 1996

"PAIN LINGERS FOR TWA 800 FAMILIES"
– Susanne Youmans, *Greenwich Time*, September 22, 1996

I had no stomach for entertainment during the aftermath of TWA Flight 800, but summer moviegoers attempting to escape the heat in a theater's air-conditioned comfort had a wide range of choices depending on how far they wanted to drive in the southwestern corner of the state. Jim Carrey starred in *Cable Guy*, Will Smith in *Independence Day*, Tom Cruise in *Mission: Impossible*, Demi Moore in *Striptease*, Eddie Murphy in *The Nutty Professor*, Helen Hunt in *Twister*, John Travolta in *Phenomenon*, Denzel Washington and Meg Ryan in *Courage Under Fire*, and Disney released an animated version of *The Hunchback of Notre Dame*. Big screen entertainment seemed to have pulled out all the big names and artillery for the sunny-season dollars. All I wanted to know was who and what brought down TWA Flight 800 as a giant red-orange fireball. Everywhere there was speculation and reports of a missile, including numerous witness reports. Did some form of ordinance or artillery cause it?

Lots of explanations for TWA Flight 800 made their try-outs on the news. Each one gathered its own fan base within the American public. First up was a theory that the air conditioning packs overheated and caused the center tank to explode after sitting on the ground for two and a half hours during a ninety-degree evening. That sounded plausible to the uninitiated, but it was laughable to anyone with an understanding of aircraft systems. Delayed takeoffs are an everyday summer occurrence. Additionally, the adiabatic lapse rate cools our atmosphere at approximately 2.7 degrees Fahrenheit per 1,000 feet rise in altitude. Translation: air gets thinner and cooler at increasing altitude at a predictable rate. At nearly 14,000 feet, the outside air temperature would have been about fifty-three degrees, hardly a workout for an air conditioner certified for extreme conditions over a thirty-year service life. Your refrigerator has as much chance of exploding in your kitchen just because it is plugged in and turned on.

Another theory that gained a lot of interest was that a center fuel tank scavenge pump sparked and caused the explosion. More plausible than an overheating pack for sure, but still on the level of your electric stove exploding on its own. Jet fuel is essentially kerosene, and it's very hard to ignite. In that respect it's not like your automotive gasoline at all, even though they are both refined from the same crude oil. We all know that pouring gasoline on a fire makes it flame up in a whoosh. But drop a lit match into a tank containing Jet A —pronounced *kerosene*—and the match will extinguish just the same as if you dropped it into a fish tank full of water.

A big deal was also made that the 747's center fuel tank was empty, making it full of combustible fumes rather than liquid jet fuel. I currently fly MD-80 aircraft, and we drain our center tank dry in the air on almost every single flight—a full seventeen years after TWA Flight 800 exploded. By procedure, we don't turn off the center tank fuel pumps until they are cavitating in an empty tank, and hundreds of my airline's aircraft—possibly thousands of MD-80s worldwide— all do this several times every day. When I fly the long-range MD-80s with two additional auxiliary tanks, we burn that fuel first and end up landing with three empty tanks. And countless other types of aircraft fly with empty tanks as well. Am I worried about blowing up because of this? Not unless my center fuel tank is hit by a missile.

What caught the public's attention about this investigation were two critical things: no official explanation could be proved—even in the NTSB's eventual final report on August 23, 2000, over four years after TWA Flight 800—and the numerous eyewitnesses who reported seeing a missile streaking across the sky. The FBI initially interviewed 670 eyewitnesses and then attempted to publicly discredit every one. Some of those witnesses were pilots, and at least one had seen missiles in flight during wartime. According to the *Fairfield County Weekly*, Major Fritz Meyer of the 106 Rescue Wing of the Air National Guard was flying a Sikorsky helicopter with Captain Chris Bauer and Sergeant Dennis Richardson and reported seeing a "streak of light" before the explosion. World Net Daily writer Julie Foster quotes Major Meyer as having seen, "a trail of white headed for the plane and then four explosions before the ultimate fuel-tank explosion that erupted into a fireball." Awarded the Distinguished Flying Cross for his forty-six rescue missions in Vietnam, a single FBI agent *honored* Major Meyer with a five-minute interview to take his missile statement and took no written notes.

Unnamed sources also backed the missile theory.

"A MISSILE," *The Washington Times* National Weekly Edition, December 29, 1996

An official with the defense Intelligence Agency, spy arm of the Pentagon, has informed congressional staff members that, in his opinion, a shoulder-fired missile brought down T WA Flight 800.

THE EYEWITNESSES DID NOT SEE A MISSILE. Those are the words the Central Intelligence Agency's animated video prominently displayed on November 18, 1997, as FBI lead investigator James Kallstrom released it on simultaneous multi-network live TV to discredit all of the eyewitnesses who saw a missile shoot down TWA Flight 800. You can still find this video on YouTube today and see for yourself its polarized, political nature as the words appear and remain on the screen. The video claims that witnesses saw the Boeing 747, after its nose was blown off, climbing while on fire — not a missile rising, but the crippled aircraft itself. Their speculation, based on NTSB computer simulations and FAA radar tapes estimating the flight path, shows the remaining nose-less hull pitching up while rolling to the left and climbing to a maximum altitude somewhere between 15,000 and almost 17,000 feet — more of a trajectory than a flight at that point.

Courtroom defendants have been convicted of felonies based on a single eyewitness report. The FBI and the CIA found a way to sweep aside more witnesses than dead passengers and crew.

One witness attending a fundraiser in East Quogue on Long Island captured a "long, cylindrical object in the sky" in one of her photos taken just before TWA Flight 800 exploded. Linda Kabot's photo was published in *Paris Match* magazine next to a photo of a cruise missile with amazing similarity, but when she reported it to the FBI — and they determined that she was facing north, not south toward the ocean when the photo was taken — they confiscated all of her film including the negative. The distressing component of that realization is that if her object was a missile — that nobody saw launched from very populated Long Island — then it would have had to have been launched at sea, posed for her camera over land, and then turned around to track and destroy the doomed 747. That would indicate a missile with a sophisticated tracking system — one launched from a military platform, not a terrorist's shoulder. As a parting shot at the confiscated Kabot photo, the FBI discounted her object of interest as a discarded cigar, in lieu of a cruise missile — and they somehow did it with a straight face.

"THE ANTI-CONSPIRACY THEORY"
– Mark K. Anderson, *Fairfield County Weekly*, December 26 -January 1, 1996

THE FBI'S EXPLANATION: "THIS COULD HAVE BEEN A CIGAR
THROWN AWAY BY A GUEST."

Already I was angry the FBI had taken the investigation lead away from the
National Transportation Safety Board — the agency normally tasked to investigate aircraft accidents.

"FBI REPORTED READY TO TAKE OVER BLAST PROBE"
– Mark Mueller, *The Boston Herald*, July 20, 1996

> *The* FBI *plans to take over the investigation into the fiery downing
> of* TWA *Flight 800 off the Long Island coast, conducting a massive
> criminal probe into what authorities increasingly suspect is a terrorist
> bombing or missile attack, two news agencies reported.*

With terrorism a possibility, that decision had some reasonable justification
at first, but they never let go even after they publically claimed that foul play
hadn't occurred. And what business did the CIA have in a U.S. registered aircraft investigation, and why did this normally clandestine organization (tasked
with foreign intelligence gathering) become the domestic live broadcast dele-
gate?

With all of the eyewitness reports brushed aside, any further evidence that
refuted the burning, zoom-climbing, severed-aircraft scenario after the initial
explosion was discredited.

Air Traffic Control radar plotting tapes that revealed a primary target that
could possibly be a missile — radar returns not enhanced by onboard equipment
called transponders that help identify each aircraft in the air — were written off
as anomalies.

" 'POSSIBILITY OF CRIMINAL ACT,' SAYS U.S. AVIATION OFFICIAL"
– Lawrence Malkin, *The New York Times*, July 20, 1996

> *Investigators were particularly perplexed by a small blip that appeared
> near the jet on radar screens just before the crash. Experts said it was
> most likely an anomaly.*

In 2006, CNN produced a show titled *No Survivors: Why* TWA *800 Could Happen Again* that reiterated the no-missile theory. Soon afterward, the Discovery

Channel aired a show *Best Evidence* that calls TWA Flight 800 "a disturbing mystery." It reported accusations of the FBI removing aircraft pieces from the reconstruction hangar and lead investigator Kallstrom calling such removal "a normal investigative procedure." At first the FBI reported traces of PETN and other explosive residue, but suddenly those reports stopped, and the few existing findings were explained away as a result of the parts having been transported from the ocean to the aircraft reconstruction hangar in Calverton, New York—formerly the Grumman Aircraft facility that became host for the most costly air disaster investigation in U.S. history—on active military vessels. In an attempt to rebuild the destroyed Boeing 747 to find the source and cause of the explosion, over ninety-five percent of the Boeing 747 was recovered by federal, state, and local agencies plus contractors using side-scan sonar, remote-operated vehicles, and eventually scallop trawlers to rake the debris fields.

"TRACE OF CHEMICAL –
COMPONENT FOR BOMBS AND MISSILES CAME FROM WRECKAGE"
– Don Van Natta Jr, *The New York Times*, August 23, 1996

> *Chemists at the Federal Bureau of Investigation crime laboratory in Washington have found traces of PETN, a chemical in plastic explosives, on a piece of wreckage retrieved from the jet's passenger cabin between Rows 17 and 27, according to three senior officials deeply involved in the investigation. They spoke on the condition of anonymity.*

Bodies that were recovered went to the Suffolk County medical examiner's office in Hauppauge, New York where Don "Skypig" Foldy—one of my TWA pilot friends—was assigned by our union to assist the NTSB's medical aspects investigation team. Their assignment was to identify the bodies, but they also examined shrapnel patterns in an effort to identify the explosion source. Susanne was identified within a week. One of my closest friends, "Cool" Mark Boudreau, drove Susanne's dental records from Connecticut down to the office on Long Island for verification, but it took over ten months to identify the 230th victim.

"OCEAN OF TEARS" – Associated Press, *Connecticut Post*, July 23, 1996

DIVERS RECOVER 6 BODIES FROM FUSELAGE SECTION

"East Moriches, N.Y. – Divers reached a large section of downed TWA
*Flight 800 on the ocean floor Monday, pulling out six bodies from
their watery tomb and searching for any evidence of what caused the
disaster."*

I became a simulator instructor and check-airman in the years that followed,
and was bestowed the honor of re-qualifying one of our TWA captains who
had been grounded and investigated for removing from the Calverton hangar
a swath of seat-back cloth covered in what he believed was missile residue. He
attempted to have it independently tested through private investigator James
D. Sanders, but the FBI confiscated it and insisted the substance was glue used
in the manufacturing process. James D. Sanders wrote the book *Altered Evidence*
about his struggle with authorities during his investigation.

I know that claiming the government covered up the truth, for whatever
reason, lumps me in the category of every conspiracy nut ever to walk the planet
— from UFO believers, to JFK assassination theorists, to the Flat Earth Society
whose members believe the Apollo landing on the moon was a hoax. Throw in a
Bigfoot or Sasquatch reference, and it's easy to see how anyone claiming that a
missile shot down TWA Flight 800 can have their reputation smeared by completely unrelated events.

Media spin is a powerful tool — from the mid 1960s through the mid 1970s
nearly sixty thousand American deaths occurred in southeast Asia while we
were *winning the war against communism* — and I believe that somewhere way up
at the top of the 1996 political line, a decision was made to produce an official
theory rather than conduct an honest investigation. The term *Pierre Salinger Syn-
drome* is derived from the ridicule directed at the former White House press secretary after he went public speaking in favor of the missile theory. The term is
now used to describe someone who believes everything on the Internet is true,
as it was the uncontrolled news source for theories alternative to the official
diatribe. The *Times* described Salinger as "a doddering fool who'd been suckered
in by that infernal Internet contraption." The *Fairfield Country Weekly* claims the
FBI, NTSB, and the Navy have discounted that friendly fire brought down TWA
Flight 800 and "they've painted Salinger as a loose cannon, a few baguettes
short of a dinner party."

"A THIN WHITE TRAIL RISING UP..."
– Mark K. Anderson, *Fairfield County Weekly*, December 26–January 1, 1996

THE ANTI-CONSPIRACY CONSPIRACY — IS PIERRE SALINGER A NUT,
OR COULD AN AMERICAN MISSILE HAVE DOWNED TWA FLIGHT 800?

*Call it conspiratorial. Call it as the FBI's James Kallstrom did at a
recent press conference, "absolute, pure, utter nonsense." Tar it with
whatever brush you will.*

Over the years I have flown with many former TWA pilots, and they have
told me many tales about TWA Flight 800 that have made me sure there was a
cover up at a very high level. Some were direct accounts from our airline's volunteer investigators who privately confirmed the public accusations that the
FBI was removing aircraft pieces from the reconstruction hangar. This activity
was finally revealed in the July 17, 2013, Epix documentary about the flaws of
the TWA Flight 800 investigation, which adds that the FBI was caught ham-
mering pieces into new shapes in the middle of the night — presumably to make
them fit their center tank explosion theory. Other coworkers flew with Major
Fritz Meyers in the Air National Guard and echoed his missile-recognition credibility. These accounts, and others, were revealed to me under the condition of
anonymity. Two stories involve the Navy SEALS.

A TWA pilot — who also served in either the Air Guard or the Air Force
Reserves — flew Navy SEAL Team 6 on a mission some time after TWA Flight
800. Team 6 is the DEVGRU, or Naval Special Warfare Development Group. They
represent the Tier One Special Forces arm of the U.S. Navy that performs black
ops at the direction of the Commander in Chief. They used to be more covert,
but recent books and movies about them have made their identity a household
name. This fellow TWA pilot asked one of the SEALS on his military flight if he'd
covertly retrieved missile parts while diving the Boeing 747 wreckage during the
initial forty-eight post-tragedy hours. The SEAL's official reply was a spoken,
"No," but accompanied by a vertical head nod. The pilot's interpretation was
that the SEAL was honoring his oath not to speak about his mission, while
informally acknowledging the truth. Like the SEAL, this TWA/Air Force pilot
wouldn't publicly commit to his story at the time for fear of reprisal and only
indicated man-to-man what he couldn't reveal in the open. Now, he doesn't even
want to discuss what he told me in that crew briefing room over a decade ago,
so I can't confirm what my distant memory recalls. I'm disappointed, but I can't
blame him. Not everyone has the loss of his fiancée to galvanize his unwavering
search for the truth. Instead, he chooses a quiet life free from federal scrutiny.
And how convenient is it for our former administration that if I did somehow
manage to locate one of the former DevGru Navy SEALS in order to ask him in

person about the team's dive missions immediately following the TWA Flight 800 disaster, the long and seemingly infinite reach of the executive branch still lawfully muzzles him.

These stories are all part of my accumulated secondhand knowledge of the aftermath and investigation that would certainly be considered hearsay in a courtroom — and probably dismissed by objection — but inside my personal TWA universe, they are the lore of reliable peers and mentors. Do I have the smoking gun to reveal to the world? Unfortunately not. My perspective is personal, not investigative. But based on all I have heard, seen, and experienced along with my former TWA family, I strongly believe that not only was *something rotten in the state of Denmark*[5] (according to Marcellus in William Shakespeare's Hamlet), but something is also rotten on a federal level with the investigation of my fiancée Susanne's final flight.

There is one coworker willing to stand by his personal account. Recently I flew with another former TWA pilot who also served in the U.S. military. Marine Major Lance Stewart retired from the Corps when he was hired by TWA in May 1990 as a Boeing 727 flight engineer. When he was subsequently furloughed by the airline in January 1991, he returned to active duty with the Army Utah Air National Guard (UTARNG) and became a Chief Warrant Officer (CW2). He has allowed me to reveal his post-accident story that I present here with minimal grammatical editing:

The following account of an occurrence related to the downing of TWA Flight 800 is recorded from my best recollection. Dates, times, and people involved (are) based on my memory from being there. Fall 1996, approx. October time frame, I was a pilot on a C23 (Sherpa) cargo plane. Our location was at the Marana Airfield located south of Phoenix, AZ. We had orders to support a Navy SEAL team that was stationed at the Marana Airfield. Our specific assignment was to give air support in the form of paradrops from our plane. Each morning we would take SEAL Team members to an altitude of approx. 14,000 to 18,000 feet where they would exit the rear of the airplane. We did this about 5 to 6 flights each day to assist the SEAL Team in their training.

Our flight crew was informed by base ops one morning that the airfield would be closed the next day for security reasons. The next day we observed a large gathering of media (newspapers, radio, TV) assembled several hundred yards away from the Navy SEAL base. Their attention was

---

5 Shakespeare, William, and Harold Jenkins. *Hamlet*. London: Methuen, 1982. Print.

focused on an old, mothballed Boeing 747 located on the Marana Air Base. Marana had about 70 old mothballed, former airline passenger jets positioned west of the runway. This particular 747 of interest was for a demonstration. Officials from the government were going to present their best explanation of what had caused the downing/explosion on the TWA 747 known as Flight 800.

The old 747 parked in the desert was partially fueled and had been connected to a portable electrical cart. The cart was a typical aviation piece of equipment used to provide electrical power to airplanes, capable of dispensing a significant amount of power. With cameras rolling, the power cart was started and then on cue the power was fed to the center tank on the old 747. Nothing happened! No explosion, not even a murmur.

I was on the roof of the SEAL Team building, located about 300 yards from the 747. Along with half a dozen Navy SEALS and my flight crew. We observed the failed attempt to demonstrate the government's supposed explanation of what happened to TWA Flight 800.

The following day a second demo — with the news media present — was scheduled. Again I, along with SEAL Team members, were observing the event. The electrical cart was started and power was sent to the center fuel tank on the 747. That second demo went as planned and the 747 fuel tank exploded, causing the fuselage of the aircraft to break apart like a peanut shell. The cameras caught the entire event on film that has been replayed many times over the years on cable TV.

That day as I witnessed the explosion on the tired old 747, the Navy SEAL standing next to me explained that the 747 had 3 sticks of dynamite placed in the belly of the aircraft. The dynamite was put there the previous evening to make sure the demonstration the following morning would go as planned! This particular and significant fact was not made public.

I have the highest respect for Navy SEALS, and I have met three personally—one was a TWA pilot. These men are trained to perform extreme tasks and sworn to maintain national secrets. But it is now seventeen years later, and it is my hope that once they've retired from military service, at least one will decide that he'd signed up to serve the American people and not the philandering former American president deserving of his impeachment — and our proud warrior will seek to clear his conscience, even though our then President signed Executive "gag" Order number 13039 [6] (less than a year after TWA Flight 800) that spe-

---

6 Clinton, William J., "Executive Order 13039 – Exclusion of the Naval Special Warfare Develop-

cifically excludes the Naval Special Warfare Group from whistle-blower protection. Considering the intensity with which these men earn their tridents, and both the political and personal risk involved with coming forward, I think the likelihood is remote. It would take someone highly respected like a Navy SEAL to bring credibility to cover-up accusations. But whatever way the truth eventually leeches to the surface, I hope that I live long enough to see it.

Navy SEAL Matt Bissonnette wrote *No Easy Day* about the Bin Laden raid, and then the Pentagon threatened him for violating his nondisclosure agreement. Edward Snowden is living overseas in exile for whistleblowing against the NSA. Mr. Snowden revealed widespread surveillance of U.S citizens because he felt he was serving the people, "so what affects all of us can be discussed by all of us in the light of day, and I asked the world for justice." Revealing covert actions protected by secret executive orders would not be an easy step, even for a brave and patriotic Navy SEAL, or anyone with inside information. I applaud the filmmakers, participants, and especially the six former investigators who recently stepped forward in the Epix documentary. Following the airing of this documentary, former FBI lead investigator James Kalstrom said on CNN News, "It seems like they've comfortably waited until they have their pensions before they became whistleblowers."[7] It may seem that way to him, but his words seem to demonstrate that federal retribution against anyone contrasting the official theory is still alive and well.

I try to keep in mind that Galileo sought the truth, was condemned for vehement suspicion of heresy, and was confined to house arrest. Jesus was nailed to a cross for blasphemy or speaking out against the official beliefs of his time. Remember Julius Caesar's last moment before the Roman Senate slaughtered him, "Et tu, Brute?" Truth is sometimes subverted for power. For a modern cover-up example, Google *Pat Tillman* and *friendly fire* and your eyes will open. Jon Krakauer explores Tillman's friendly-fire death and the military's resulting duplicity in his fifth book: *Where Men Win Glory*. And this is not an isolated case. Carol Burnett starred in the 1979 movie *Friendly Fire* about a similar cover-up during the Vietnam War based on the real-life story of Peg Mullen, as revealed in the book by C. D. B. Bryan.

But why would the U.S. government conceal the true cause of the TWA Flight 800 disaster? That's hard to answer, because there is no revealed truth from

ment Group From the Federal Labor-Management Relations Program," March 11, 1997. Online by Gerhard Peters and John T. Woolley, *The American Presidency Project*. http://www.presidency.ucsb.edu/ws/?pid=53855.

7 Tapper, Jake. "Investigator: New TWA theory Is 'bull'" *The National Lead*. CNN. 19 June 2013. Television.

which one can work backward. Several speculative reasons still cross my mind. The first is political. Our president, the one who *didn't inhale* and who *did not have sexual relations with that woman*, was running for re-election less than four months later. In hindsight, we know what happens to our economy when terrorism lands on our shores or, more accurately, crashes into our buildings. We also know what happens to incumbent presidents when our economy tanks.

Another theory involves the active warning areas W-105 and W-106 over the Atlantic near where TWA Flight 800 went down. It's no secret that the military had cordoned off that airspace for their use. What do our armed forces do out over the ocean—sail around and wash the decks?

"THE ANTI-CONSPIRACY CONSPIRACY"
– Mark K. Anderson, *Fairfield County Weekly*, December 26–January 1, 1996

> *...both Aerospace Daily and New Amsterdam magazine have reported that* TWA *Flight 800 was on a flight path skirting a Navy "hot area" that was reserved for the evening. While the Navy has never come clean with its reasons for roping off the "hot area" that night, such warning zones are typically activated to keep civilian traffic clear of military activities.*

> *...The Navy admits a* P-3 *radar tracking plane was only 15 miles from the crash.*

Of course the military tests new and experimental weapons and defense systems. Staying the leader in technology is how the U.S. military remains the dominant force in the world and projects its military power. All the reports that I watched about missiles in the wake of TWA Flight 800 compared the ranges and capabilities of various surplus military weaponry. That information attempted to rule out a shore- or small-vessel-launched shoulder-fired weapon like the variety our own CIA and Department of Defense supplied the Taliban to fight the Russian helicopters in the Soviet war in Afghanistan before the Taliban began focusing their hatred on us.

But that didn't rule out friendly fire. Our military doesn't float an armada, or even a small task force, to launch bottle rockets. The technology being tested in 1996 was rumored to be the Aegis Ballistic Missile Defense System. Computerized missile tracking and control allows one ship to fire a defensive missile while another guides it. Remember our Patriot defense batteries knocking down incoming Iraqi scud missiles during the first Gulf War? Now imagine that scenario playing out at sea. Since radar can't see over the curvature of the earth, this is a way to network Navy ships in order to protect each other. In theory it's a good thing, but in practice, have you ever seen a computer crash or malfunction? Who hasn't? Perhaps it was determined at the highest level that revealing live-missile firing and intercept exercises — even practice missiles without explosive warheads — so close to commercial air traffic, would not serve the American public's best interest, especially during an election year.

Has an airliner ever been shot down by friendly fire? Can that sort of thing even really happen? The Soviets shot down Korean Air Flight 007 — coincidently also a Boeing 747 — on September 1, 1983, over the Sea of Japan causing 269 fatalities. Our own Navy's missile cruiser, the USS Vincennes, shot down Iran Air Flight 655 — a widebody Airbus 300 — on July 3, 1988, over the Persian Gulf, causing 290 casualties.

Another cover-up theory involves even more advanced weaponry. President Reagan created the Strategic Defense Initiative back in 1983 to use ground and space systems to intercept incoming threats including ICBMs — intercontinental ballistic missiles. Thirteen years before TWA Flight 800 — our president claimed this system was already in place. Critics nicknamed the program Star Wars and feared the technology could be used to support cold-war doctrines and lead to mutual assured destruction. Federal funding for this project is typically off budget and considered a black operation where secrecy is valued over public interest. Any use or experimentation of this system would be kept out of the public eye at all costs.

Since TWA Flight 800 exploded off the Long Island coast with no official explanation and lots of unconfirmed speculation, I have more questions than answers. I feel like an angry goldfish staring through my limited bowl at the smiling cat in the room that got away with eating my fiancée.[8] All I could do was channel my hardened feelings into lyrics — my emotional outlet of choice. Deep into what my company-assigned psychologist would call the anger phase, I wrote this song: "One Day."

> *They're not here for you*
> *They're not here for me*
> *They're just here for themselves*
> *As you will see*
> *They look up to no one*

---

8 In the years following TWA Flight 800, I joined the Flight 800 Independent Research Organization — FIRO — from roughly 1999 through 2005. A website dedicated to the group's findings is: http://flight800.org/

They look down on you
Everything that they say
Everything that they do

Oh, one day
One day we will see
Oh, one day
One day we will be
Just a product of our complacency
Nothing left for you and me
Oh, one day
One day we will see

I believed they were good
I believed life was fair
That my water was clean
That I could still breathe the air
But these aren't rights that I own
They've all been taken away
Now that I've opened my eyes
I see it every day

Oh, one day
One day we will see
Oh, one day
One day we will be
Just a product of our complacency
Nothing left for you and me
Oh, one day
One day we will see

As I forge ahead
I wonder where I'll go
They won't let me stay
Now that they know I know
They still hold all the cards
They still run the show
Maybe soon there won't be
Anywhere else to go

Oh, one day
One day we will see
Oh, one day
One day we will be
Just a product of our complacency
Nothing left for you and me
Oh, one day
One day we will see

They're not here for you
They're not here for me
They're just here for themselves
As you will see
They look up to no one
They look down on you
Everything that they say
Everything that they do

Oh, one day
One day we will see
Oh, one day
One day we will be
Just a product of our complacency
Nothing left for you and me

Oh, one day
One day we will see
Oh, one day
Oh, one day
Oh, one day
Oh, one day
Oh, no day like today

33 | GOING SOUTH IN EASTERN EUROPE

I Escaped Into a Dream

LIKE IT OR NOT, life went on without her, and I noticed her absence in little things, like music. "If You Could Only See" by Tonic, was the first song after Susanne's death that I thought she would have loved, and it often played on the radio in the years following that awful summer of 1996. I realized by degrees that there would be no more sharing new music, personal opinions, or daily interludes with Susanne. There'd be no more looking into her blue eyes as suggested in Tonic's song — Susanne's as deep blue as the North Sea water of her homeland. There'd be no more reading her thoughts or emotions, no more running my fingers through her long blonde hair so pure it was white with almost no trace of yellow, and no more experiencing anything together.

I could handle casual interaction with well-meaning friends and coworkers, but an embrace often broke my protective shell. In the years following TWA Flight 800, so many of us were reeling from that flight's demise that a hug became known as the TWA handshake. Since TWA was bought and consolidated in 2001, and many of my fellow pilots were furloughed post-9/11 and subsequently hired at many other airlines, there's a good chance to this day that two uniformed crewmembers seen hugging in a terminal are both former TWA employees reuniting in passing.

For the next couple years following TWA 800, I buried myself in my work. Yes, I still occasionally went flying as a first officer in Boeing 767 aircraft — making position reports across the Atlantic Ocean all the way to Europe and back. I avoided trips to Paris — Susanne's intended destination — flying instead to Milan, Rome, Berlin (no longer divided by the notorious wall), Frankfurt, Athens, Tel Aviv, Cairo, etc. But I also found a new challenge teaching other TWA pilots, at our small training facility at JFK, in the simulator of my old favorite Jurassic jet — the mighty Pigship, a.k.a. the Boeing 727.

As an instructor and check-airman, sometimes I would give full crews their annual recurrent training, but mostly I flew the 727 simulator solo while flight engineer training was conducted on the sideways panel of knobs, switches, and dials behind the two flying pilots. I was a filler pilot for their F/E training. If you thought flying a jet was difficult, try doing it as a captain—before my seniority could actually hold that exalted title—alongside an empty copilot seat, while a team of flight engineers-in-training worked through every imaginable emergency.

First an engine would fail just after the takeoff roll. Then, after we'd secured that situation and prepared to make an approach back to the departing runway, a second engine would catch on fire. I'd fly the plane while working with the flight engineers to extinguish and shut it down, and then work through a slew of checklists to set up for a single-engine approach in a formerly three-engine jet. The flight engineer instructors loved to load us up with emergencies—failed hydraulic systems, stuck landing gear, duct overheats, iced-over instruments, and electrical failures. The worst one was the interior fire/smoke checklist that guided us to don oxygen masks and smoke goggles while shutting down almost all of the ship's power—performing much of the lengthy checklist in the dark. But honestly, that's what the simulator is made for. I have more simulated single-engine landings in the Pigship than I care to remember—sometimes four, six, or even eight of them in a single session.

This new challenge of teaching 727s while flying 767s kept me busy and my mind occupied for a couple years. But once these challenges finally became routine through significant repetition, my old friend wanderlust came knocking again.

Focusing on my cockpit duties allowed me to feel like I had one piece of my life back in order. My 727 instructor/check-airman position was an entry-level opportunity into management circles if I decided I wanted to pursue that career path. My friend and earliest TWA mentor Captain Ken Cook was a fleet manager for the Boeing 727 before he died of pancreatic cancer. It occurred to me, however inadvertently, that I was following in his footsteps. TWA's higher management was finally off of my back—no more proving I was emotionally fit to fly since the 747 explosive disaster. In fact, I was rising up on their radar in a leadership role this time, but the whole work experience felt hollow. I no longer looked forward to my formerly anticipated captain upgrade that—based on seniority projections and expected retirements—was now only a year or two away. I still looked forward to flying and teaching, but without Susanne in my life simultaneously climbing her career path towards vice president at GE Capital, my enthusiasm for success must have leaked out through the hole in my heart.

Nancy told me, before we parted ways, that grief could often be cyclical. Healing after losing a life partner is not a linear journey. If old feelings—ones we'd worked through in the first year after TWA Flight 800—came back to haunt me, that's normal.

I don't know what the initial trigger was. Maybe it was an aircraft walk-around—the preflight required before accepting an airplane for a trip—when my Boeing 767 was parked between two giant red and white Boeing 747s, both identical to the one that rained down in pieces into the Atlantic. Maybe I saw a dark blue Saab convertible sedan, like Susanne's former pride and joy, on my way to or from the airport. Or maybe I'd just kept myself so distracted with double duty at work that while I was wrapped up in the comfort of everyday living, Susanne slowly slipped more and more back into my daily thoughts. Tonic still sang, "If You Could Only See," periodically on the radio, and that song still reminded me of Susanne even though she'd never heard it, and I wondered what she would be yearning to see, hear, and experience if she could. Restlessness set in.

At some point, the weight of my situation—looking backwards at all that I'd lost instead of the opportunities waiting for me up ahead—felt almost too much to carry again. I was haunted by an urge to escape all things familiar. I was an adult, but I needed to run away.

So, I adopted old habits and began planning to trade my routine and responsibilities for the manageable weight of my backpack as soon as I could secure the necessary time off. My next adventure became my obsession: away-away—as in really away. I'm good at forgetting—pretending the dark situation of my life isn't real—by departing for the unknown.

Time kept elapsing, and I kept moving but not moving on. I was stuck, but at least I recognized it. I hoped the challenges of recreational, international travel would help restore some kind of personal perspective. Maybe some people turn to drugs and alcohol to modify their feelings, but I was lucky to have airline passes and jumpseat privileges as my form of escape. These excursions were usually therapeutic, but sometimes they didn't go so well.

Before I was free to explore new lands, I moved to St. Louis. My New York roommates were on the verge of getting married. Even my blunted brain recognized that three was about to become a crowd. Also, TWA decided to consolidate the training department by moving the JFK-based 727 simulator to the airline's primary training center in St. Louis. It's ironic that aircraft simulators project the world's airports on their cockpit screens, but they never actually go anywhere—they remain rooted on top of their spider-like hydraulic jacks inside of garage-like bays, flight after simulated flight. When the Boeing 727 simulator I worked in was crated to the Midwest, I went with it—not in the actual box of course, but my primary job was transferred.

My new St. Louis neighbors biked across the Czech Republic. When they returned, I sat through their post-adventure slideshow over cocktails. Unlike most vacation photo sharing, this wasn't a painful experience. They showed me Eastern Europe at ground level instead of my usually impersonal birds-eye view of the world from the cockpit. I was still thinking about planning a serious trek, but I could see from their presentation that biking would allow me to cover more ground than schlepping a pack. Their post-adventure enthusiasm helped me decide that this is what I now needed to do, so I begged for their itinerary. It was the best plan I could come up with to drag my obsessing mind out of the past. Their travel log became the rough draft for my own trip, and I learned how to mount new panniers on my mountain bike and stuff them with wrinkle-resistant, waterproof travel clothing in order to escape. This was the modern, 21-speed pedal version of packing all my necessities into a handkerchief at the end of a long stick.

One of my fraternity brothers referred me to an Austrian tourist he'd met during his travels. Email was still new, and I typed a request to this friend of a friend who lived in Vienna, near the Czech border, instead of writing on lightweight Airmail stationary. The last time I met up with a friend of a friend, I ended up in San Juan. This time I ended up in a much darker place. Let's call my new contact Freddy. His name has definitely been changed.

Freddy agreed to let me ship my mountain bike to him, and I was able to put together a little more than two weeks off from my airline through careful bidding. TWA had great work rules. When I really needed some time off, I could obtain them. I was almost ready to depart for my much-needed Eastern Euro-emersion — reviewing my inventory of specially ordered AAA maps, a *Lonely Planet* paperback guide, a compass, and much more — when the phone rang.

"Mark, what are you up to?" Dana asked.

She's a former girlfriend — one of the first I eventually tried to date after losing Susanne. I'd met her on a British Virgin Islands sailing excursion — another emersion vacation escape that I'd attempted in order to clear my head — and we had seamlessly navigated through being friends, to being involved, and back to friends again like we were tacking and jibing in a gentle wind. Actually, I really liked Dana, but after a few months of long-distance dating she dropped the bomb: *I want four kids and I'm ready to get started.*

I ran from that request like I was escaping the fallout from a nuclear attack. That was too much commitment way too fast. I was still fragile. Maybe I wasn't even ready for dating and had forced it. Maybe the recent years felt like merely thirty emotional seconds. Maybe Dana's long, straight blonde hair reminded me too much of Susanne's. Or maybe the idea of settling down made me feel like she wouldn't last, either — that something tragic would happen to her if I became too attached. I'd wrestled with those confusing feelings several months before this phone call and lost. I didn't have Nancy — my personal, airline-sponsored counselor — to talk to about this kind of thing anymore, so I just let all of my confusing feelings go. I told Dana over the phone that I was working on a project on my computer.

"Do that later," she said. "Take me out for dinner."

"You're in town?" I asked this because she lived in Phoenix, not St. Louis, but she was a Southwest Airlines flight attendant, so anything was possible.

"I just landed. Come get me." She knew me well, and I was on my way.

We shared dinner, Mexican chicken and steak fajitas with lime-topped Coronas, at a delicious dive near the airport. I told her about my impending trip, and she nodded with what appeared to be a feigned interest. Maybe I never learned how to read her well, or maybe her stunning Arizona-sun beauty short-circuited my otherwise strong intuition. I could picture her right at home in the centerfold of a men's magazine, but apparently I misread all of her signals.

I kept the beer drinking to my sober driving limit, avoided all invitations for tequila, and eventually dropped her back off at her hotel. I made no attempt to kiss her, much less try to invite myself up to her room. She was gorgeous, yes, but I looked at her as fully loaded. I needed to keep my sperm to myself, unless I wanted to put it through college.

A few days went by, and my imminent departure for Vienna loomed when she called again. "Mark, where do I ship my bike?"

"Hellooo? What?" The robot from Lost in Space began waving his slinky arms and broadcasting *Danger Will Robinson!* in the back of my mind.

"My bike," she said. "Where do I ship it? I'm going with you."

Hmm, I didn't invite her over dinner, did I? No, I'm almost sure I didn't, but there was no time to ponder this sudden situation — what to do, what to do, what to do?

"Mark, I've boxed up my bike and I'm heading over to Fed Ex with it. I need that address for your friend's friend in Vienna."

Dana's a cool gal and hot at the same time. There seemed to be no post-dating fallout between us. I made a split-second decision and welcomed her aboard, platonically. She'd be a solid travel buddy, and there was the added bonus that she'd also be easy to look at.

Here's where the prospective itinerary became an issue. She still had one short trip left to fly for her airline before she could leave. I was ready and anxious to depart. About that time Freddy called, long distance, from overseas. This was before the new millennium, and long-distance phone calls were still an expensive option.

"Mark, I have tickets to the Grand Prix in Hungary," Freddy said. "Let's go there before you go biking."

I'm not that into auto racing — Formula One or otherwise — and I'd worked several Daytona 500s plus numerous other races selling beer and catering infield skyboxes for my fraternity back during my undergraduate college days in Florida, but this seemed like a spontaneous international opportunity, so I said, "OK."

Freddy picked me up at the Vienna Airport in a street-legal racecar. Low to the ground and streamlined like a dart, it was a candy-apple red rocket ship. I don't believe he had an onboard navigation system, but the stereo was inter-active and scrolled each song title digitally — a new fascination for me until memory-jogging tunes began to play. I thought to myself: *Please no Tonic, please no Tonic, please no Tonic.* Freddy shifted each gear late, letting the RPMs spike the high-speed, redline limit with a revving whine between each stomp on the clutch. Auto racing was very much one of his favorite sports. Through his wind-shield, I became reacquainted with the Vienna streets as they blurred by. I'd briefly been based there with TWA — one of the many European satellite domi-ciles I bounced through after the Berlin Wall came down and TWA's European crew bases were moved around in search of a profitable replacement to the inter-German service we'd been providing.

Freddy and I made a pit stop at his shop, and I assembled Dana's and my mountain bikes with tiny travel tools. With the Czech trip now ready to go as soon as Dana arrived in a couple days, Freddy and I headed down into rural Hungary in his Honda that looked like a Ferrari.

> *The Formula One*
> *Was waiting for me*
> *Just an autobahn ride*
> *Down to Hungary*
> *Freddy and I*
> *In his cherry sports car*
> *Left Vienna one day*
> *At two hundred per hour*

Austria has many vineyards, and parts of it reminded me of the Napa and Sonoma valleys in California. As we crossed the unmanned border into Hun-

gary, the scenery became more flat and Midwestern in appearance with continuous plots of corn and soy crops — maybe some wheat, too. I'm a city boy
at heart and not versed in agriculture, but I know an extremely rural setting
when I see one. I expected Freddy's map to say, "Here There Be Dragons," except
the surrounding sea was made of waving stalks and grains. On either side of
the isolated pavement was an endless view of plants deliberately being grown.
During our steady course through the furrowed fields, he told me we were
going to meet some really nice girls.

"Really? I thought we were headed to the big race."

"Yes, the race, too, but I bought extra tickets. There's a girl I met — we're
taking her. She has a twin sister. Fraternal, not identical, but I think you'll like
her."

This was starting to sound like a true European adventure with all the trim-
mings. Freddy was a lean, blonde, almost metro-sexual member of Vienna's
see-and-be-seen crowd. I imagined that he didn't spend a night alone unless
he wanted to. He was picture-perfect for the Aryan race and spoke the Queen's
English like he was educated at Oxford, but with an Austrian accent. Trucks
were lorries, a flashlight was a torch, but he was quite understandable. I asked
Freddy to tell me about these twin Hungarian dates that had me intrigued and
him so enraptured.

"Well, Mark, they're young. I really want to start a family so I've been looking
for the right gal."

I immediately thought of Dana. She also wanted a family right away. I told
him about her and that she and I were just friends — she's single and available.
She'd look great in his red sports car with her blonde hair blowing in the wind
on the autobahn. With Freddy's fluent English, Dana would have all the time in
the world to eventually learn Austrian German. She'd fit right in over here — *eine
schöne frau.*

"How old is she?" Freddy asked with a hint of skepticism.

Freddy and I were both about thirty-four. I replied, "She's a little younger
than we are."

"Good, because I like younger girls."

"I think she's thirty. Picture a full-size Barbie doll without the metal joints in
her movable limbs revealed, except she's even more beautiful."

Freddy's expression soured. "Oh no, that's too old for me."

"What do you mean too old? She's a good four or five years younger than you
are. She's totally cool, and smart, too. With her airline pass benefits she can hop
back and forth to Vienna while you get to know her."

Freddy frowned. I was surprised he could turn her down so quickly. After all, if not for the rush for kids, I could have been happy with her. His next comment surprised me even more.

"I'm looking for a virgin. It's important for me to be the only guy she's been with."

Did we just drive back into medieval times? Freddy's sport car wasn't a plutonium-powered, polished-metal DeLorean, but I suddenly felt a need to get back to the future. I was confused. I'd lived many places in Europe and knew a lot of the cultural differences, or at least I thought I did, but I hadn't come across this primitive instinct in an educated man before.

"We're going to meet some virgins," Freddy said. "You'll like them. You'll see."

"Are you kidding me? How old are these gals we're taking to the Formula One race? Twenty-five?"

"No, they're younger."

> *We're meeting some girls*
> *He confided in me*
> *I know that you'll like them*
> *Just wait and see*
> *They're young little virgins*
> *And Schumacher fans*
> *I've arranged everything*
> *I've made all the plans*

"Tell me they're at least twenty-one, please."
"No, Mark, they're *virgins*."

> *"Virgins," you say?*
> *Did I hear that one right?*
> *I wanted out of the car*
> *But there was nowhere in sight*

"You've got to be kidding me," I said. "We're picking up a couple of eighteen-year-olds? And now that I think of it, how are we getting them to the race? This made-for-speed car only holds two people."

"They have their father's van that we can use—and they're fourteen."

"Stop the car."

> *"Fourteen," did he say?*
> *Did I hear that one right?*

I wanted out of the car
But there was nowhere in sight
I've gotta escape,
But I can't see the light
I wanted out of the car
But there was nowhere in sight

Scenes from *Midnight Express* flashed through my head. My future Hungarian cellmates would have their own version of Turkish revenge ...

I escaped into a dream
Dreaming I'd run far away
Only in my dream
Could I make this go away

...Or maybe in Hungary they didn't even bother with non-lethal stabbing below the waist. They'd have their own worse fates planned for suspected child molesters. Traveling with Freddy, I'd be guilty by association. I didn't want to go to any jail, much less one in a third-world country. I doubted Dana would smear her bare breasts on the bulletproof glass for me during my annual visitation day, like the girlfriend in the movie.

I had nowhere for Freddy to let me out; we were in the middle of endless agriculture in the heart of a foreign country. Farmers' fields hosted the occasional windowless equipment shed, but there were no houses as far as I could see. I would have spent days searching for a train, or any kind of transport that didn't need to be fed grains and involve a cart. I was Freddy's captive.

"Freddy, I'm an American. I don't know what the rules are in Austria or Hungary, but I'm pretty sure mating with a fourteen-year-old is a punishable offense. Even if it's somehow not against the law here, it's just plain wrong."

"I need a virgin," he said, "to accept my seed."

I thought of King Henry VIII and the fates of his wives who didn't produce a male heir. Was some poor Hungarian child headed for a beheading at Freddy's hands? Maybe if I played with the car's radio I could dial us back to the year 1999. Of course there was still the problem of where I was going to find 1.21 gigawatts of electrical power needed for time travel.

These girls fulfill my need
Freddy said through my haze
So I can spread my seed

His words seemed cra-zy
"Seed," did he say?
Did I hear that one right?
I wanted out of the car
But there was nowhere in sight

"Besides, she's finishing Gymnasio," Freddy offered as an explanation. I later learned this is something like our American junior high school. The thought of this thirty-four-year-old cruising Eastern European primary schools for a place to plant his seed brought on a toxic compound of emotions: revulsion, contempt, and a little fear. What is he truly capable of?

I escaped into a dream
Dreaming I'd run far away
Only in my dream
Could I make this go away

When we eventually reached the village where the girls lived, Freddy showed me the photo collage of Gymnasio graduating classes posted in various storefront windows — most likely by proud parents. An overwhelming thought occurred to me: *this was Freddy's menu.*

He showed me the photo within the poster collage that displayed his girl. I was so far out of my comfort zone that I looked around for the hidden camera. I just knew that I was the victim of some European sordid reality TV show, but I wasn't. Once back in Freddy's car for the final short drive to this underage princess's home, I looked out the window so he couldn't see my pre-puking expression.

"I'm not going anywhere near them," I told him. "Sorry, but there's no way."

I wish I could say that I started walking back to Austria, that I left that hamlet in the middle of nowhere and rode in an oxen-powered cart for part of the way, that it took my full two weeks off from work to return to civilization, and this extraction became my day-to-day, live-in-the-moment adventure that cleared my head. Instead, Freddy and I reached a compromise. I was his captive traveler, but he agreed that we'd take the girls' father with us, who seemed very excited to see the race when Freddy invited him — and dear old dad even drove his own van. My reluctant journey continued inside a near replica of Scooby Doo's Mystery Machine — without the flower-power paintjob — and it was a stick shift, yet another sign that I'd traveled back in time.

The girls were as close to being identical as sisters of the same age can be.

They were giggly and had both spray-painted the Ferrari standing-stallion logo into their long, straight, light brown hair. They were big Michael Schumacher fans, in the adoring way of girls just discovering there were two different sexes worshipping their first sports celebrity idol. My overwhelming impression was that I should have brought some *Mad Libs* or *Highlights* magazines with the magic yellow pen with me. Language barrier aside, surely these staple early-reader publications existed in Hungarian.

"Aren't they beautiful?" Freddy asked.

"Sure, like kittens are beautiful, or puppies," I answered. Certainly not in any sexual kind of way, which was what I fathomed he had on his mind. This pre-biking adventure into Hungary had totally spun out of control, and although I could usually recover from a spin, this one wasn't in an airplane.

Introductions were brief, and off we went. I claimed my space among a hundred thousand race fans on the grass along the side of the track, coated myself in SPF 50 sunblock, and watched a few laps of the Formula One as the drivers jockeyed for position. We could only see part of the speedway, and the thunderous motors were rock-concert loud as they roared by.

I don't know how anyone could tell who was who without the loudspeaker announcer's diatribe, which I think was in Hungarian but might as well have been in the beginner's trombone dialect of Charley Brown's parents for all the distortion. The girls yelled and screamed against the crash-protective screen whenever the cars appeared as multi-colored blurs — visual smears to compliment the world-inside-a-lawnmower noise that raged inside my head.

Then, against this surreal experience that I was committed to ride out to its Viennan conclusion, I began falling asleep in the hundred-degree heat. Excuse me; we were in Europe, so the thirty-eight-degree Celsius heat. The surrounding fanatics — with favored driver's logos and numbers painted on their bare beer bellies — tried to ridicule me for missing the race. Freddy translated their heckling, but I ignored them. Sleep seemed my only escape.

> *I escaped into a dream*
> *Dreaming I'd run far away*
> *Only in my dream*
> *Could I make this go away*

Through my haze, mixed German and Hungarian commentary seeped into my thoughts — most of which went over my head. I would have preferred all of it that way too, except Freddy translated the part that made him the most excited.

"Her dad says we should wait until she's sixteen to get married, and no relations until then. But I think he'll soften after we're together a few months."

Get me the hell out of here.

> *Only in my dream*
> *Could I make this go away*

Finally, the race ended and we went back in the mystery van to our Hungarian hosts' house. The girls' mother had remained home and offered us some snacks on a tray. She was very humble and polite. No communication was possible without translation, and I didn't ask for any. I wondered if the family was discussing a dowry. Would Freddy get to keep it if his seed didn't take? Or maybe since Freddy was the one from the country of means, was he offering to buy his pick of the litter? Did she come with a money-back guarantee? Did she have all her shots and papers? It wouldn't have surprised me if Freddy stuck his fingers into this poor little girl's mouth to check her teeth and gums. I felt like she was being traded straight from puberty to pregnancy. I had no idea how much of this she understood. I imagined Freddy saying, *I'll give her a good home, a comfortable life, and I plan to breed her right away.* For once I was glad for my lack of local language skills—I just didn't want to know.

> *Twin girls offered up by their father*
> *Each one barely fourteen*
> *Their giggled misunderstanding*
> *At what this all could mean …*
>
> *I escaped into a dream*
> *Dreaming I'd run far away*
> *Only in my dream*
> *Could I make this go away*

Freddy and I eventually drove back to Vienna, time-traveling back to meet Dana's flight. I didn't mind putting her on my lap—Dana is a woman, not a girl. I'd long given up on trying to set Freddy up with her. She'd kill me if she knew I'd even considered it.

Dana and I spent a single night together in Vienna in order for her to shake off her jetlag. Freddy confided in me, "She's way too old."

In the morning, Dana and I hustled onto the train for Breclav with our loaded-down bikes. I carried a plastic bag containing breakfast muffins while balancing two hot chocolates, ready to begin our journey into the southeastern part of the Czech Republic.

Our plan was to ride west to Ceski Krumlov, and then north up to Prague in nine days. That's another story — a more fun, benign, and tolerable one: two friends pedaling into new territory — defined only by a highlighted line along barely pronounceable street names. I was escaping more than I had originally planned and was happy to be living in the moment again, forgetting about everything except the immediate travel tasks — how many kilometers to ride each day, when to stop for meals, and always remembering to refill our water bottles.

There was something about pushing a bicycle plus a balanced pair of panniers full of gear through the summer heat, not knowing where we were going to stay each night until we found an open inn or guesthouse (nestled within some small town along the way) that had a special way of keeping my mind in the present. And that was the true objective of this trip.

As Dana and I divided blueberry and banana-nut muffins according to our preferences and mixed powdered Gatorade into our water bottles for our new adventure, she asked, "Did you have a good time with your friend at the race before I arrived?"

34 | MAKE THE RELAX

The Infinite Steps

I RETURNED HOME from Eastern Europe to an empty backpack still waiting its turn for my attention. Inanimate objects didn't talk to me, although if this one could, it would have rolled over on its back and nodded for me to scratch its belly — then whispered for me to slip just a single strap over my shoulder, and before I knew it we would be on a far-off mountaintop together. I didn't know it yet, but a mountaintop was in my imminent future, and I was also about to meet someone who truly believed that inanimate objects could speak to her.

Even traveling platonically with such a resplendent desert flower as Dana had awakened feelings I thought were comfortably hibernating or perhaps even on life support. But as time continued marching on without Susanne, frustrating me that the world hadn't entirely come to a stop with her last heartbeat, I began feeling a lonesome pull for some adult female companionship, and not anything too serious — the more detached, the better.

When the movie *The Bucket List* came out, I was painfully aware of the concept. Susanne had lived only thirty-one years, and her loss made me feel like I was already counting down my remaining breaths on earth, so I began plotting how best to use them. Bucket list items seemed like they needed a real decadence or challenge to them — items without repercussions.

Maybe my returning sex drive was a good sign — an emotional start — but I wasn't sure how to interpret it. I was not at an emotional place to make philanthropic or conscientious decisions. I scribbled near the top of my new bucket list: *having a threesome* (still an unchecked box by the way). Aside from the allure of overt sexual satisfaction, finding two adult females willing to help me shatter this taboo carried with it a degree of difficulty that also appealed to my reawakening competitive spirit.

Lust may be a poor substitute for lost love, but *wanderlust* — my trusty companion — is a compound word that combines both travel and sex — two cravings that I hoped together could pull me out of depression enough to put my life back in motion. But even as I lowered my ambitions enough to consider pursuing this particular triangular seduction, I remained true to myself with my number-one bucket list wish: *to travel all the way around the world* and see the geographical limits of what life on this planet had to offer.

Still, the days and weeks and even a few months came and went without my routine registering above a mundane level. Those who have grieved deeply know all too well how easy it is to lock up and shut down. Nancy's parting advice that grief is cyclical was right again, and I spent an unhealthy amount of time daydreaming that Susanne's fatal explosive demise offshore Long Island never happened, and all my wish thinking couldn't bring her back.

Everything at home and work continued to remind me of Susanne, and my backpack still sat forlorn and empty. I thought about the ground I had covered during my lifetime. My experience as an airline pilot had put my feet on the ground in twelve time zones. My early days flying 727s from TWA's European domiciles had taken me east as far as Cairo. Years of subsequent widebody ocean crossings had flown me as far west as Honolulu. That was the span of my world—from GMT+2 to GMT–10. I once sent a postcard from Egypt to my aunt in Hawaii and wondered which way it would travel to get there—the distance working out roughly the same traveling east or west. Yet half the planet still eluded me, and it called to my wanderlust to be explored. Well, something or someone was calling. I was sitting at home when the phone rang.

"Do you want to go trekking in Nepal with me and four other gals?" Dana offered through the receiver.

The call came as a surprise, but the offer shouldn't have. When it came to adventure planning, I'd clearly met my match. I broke out of my funk and said, "Sign me up." I envisioned her friends as Arizona sun-worshipping goddesses like her. She was throwing me a lifeline, and my life needed a little shaking up. My future felt as promising as an opossum dangling limply in a coyote's mouth, and I was finally tired of playing dead. I accepted that if I was going to chase my own tail, then I was going to do it in a big way. Going somewhere, anywhere, was always a good start, even if it was all the way around in the largest possible circle.

The training department at TWA failed to recognize the importance of my globe-circling travel plans and scheduled me for a checkride during my projected adventure, forcing me to delay my intended departure date. My five gorgeous potential trekking mates had unalterable plans and left for the Himalayas without me—along with my shot at a threesome, a foursome, or some kind of physical excitement on the trail. As it turns out, heart-thumping moments were waiting for me in the distant mountains, but not in the way I was envisioning them.

When I consulted *Lonely Planet: Nepal*, I discovered there was no way to make up three days on the Annapurna Circuit trail and catch up with Dana and her crew on their itinerary. My opportunity to explore the backside of the earth —while following a few athletic yet curvaceous feminine backsides as well— evaporated due to my unchangeable employment obligation.

"What the fuck." Tom Cruise's words of wisdom from *Risky Business* came to mind. I'd already done the extensive travel prep for this trip, and this setback would only clip my prospective travel itinerary by a few days. Sure, traveling alone wouldn't be nearly as much fun as escorting an adventurous harem, but could I still set out solo if I overcame my initial disappointment? *I'm good enough, I'm smart enough, and doggone it...* [9] Well, at least Stuart Smalley would be proud of me.

A quick review of the popular trekking trails revealed I could still complete the back half of the Annapurna Circuit in reverse and fly out Jomsom —eight days of trekking the clockwise direction instead of the full twelve-to-sixteen-day counterclockwise loop the Arizona girls were doing. This portion of the Annapurna Circuit was laid out as a separate trek in *Lonely Planet* and renamed the Jomsom Trail. If I were lucky, I'd meet Dana and her friends as they emerged from the high pass of Thorong-La and we'd all get drunk together in the Bob Marley Bar in Muktineth. And then, who knows?

My around-the-world solo adventure, with nothing more than I could carry, began right after I filled the training square at work and began my belated days off—almost three weeks to hop around on airplanes, explore Nepal, and prove to myself just a little bit that I could make it on my own again now that I no longer had my chosen life partner. It's funny how a short trip inside myself would potentially take a longer trip to the most distant point on the planet to get there. It would take space travel for me to have ventured any further away from where I started.

I put Bob Seger's "(I'm going to) Kathmandu" on my new Rio mp3 travel player that held a whopping thirty songs—I was relieved to discover this new lightweight way to carry music without dragging along cassettes or CDs—then I chose the remaining songs carefully as they would become my only constant traveling companions, and I was on my way.

---

9 Franken, Al. "Daily Affirmation With Stuart Smalley." *Saturday Night Live*. NBC. New York City, NY, 9 Feb. 1991. Television.

To get away from my grief
I went far away
I strapped on a pack
And lived day to day

Once in Nepal, and guided by *Lonely Planet*'s suggestion, I walked from the international terminal to the domestic one at Kathmandu Airport and bought a roundtrip ticket to Pokhara, the staging town for numerous trailheads — skipping the nation's capital for the way back. I was anticipating that the trekking portion of my trip would be the hardest to gauge time-wise and wanted to get right to it. This proved to be a lucky break as I later learned that one in four tourists contracted dysentery in Kathmandu. I discovered this from someone whose hand I was reluctant to shake, for obvious reasons. This affliction was miserable enough to watch. It made the sufferer intimately acquainted with the scrub along the sides of the trail, as the need to squat arrived often and without warning. But I was blissfully unaware of potential physiological meltdowns as I prepared for long days under a pack. I was giddy with impending adventure and a little hypoxic while sucking deep breaths of the cool, thin mountain air at the gateway to the Himalayas. I had everything I could possibly need in this world suspended from the straps on my shoulders, and the ardor of independence felt like waking to an unexpected kiss.

In Pokhara, a light pack is a happy pack. Even so, mine was still gloriously overstuffed, which was a typical rookie mistake. I thinned it down to forty-eight pounds at a small hotel by Phewa Lake by dropping off my non-revving attire — a hound's-tooth sport coat, black dress shoes, and dark socks that wouldn't be needed at remote tea houses — as well as everything else I considered non-essential. My pack now weighed less than a quarter of my body weight, and I thought that was a good rule of thumb. I later found out that experienced trekkers carried no more than fifteen pounds. Some even cut the handles off of their toothbrushes.

I caught the bus to Naya Pul where I met my first two trail companions — a couple of nineteen-year-old Danish gals whose hike up Annapurna IV overlapped my Jomsom Trail for the first two days. One was blonde and the other brunette. They both had ivory skin and high cheekbones. I couldn't tell if they were sisters, friends, or lovers, but they were definitely Scandinavian. Their backpacks were probably full of schoolbooks only a few weeks before. Normally these gorgeous young ladies would excite me, but they were Danish. Susanne had been Danish. On the far side of the world I wasn't getting any farther away from my memory of her loss. I tried not to hold them accountable for my emotional insecurity, and they were going to need me for their personal security, but none of us knew it yet.

We signed into the national park—the Annapurna Conservation Area Project (ACAP)—a requirement of our trekking permits, and hiked as far as Tikedungha the first day while crossing pedestrian suspension bridges and stepping aside for passing long-horned yaks hauling loads for the locals. The next morning, the three of us started out early for the long climb to Ghorapani and Deorali. Trekking begins at first light to avoid navigating unlit and unimproved trails at the end of a rigorous day in the mid-afternoon darkness. The sun sets early in the mountains.

After passing the hamlet of Hille, we began ascending *The Infinite Steps* as we continued north. This is a grueling, nine-hour, uphill climb for healthy hikers.

> *When I'm wearing a pack*
> *Every step is a chore*
> *But with every step*
> *There's another step more*

But one of the Danes was experiencing stomach problems. She was on medication prescribed by a doctor in Kathmandu where she'd become the unlucky one-in-four. We made frequent stops for her, guarding her pack while standing close with our backs turned in a lame effort to offer her a human privacy screen, and began falling behind the pace of other trekkers. A rotation of her underwear was perpetually bungeed to the back of her pack in order to dry in the sun, and she frequently washed them out whenever we passed a stream or usable water. It was painfully obvious to even the most casual observer that her insides were grinding and leaking, and our pace slowed even further due to her intestinal suffering.

> *The Infinite Steps*
> *Continued on and on*
> *As far as I can see*
> *And I've been climbing since dawn*

With still over an hour to Ghorapani, it became apparent that we were going to finish the day's trek in light rain and mountain shadows. We'd already stopped seeing other trekkers altogether when we entered the upper wooded area.

Nine hours of climbing
A 3000-foot rise
The last thing I needed
Was a scary surprise

We passed a small trailside home and a little dark-haired, grinning boy began following us. I'm guessing he was between five and eight years old. He stopped where we stopped, continued when we continued, and he wouldn't leave us alone in spite of our sign language and English requests for him to return home. He reminded me of my own elementary school days while hanging out with my neighborhood friends on the weekends. Someone's kid brother always tried tagging along—pretending not to. He'd hang back, kick a pebble as if dribbling a soccer ball, and pretend to be happy in his isolation. I was tempted to sing the lyrics immortalized by *The Sweet*, "Little Willy, Willy won't, go home,"[10] but I was too thirsty and dry-mouthed. Also, this Nepalese kid didn't reek of need or loneliness; he somehow radiated an aura of an undersized predator. He was tracking us.

He began whistling loudly. Then we heard other whistling in the form of poor birdcall imitations echoing from the woods. My best friend back home and his wife each make wounded-owl screeches, barely related to whistling, in order to locate each other in oversized shopping warehouses like Home Depot and Sam's Club. These trailside birdcall attempts were even worse and, moreover, obviously fake. Black and white TV movie memories of westward venturing cowboys stumbling through sacred Indian burial grounds, with tomahawk-wielding, body-painted braves sneaking up on them from all sides, ran through my mind. The birdcalls and my increasingly uneasy feeling continued for some time.

Whistling in the woods
That can't be good
Am I being followed?
I froze where I stood

Finally, when we had to stop and take off our packs and rest for the girl with the stomach problems, we exchanged worried looks and then a few cautious words. The trepidation was unanimous — we were about to get jumped on the

---

10 Chinn, Nicky, and Mike Chapman. "Little Willy." Rec. 1972. *The Sweet*. The Sweet. Bell, 1973. Vinyl recording.

trail. In a horror movie, the creepy theme music would begin playing softly now and then slowly build in volume and intensity. The trees would begin to shake, and the wind would pick up in order to carry away our screams. The actual rustling from off-trail was subtler, but I had that sixth-sense foreboding of danger that some people describe as the hair standing up on the back of their necks. For me it was more like a chill blowing through my sweat-soaked nylon outdoorsman clothing. I think the clincher was that the wooded birdcalls, very close but still just out of sight a moment ago, suddenly stopped. Both of the girls instinctively huddled together and told me they were scared. The thought occurred to me that this was my last chance to act, or accept the reacting role of a victim.

> *Those birdcalls are fake*
> *And even though I ache*
> *If they decide to attack me*
> *They'll learn their mistake*

> *I'll fight 'til I'm dead*
> *I have nothing to live for*
> *If you want a fight*
> *I'll give you a war*

I moved over to where the little boy was still whistling loudly and picked up two heavy, fist-sized rocks. My shoulders were sore, and my legs were inflamed and close to quivering from the day's long uphill excursion. The last thing I wanted to do was add weight to my load after our brutal climb that was not yet over. But I put one rock in my pocket, and I gripped the other in my free hand, the one not carrying my brightly painted bamboo trekking stick.

> *I picked up a rock*
> *And resigned to my fate*
> *Nowhere to run*
> *So I stood up straight*

> *I can't afford*
> *To be easy prey on the trail*
> *They'll want a soft target*
> *But they're gonna fail*

In as commanding a voice as I could manage, I yelled at and past the girls, "If we do get jumped, the little kid's going to get it first!" and watched for the twerp's reaction. He stopped whistling immediately. After what felt like an eternity but was probably less than a full panting breath, the whistling in the woods resumed, but our juvenile shadow no longer *answered* it. His eyes never left the rock in my hand, as the girls and I packed back up and continued on in silence.

I could hear them
Just off to my right
Making noise in the woods
Just out of sight

The Infinite Steps
Continued on and on
As far as I can see
And I've been climbing since dawn

The little boy still followed us, though at a greater distance — stopping in his tracks and glaring at me with what I hoped was fear, or at least uncertainty, every time I turned my head enough to see around my pack. The girls and I made it to the outskirts of Ghorapani at a near-crawling pace, where the sick Danish girl needed the first outhouse. I was relieved that she could hold on until reaching one this time, as an inopportune trailside squat would have made us unfathomably vulnerable. While the other girl and I guarded her pack, four late-teenage boys came out of the woods on a side trail carrying sticks and ropes, plus a bow and arrow, and then disappeared again before entering what barely qualified as a village.

When I finally
Approached Ghoripani
What did I see
Looking back at me?

Four shady boys
Staring at my hand
At the rock I was holding
That spoiled their plan

So they slipped away
Avoiding the village
To wait another day
For a trekker to pillage

I believe we were spared becoming crime statistics because I still had a little fight left in me at the end of the ascent that took us over eleven continuous hours. The birdcall imitations were over, and the horror movie soundtrack that I'd imagined was replaced by an almost silent reverence for having climbed to a trekker's base camp renowned for its view of the top of the world. Above this village, travelers from a variety of intersecting trails gathered to experience the sunrise over Dhaulagiri I, Annapurna I, Annapurna South, Machhapuchhare, and other towering Himalayan peaks.

The risk was behind me
The view my reward
Was it worth the climb?
I'd reached an accord

I couldn't go back
To before my gal's death
But just like on the trail
I could count every breath

And reach for the sun
Climbing over the range
And decide what I could handle
And what I couldn't change

The Infinite Steps
Went on and on
But tomorrow I'll see
The Himalayas at dawn

I slept that night in a tiny teahouse room that was no more than a thin plywood closet with a single mattress. If the flimsy wall had a missing knothole in it big enough for my finger, I could have poked the Danish girls in the room next door — they were that close — but I didn't want to. The noises of dysentery suffering and biological malfunctions coming from their room didn't conjure any fantasies of threesomes — as much as that would have satisfied both my travel and sexual exploration objectives, defined by my wanderlust, here on what might as well have been the dark side of the moon. Thankfully the plywood was intact and mostly kept out the smells I imagined must accompany those writhing sounds. I considered putting a thin, defensive line of Old Spice *Original Scent* deodorant under my nose, just in case, but quickly fell into the kind of deep sleep that only a full day of carrying too much weight uphill—plus a nearly violent attack and post-crisis relax—can deliver.

In the morning, I woke before dawn to the sizzle and smell of fresh, local eggs and the anticipation of hiking up to the spectacular Himalayan viewpoint. Breakfast was always provided in a teahouse stay. The Danish girls slept through this o-dark-hundred meal, apparently content to sit out a day of trekking to recover. This was surprising because nobody hiked to Ghoripani without climbing Poon Hill for the sunrise.

I left the bulk of my pack in my room and scrambled up the well-worn path. At the top, I experienced first light with a small international crowd and listened to gasps in a dozen different languages — none of them Danish. All of us mountain trail followers appreciated the sun's climb over the tallest peaks.

When I returned to my room for my pack and to say adieu to the owners who see all of their guests off to the trail, the girls were still hibernating. So I slid my contact information under their door and headed out. Our pre-selected trails split later that day anyway.

I never heard from them again, even though I'd kept them from getting mugged or worse. I suspect they wanted to forget the whole grueling, dangerous, and in the case of the sick girl, miserable experience. Much like the reaction I received from some of Susanne's closest circle following her death, I must have become a reminder of painful times. For some, it's better to leave me in their past — as disappointed as that makes me feel.

Looking forward—as this trip was supposed to help me relearn to do—I felt the need to stay on schedule, and the thought of catching up with Dana and her entourage as they emerged from the high pass into Muktineth kept me motivated. I briefly joined a variety of small groups along the trail, but the next trekkers that stuck with me were a pair of crunchy Kiwis. I'm not trying to be culturally insensitive—that's what they called themselves. One had matted sandy hair bordering on dreadlocks, and the other had shaved her head bald while experimenting with Buddhism. They ate nothing but dal bhot — the local rice-with-leftovers dish that's famous in Nepal. They were also experimenting with a lesbian lifestyle. Their talk of kindred spirits conspiring to align them wore me out more than the trekking.

It was the gay girls who found the gay guys from Britain. Our party grew as we reached our final days on the trail. The English chaps loved to haggle with the Tibetan refugee craft ladies, and they were buying up trinkets to decorate their new London flat. Whenever one would get too excited over a purchase, the other would say, "Make the relax." This was their favorite phrase from an ESL yoga class they'd taken on their trip. I love English as a second language because of the honesty derived from basic translation, and I now often use that well-intentioned yoga phrase as my own. Maybe I came halfway around the world, fought off a potential mugging, and exhausted myself on a grueling trail just to learn those three words.

Our new larger group made it through Jomsom, where the tiny airport was located that we would all return to the next day. We continued trekking to Muktineth — the frontier to the Mustang region of Tibet and the end of eight days on the trail — where I was hoping to find Dana's name and today's date in the trekker sign-in book. When I could hear music coming from the Bob Marley Bar, I was more than ready to put away a few too many beers — I'd earned the calories in spades to the tune of roughly six thousand burned each day. Alas, the American gals didn't make it that far and instead flew out of Hongde before reaching the high pass, but I didn't learn about that until weeks later, after I was home.

Even though Dana and her clan's path never overlapped with mine, the concept of catching up with them on the far side of the world had lured me into a backpack. Also, my assortment of trail mates wasn't the harem I'd anticipated, but at the end of the journey, the lesbian and gay couples and I did have fun playing Three Killers, a card game they taught me. An Australian couple — that joined us while in the process of breaking up — added melodrama to our final evening. Even though it was all just an amusing occasion in a far away place, I eventually realized I wasn't looking forward or backward, and it had been a long time since a simple social gathering held my full attention. I was simply enjoying the moment and a bottle of prune whiskey I'd bought from a local distiller. We held face cards to our foreheads and passed libations around to the murder victims as they were eliminated from each round of the role-playing card game. I fought to stay in play with the same intensity that I'd mustered to face the threat on the trail. Eventually the cards killed me off, and my new friends laughed. Their laughter was contagious, and I finally let out a few overdue chuckles of my own.

This reflection still seems somewhat magical, because I remember that I was genuinely smiling instead of faking it. The far side of the world was far enough to finally allow my brain to shift into the present, at least for a while. I was "making the relax."

* * *

In the morning, the hike back to Jomsom was thankfully downhill, and we all flew back to Pokhara on separate flights. That evening we met for drinks at the Amsterdam Club to celebrate the completion of our treks. One of my new English buddies claimed to be Margaret Thatcher's nephew and attracted the interest of several younger English chaps playing pool. We swapped trail stories, and I quickly learned that only a few days after my Ghoripani experience, one of their mates had not been as lucky as I had. (I never say chaps or mates back home in the United States, but the Queen's English of the two queens I trekked with, plus the accents and dialect of the Aussies and the Kiwis, were rubbing off on me.)

The chap who seemed the youngest, barely twenty, said, "As we were approaching Ghorapani from the east, six of us were a bit spread out. Alastair Donaldson was alone, with the rest of us just out of view ahead or behind him. Alastair later told me that he'd walked past two Nepali guys who were loitering on the trail. After he passed, they hit him on the back of the head with a stick and then with the hilt of a knife, splitting his head open and causing a lot of blood loss. I was following and found him on the side of the trail covered in blood — practically naked except for his T-shirt, boxers, and boots. The attackers stole his pack, passport, money, and everything else. I initially believed him to be dead. I called out to my mates, and we eventually helped get him to Ghorapani where he was airlifted by helicopter. We asked an official in Ghorapani to initiate a search party for the attackers, but there was no success locating them."

I learned enough from this account to know for sure that I'd narrowly escaped harm. This inspired me to send a letter to *Lonely Planet*, urging them to update future guidebooks: *I believe the area near Ghorapani is a continuing spot for trouble. Many trekking trails lead there for the amazing climb to Poon Hill (or Pun Hill; I've seen it printed both ways) where travelers gather to experience the sunrise over the area's most prominent mountains. The brutal uphill trekking from all directions, and the high wooded area for escape, makes it a prime location for thugs. Most trekkers don't have an energy reserve at this stage of their day and make easy targets, especially alone or in small groups.*

My survival instinct had been tested, and this near-criminal experience gave me what I'd really come to Nepal for, in a way that was totally unexpected. It wasn't exotic travel or erotic sex that renewed my interest in feeling alive — it was the tickling of my primitive fight or flight response that ultimately woke me up. And then relearning to just enjoy the moment.

* * *

Following a good night's sleep, my long return journey home began. Arriving in Kathmandu left me in a quandary. The ticket agent told me I needed to connect straight through to Bangkok or become stuck in Kathmandu for at least three days, due to oversold flights. So I took the first flight out and missed Nepal's capital city once again — the chance to see the Monkey Temple, play one-in-four dysentery roulette, and maybe even catch a glimpse of the royal family before they were massacred a month later. That's an event that crushed tourism, dynamically altered the political climate of Nepal for years, and is probably why Lonely Planet never answered my letter. To put it succinctly: Nepal tourism was overcome by events.

On the flight to Bangkok, Thailand, I met a crazy Canadian registered nurse. We wandered up and down Khao San Road together, exploring Thai culture and food with my last few days of freedom before I had to report back to work. She was another Barbie blonde with a passion for travel, but far less of a penchant for self-preservation than Dana. She claimed to have just escaped a cult and was recovering from drug-induced hallucinations about statues coming to life and dancing with her. I couldn't resist asking, "Are dogs telling you to kill anyone?"

She said, "No," but I paid for my own room just in case. Hers was two dollars per night, and she made fun of me for spending ten dollars for an air-conditioned upgrade. Unlike many of the travelers I met on my journey, I had a steady job. She was a traveling nurse in the sense that she'd earned a nursing degree and was traveling, but she hadn't worked anywhere for a while and her budget was tight. Like many of the people I met in Nepal, we all seemed to be finding ourselves in some way. She had taken this challenge more seriously than most by experimenting with a cult — a mistake she was still coming to terms with.

I probably could have enticed her into the comfort of my climate-controlled room, but my mood still wasn't far from survival mode, and I didn't want to wake up inside a slasher movie. Bangkok is full of stray dogs, and any one of them could start talking to her at any moment — Son-of-Sam style. My previous experience with auditory hallucinations and delusions was limited to the media coverage of David Berkowitz' New York City killing spree back in the 1970s. Besides, there was only one of her, and experiencing her bedside manner wouldn't have crossed anything off of my bucket list — unless we included some of her imaginary friends. I behaved like a gentleman, and just in case she heard any inanimate commands during our brief traveling companionship, I kept an ear out for the return of the horror movie soundtrack I'd recently imagined the last time danger loomed.

* * *

I flew back home through Narita, Japan, and did make it all the way around the world. My bucket list now has one less item. More importantly, I think that through the threat of violence, rather than the lure of ménage-à-trois sexual conquest, I'd excited my survival instinct. That's what I was going to need to re-engage everyday life without Susanne. I'd had enough running away from myself and realized that I was a fighter after all—yet one also capable of making the relax.

35 | MY VANILLA SKY
Cathedral Steps

ANOTHER THING on my bucket list was building or rebuilding a home, so I bought a house that needed a gut rehab. I didn't consciously realize it at the time, but it was clearly a metaphor for rebuilding my life. I enjoyed the hands-on activity and admired the beauty of each step of the restoration as it was completed. When I finally looked at the paint-stripped, sanded, stained, and urethaned hundred-year-old oak and pine baseboards, crown molding, solid six-panel doors, and trim, I could feel the years of sweat and effort that went into the now-polished appearance. Like my house, I hoped I was rebuilding myself from the inside out. Nevertheless, my home and my life were single-occupancy-only for much of the time after Susanne's passing, with limited allowances for beautiful, distracting visitors, usually dated at arm's length. I'd built a comfortable nest, but I still spent as much of my time as possible in cockpits with my peers.

"Thank God you're all right. Thank God you're all right." I'd just stepped out of the shower on a layover and started shaving using shampoo from a mini bottle. My travel shaving kit had run out of the real stuff the night before in another city. I'd been losing the battle of wiping the steam from the mirror when my cell phone began ringing. I had a towel wrapped around my waist and I looked at the clock to decide how much time I had to talk as I was answering. The hotel van was scheduled to take me to the airport with my crew in less than thirty minutes when my former girlfriend Kelly—another beautiful yet short chapter of my life—uttered those words through short breaths through the receiver.

"Killer, what's up?" That was her nickname bequeathed by her dad. I think she was a fearless child, and her dad was sure her unbridled enthusiasm for life was going to give him a heart attack before she grew up. They both survived. She'd become an advertising VP and lived in midtown Manhattan. She and I were briefly but no longer romantically involved, and like Dana, still good friends. She felt that what we had tried relationship-wise was strained by long distance, but I knew that I gave gals who were interested in me nothing emotional to hold onto. Although I lived in St. Louis, I was in Portland, Oregon, at the moment.

"I'm glad you weren't flying," she said between forced breaths. Her voice was elevated in pitch and an octave above normal.

"I'm about to. I need to get moving. I'm on a layover getting ready for pick-up."

"You're not going anywhere. Turn on the TV. Airplanes are hitting buildings here in New York. Call Warren. The World Trade Center is on fire."

"What?!" was my first reaction. Warren is my best friend, and he worked on Wall Street, in the shadow of the Twin Towers. As I hung up with Killer, I wrestled with my phone—resetting it several times as I fumbled the speed dialer in my rush to find his number while simultaneously trying to turn on the TV. Even as my dexterity returned and I managed to hit the right combination of buttons, the circuits were down. This can't be happening. I felt like I was stuck in a movie. This kind of thing doesn't happen in real life.

I've never met Tom Cruise, but he and I have a long history together through his movies. When he made *Risky Business*, I loved that old time rock 'n roll, too, and hadn't switched from tighty-whitie briefs to boxers yet, either. I threw a huge party, minus the prostitutes, for three hundred high school friends as I left for college, and then left the mess for my parents. His character, Joel, one-upped me by cleaning and arranging his parents' house back into its original order before they returned home. Then Tom made *Top Gun* and trained with the Navy in F-14 Tomcat fighter jets as Maverick. I went to Embry-Riddle Aeronautical University where I learned to fly in single-engine Cessna-172 Skyhawk training aircraft. My fellow flight students and I saw *Top Gun* many times and often repeated Tom's famous line, "I feel the need, the need for speed."[11] I've also seen him on TV. I haven't jumped up and down on Oprah's couch yet like he did, singing praises because he'd fallen in love with a new gal after losing Nicole Kidman, but there's always hope—both for finding the second love of my own life, someone after Susanne, and the invitation to sit or jump up and down on Oprah's couch or her successor's. As I wrote this section a couple years before the 17th anniversary of TWA Flight 800, Susanne had been gone for fifteen years, and I felt like it would take Oprah to open me up to someone new. But I'm digressing from my *Vanilla Sky* moment, my next parallel to Mr. Cruise's career. Film after film, sometimes I've felt like I've been living each of his character's lives.

---

11 *Top Gun*. Dir. Tony Scott. Perf. Tom Cruise. Paramount, 1986. Film. Tom Cruise's character Maverick's dialog.

Everyone's tragedy is his or her own, and there are many more severe than my experience on 9/11/2001, but this is how that day affected me. I knew a fireman, Kenny Marino, whom the collapsing towers crushed. He left a wife and three children behind. I went to Washington, DC, for the funeral of David Charlebois — the Boeing 757 copilot whose aircraft hit the Pentagon. We had worked together as flight instructors in our early aviation years.

And then there was Battalion 9 Chief Brian O'Flaherty (and former Rescue 1 captain) who was special detailed to Safety Battalion 1 that day. It took a long time before even his family knew he wasn't killed in the line of duty. He was in the lobby of the Marriott when the South Tower fell on top of the hotel and was blown off his feet from the force of the collapse. Severely injured, his peers ordered him out to seek medical assistance. He was in a street choked by a blanket of dust and debris while asking for directions to the medical station when his fellow commanders were buried under the North Tower when it fell.

All this was happening as I sat on the hotel bed and located the first news channel to pop up while I scanned from the initial welcome channel message, *We hope you have a nice stay. Thanks for choosing Holiday Inn* (or Ramada, or wherever the hell I was). I didn't know it then, but I would spend four extra nights in this room. While my passengers were fighting over rental cars and finding ways to complete their journeys on the ground, I was stuck on duty in this Portland airport hotel. Airplanes were going nowhere until the nation figured out what to do.

Those families have real grief to vent and loss stories to tell. Like you, most likely, I was affected in a peripheral way — a little more so since I'm in the aviation profession and lived in and around the New York area including Connecticut for much of my life. I was on the West Coast and far away from the destruction when it was happening. The TV was my lifeline, and not for the first time I watched the things I took for granted dissolve — aviation safety, our nation's security, and the expectation that everyone I knew would all still be here, alive and healthy at the end of the day. Feeling an emotional chill, like a ghost had just walked through me, I dressed slowly while watching the same horrific newscasts that every American and much of the world were absorbing.

I called Warren many more times that day. I failed to connect with him until after he eventually made it home, and then he told me how he was stuck in his office at the heart of the disaster as events unfolded:

> I was on the phone with a client who said the north tower just got hit. An airplane flew into it. I had heard the impact and it made me nauseous. I didn't know why yet, but I just knew it didn't feel right. This wasn't a

normal thing. Of all the truck and construction noises this city makes, this was something new. The guy next to my client yelled over the phone, "My line with Cantor just went dead." Someone in my office said, "It's Cantor Fitzgerald's floor." Just weeks ago several guys from my office quit to go work over there. We all looked at each other incredulously. Through the windows I could see tons of paper flying, swirling, falling everywhere. It was like a ticker tape parade but someone forgot to shred the paper. These were full sheets. Inside someone yelled, "We gotta get out of here." I told everybody, "No. It's not safe. I don't want anyone getting hit by debris. It's everywhere." We argued and yelled about the best thing to do. Some people made their own minds up and left. Then the south tower was hit. I reversed my opinion and said, "Everyone needs to get out. It's your own decision, but it's not safe here." I didn't know it until later, but an aircraft engine hit our building at the ninth floor.

Some people got out through the basement of our building. I exited out the west side and into the debris. I looked up to make sure I didn't get hit by something big. I saw people falling. They were still alive. Arms were moving and legs were flailing. I looked down. I didn't want to see them. I didn't want to look, but my survival instinct made me. I had to. I saw two people holding hands as they fell — then three people at once. I wondered, "How bad could it be up there that people would choose to do that?" Then I heard the worst noises of my life. I can't describe it out of respect. Sometimes I still hear it.

Wall Street is as tight a community as the airline industry, and Warren and I both felt this disaster cut away the lives of people we knew and worked with. Both of our professional passions collided in a way previously unimaginable — commercial aircraft into financial office buildings. I later tried to be the compassionate friend for Warren that he has been for me following the loss of my mom in 1989 and my fiancée in 1996. Our history is very deep. At some point there were just too many funerals to go to, so I sat with him as close as he could bear to be to the services. We parked our butts on many cathedral steps self-medicating from a silver flask. We heard the music from the organs but not the words of the speakers — family and friends of those who were leaving each altar in another mahogany or pine box, perhaps only symbolically as many bodies were never recovered. But all that was still to come.

> *Sitting on cathedral steps*
> *Self-medicating from a flask*

Why did this have to happen?
Is that so much to ask?

Sitting out another sermon
Drinking away another day
Can't look at New York City
And see things the same old way

9-11 are just numbers
Carved on stones, the numbers of the dead
9-11 are just numbers
But they burn, they burn inside my head
9-11 are just numbers
Carved on stones, the numbers of the dead

Too many of my friends
Are parked below those stones
But their boxes are really empty
There's nothing left—no flesh or bones

Can't say goodbye
To an empty box
And so I'm sitting here
'cause sometimes life just sucks
and now I'm waiting for hope to appear
when will hope come meet me here?

I wanted to be in New York for Warren and more of my friends, but initially I was stuck in Portland. Back in my hotel, I finally went downstairs to find my crew. We gathered in the dining room. The earlier first TWA flight of the day out of Portland was diverted back and then grounded upon landing. That crew, two pilots and three flight attendants, returned to the hotel and joined us still in uniform for the brunch buffet. The hotel needed time to find rooms for them, and the front desk was backed up with stranded passengers. The pilots told us the sky was now empty. Air traffic control told them to "Land now—nearest air-field." No explanations were given. They'd been piecing the story together from employees at the airport and the radio broadcasts in the van on the ride back.

We all wanted to know more about what was going on and positioned our-selves to see one of the hotel's TVs. Every screen was turned on to the news.

We listened together to accounts of United Flight 93 crashing in Pennsylvania. I would later have a connection to Pennsylvania as a Critical Incident Response Team member, as a month after 9/11 I was sent to North Philly on my own time to assist in a small-group diffusing of the several United Airlines volunteers who'd dealt with Victor Saracini's family—the captain on the flight that hit the south tower. He'd resided in the north Philly area. These volunteers were among the few trained CIRT employees in that entire huge airline, and they were both overworked and understaffed for the task, but by all accounts the ones I met did an outstanding job dealing with the full burden of their shared loss. They were happy that someone, anyone, came from another airline to assist them in any way, however small. I brought with me some emotional experience from dealing with my own tragedy in 1996. My Pennsylvania visit evolved from my need to try to help.

Back in Portland, sitting with my crew while pushing scrambled eggs and sausage links around our plates, we all felt uncharacteristically helpless at the time. We speculated about how this could happen and guessed how long it would be before we would be called to fly again. Most of us at first thought it would be the next day.

We all watched countless hours of devastating footage replayed by the networks and eventually adjourned. The driving force motivating us was the need to connect with additional friends back east as we realized the scope of this disaster. We all wondered who and how many people we knew were now dead or injured and imagined long lists that would unfold for weeks or months to come. It hurt to think about it, and for the most part, the concept was abstract. The morning of September 11, 2001, was too big in scope to contemplate all at once.

At dinnertime I went into downtown Portland for a change of scenery and found a microbrewery. The news on the overhead TVs was on, but unlike the hotel, it was largely being ignored. It struck me as odd that nobody seemed to be paying much attention to commentators or the replayed footage. Either these people were unaffected in their little corner of the world, or they were burned out from a full day of media overload and distracting themselves with the routine of everyday life. I wondered if anyone in this place had ever been to New York or DC or Pennsylvania.

The server placed a square napkin on my table and asked me if I needed a drink or a menu. I didn't have any idea when I would fly again, but I was beginning to feel like it wouldn't be any time soon. So I ordered a beer—one that they made on location. She was cute, in an athletic sort of way. But what I really noticed was the overall crunchy look about her. How else do you describe a white gal with dreadlocks? And her face had piercings, beyond the regular ones in her ears. She had a stud in her right nostril, a bar through her left eyebrow, and a ring through her lip. I had noticed her perky, no-bra-wearing breasts underneath her ripped-open sweatshirt when she first arrived. The neck had deliberately been ripped down the front to reveal cleavage, and she had the sleeves rolled up to her elbows. When she told me she'd be right back with my beer and a menu, I saw the flash of silver tongue jewelry. Shrapnel, I thought. Only these were voluntary accessories — her look. As she left, my eyes naturally went to her rump, which had the tone of a life of exercise, held firm in tight Army surplus fatigues. She probably rode a bicycle to work, and I doubt if she shaved her armpits. It was then that I imagined her love nest, but I pictured it as an untrimmed scraggle — the kind I've seen in 1970s-era *Playboy*.

I'm not always a pig, undressing women with my eyes, even if their fashion choices seem to beg for attention. I wondered why I was falling into adolescent patterns on the worst day in recent American history. Was my mind compensating with sex for all the death that hung in the air? Was I subconsciously appalled that these West Coast people seemed to be able to go on with their lives while I was stuck wondering who I'd just lost? The waitress represented everyone who seemed unaffected. I think my mind was saying, "Screw her for not suffering, too!" and then literally translating that message into a sexual appetite. Or I'd already entered the anger phase of this new grief, a stage I'd never completely let go of since TWA Flight 800. I sat analyzing myself, alone, while my homeland and my aviation family were burning.

I'm a pilot and I couldn't fly. I'm originally a New Yorker and I was stuck three thousand miles away. I couldn't find any answers at the bottom of my beer. Here was someone who spoke my same language but I couldn't talk to. We lived in different worlds. If, theoretically, she'd wanted to kiss me, I would first have to make the area safe by defusing her metallic defenses. I wondered how many people in Manhattan had metal being removed from their bodies right now that had rained on them from as many as a hundred and five stories up. Someone once told me that a tongue stud makes oral sex better. I wasn't really planning to find out.

It bothered me that my mind was going into these inappropriate places, so when my next beer arrived I just sat and drank without tasting it and tried to absorb the day. Having given my brain a momentary vacation, I gave the TV my undivided attention. My time-out from reality was over. Later the president ordered us all to go on with our daily lives. Don't let terrorism cripple us with fear. The waitress and the rest of the brewery seemed to be already doing that. I wasn't. I was brooding and overloaded and numb.

* * *

Aircraft aren't designed to sit for extended times; they're meant to be flown. Old airplanes, especially, like my Boeing 727—I was a captain on it now—tend to start leaking fluids if left alone for too long. Maybe they're just crying for a little attention, but someone has to insure they're airworthy for when the FAA finally reopens the nation's sky for air traffic. In Portland, TWA used contract mechanics that wouldn't touch our airplanes without a TWA representative authorizing it. Crew scheduling made it clear that I was that company representative. The other captain stuck at my hotel, who'd diverted back into Portland with this plane, must have been smart enough not to answer his phone, or maybe they called for volunteers alphabetically, or maybe his newer MD-80 didn't require as much attention between flights. Regardless, my trip to the Portland International Airport became my most surreal and remembered 9/11 moment. I call it *My Vanilla Sky*. My situation predates the *Vanilla Sky* movie, but when I saw the deserted Times Square scene I thought, *"Tom, I feel your anxiety, I've been there, too."*

Portland has a light rail named MAX—Metro Area eXpress. I took the red line from my hotel to the airport. A couple of stops before the terminals, the last of the other riders stepped off, but nobody hopped on. My years of city living made me leery of being the only one onboard. The only sound was the wheels rolling over the track, the revs of the motor, and the steady hum of the interior fluorescent lights. I rode the rest of the way in an unoccupied car and exited at a vacant airport. The thing about airports is there are always people at them. All day the terminals are swallowing people and spitting them out. Even at night, people who missed the last flights are sleeping across chairs or are curled up in a corner clutching their suitcases. Cleaners are working and the occasional security officer paces his beat. None of that was happening and it was eerie. The airport was like a postcard—an uninviting moment without life or even movement.

In the movie, Tom Cruise parks his car in the middle of Times Square during the middle of the day. He spins his head and the camera pans 360 degrees revealing that New York's busiest intersection, perhaps the most populated in the nation, is completely abandoned. It's empty—void of all things living. All the structures are still intact, advertisements shine, and the many painted lanes in the avenues lead off toward the horizon, but there are no people. There are no vehicles, no sounds, and no signs of life. It's just Tom Cruise standing in the middle of the street at the heart of the Big Apple all alone. I felt a similar form of surreal disbelief at the Portland Airport. That was my 9/11 moment. No aircraft in the sky—which did look a little vanilla with nothing in it to see—no contrails, no signs of mankind's aviation achievements. Every aircraft on the ground was asleep. And everywhere I looked—at the empty ticket counters, the unmanned metal detectors and x-ray machines at security, and barren kiosks at every gate—there was nobody. There were no passengers, no agents, and no ground crew. It was like everyone had gone underground and failed to point me to the fallout shelter entrance. Or they'd just evaporated. It was just the silent terminal and me, until finally a single police officer appeared to check my credentials. He walked me to the gate where my 727 was parked and unlocked the Jetway door for me. Then he disappeared as rapidly as he'd materialized.

Airport ramps are usually very noisy. Not today. I walked around my aircraft and noted small pools of red fluid and oil. I expected this. No real leaks, just an airplane settling in for an undetermined-length nap. After I reclimbed the Jetway stairs, there was enough light through the cockpit windows that I didn't have to turn on the battery or fire up the auxiliary power unit to see. It had been a long time since I'd been in a completely shut down and secured airplane. I signed the logbook like I was asked to do with the comment, *Traces of hydraulic fluid and oil found under aircraft. Service as necessary.* At some point a mechanic would use my authorization to pump in a quart or two here and there and make sure this bird was ready to fly—but not now. I felt like I was disturbing some great hush over the land as I let myself all the way out to the light rail and waited for an empty car to take me away from the silent, shutdown airport, letting it go back to its strange, unnatural sleep.

Sacred Watering Holes

WHEN THE NATION'S SKIES opened up again, my fellow pilots and I had jobs to do. The traveling public was wary of air travel, but it was our obligation to continue flying with professionalism while hoping we could collectively find a way to make commercial aviation safe again. Airport security went through much iteration and airlines streamlined their fleets in order to cut costs as the economy, especially commercial air travel, declined. Another airline bought mine. Three-engine, three-pilot Boeing 727s were sold or parked, and I became an MD-80 captain when I wasn't teaching in the simulator.

"I'll meet you at the office," I said to Jennifer, my blonde-haired, Scandinavian-featured first officer — with the obvious resemblance not worth mentioning — as we checked into the hotel. Be it a Double Tree, Holiday Inn Express, or the Courtyard-Corporate-Comfort-Inn-Select Suites on steroids — wherever we are tonight — it's always just the hotel. I'm not sure which sleep chain I'm in at the moment, but I know where I'll be after a quick change of clothes. Decades of pilots have called the favorite pit-stop pub at every layover city *the office,* and I first learned this term from my late mentor Captain Ken Cook. It's where we decompress, and over time these places start to feel familiar in a multi-generational kind of way. For a guy who holds on tight to his past, I can almost feel my predecessors whenever I enter these hallowed grounds. In a world full of stuffy rooms with unreliable ventilation and beds still warm from the last occupant, albeit with a set of over-washed sheets freshly installed, a little reliable comfort food and drink can go a long way to relax a constant traveler.

> *Every city that we fly to*
> *Has a special place*
> *Known to every flight crew*
> *As our office space*

The Office is our home-away
Picked long ago by our mentors
Some sacred watering hole
With late-night food and beers

This Seattle layover started me thinking about these worldwide sacred watering holes — greasy spoon and frosty mug oases, timeless places that weather countless economic storms while most upstarts fail to last long enough to earn the term establishment. And it felt great to be thinking about adult beverages for a change, rather than adult situations such as the hard times I've been through. Every few seasons the wind blows, and the names on the buildings of culinary hopefuls change like they were shaken clean in an Etch-A-Sketch. Yet every city I'm dumped in for layovers has its staple location that is much the same as the days when I was a new hire. These same mythic places where captains bought me beers during my initial five-year B-scale salary, I now fondly introduce to my own crews. I like to think that Captain Cook would approve of me passing down the airline folklore at some of the same spots I learned it.

Number thirty-six for takeoff
And the aircraft won't get cool
Passengers are all complaining
They're calling me Captain Cruel

Only three more legs to fly today
Before reaching some random hotel
But somewhere in whatever city
There's a place I know they sell

A frosty adult beverage
With my name on it
And I can't wait to buy a couple
For myself and my copilot

While descending into the northern West Coast after a three-and-a-half-hour flight, our last of several legs that day, I'd promised Jennifer some onion rings the size of gaudy bangles, seafood chowder worth licking the bowl clean, and an African-style beer she'd never heard of but I knew she'd love. But when Roasters — the promised pub across from our hotel — closed early for the Fourth of July weekend and denied us our fix of Mac and Jack Amber Ale, she and I were stuck just outside the Sea-Tac Airport in search of a place to unwind. That's when my cloudy memory recalled a spot that served food and drinks around the clock.

Linda, our server at 13 Coins Restaurant, welcomed us and revealed that this place has been open since 1976, and their downtown location opened its doors in 1967. My life only reaches back to 1965, so that's one hell of a run for a twenty-four-hour bistro. Both their bruschetta and the meatball sliders pack a powerful punch. It felt imperative that we wash them down with Alaskan Amber, our substitute for the previously promised Mac and Jack. Imperative, only if the layover is long enough, which this time it is. Our *eight hours bottle to throttle* federal aviation regulation has been updated to include *no residual effects and a blood alcohol content of less than .04 percent*, and my current airline requires a more-restrictive twelve hours of dry time before flying.

Pilots I know and work with take very seriously our duty to keep alcohol out of the cockpit, but a few isolated incidents have made the drunken pilot into a staple parody. Dean Martin and Foster Brooks made a comedy skit back in the 1970s that was widely popular. I just finished reading *Flying Drunk* by Joseph Balzer, and nobody wants to experience what his Northwest Airlines crew went through — specifically, hard time in the federal lock-up. In the twenty-seven years I've been a professional pilot, I've only known one career aviator with visible signs of a drinking problem. Although I'm no psychologist, it appeared to stem from his depression over his impending mandatory ejection from the flight deck at the turn-into-a-pumpkin age of sixty (since raised to sixty-five with the same result just displaced five years later). He was so attached to his career as a professional aviator that he couldn't cope with losing his identity. What other job inspires such commitment from its members that federally dictated retirement causes so much stress? For you, my numerous friends who have moved on, and especially those who have flown west, I'm still out here moving metal, passing down stories, sampling local delicacies, and occasionally imbibing local brews with those who are journeying with me through this seniority-driven cockpit progression.

The best-named beer that I have found is Captain Bastard. Did they name it after me? It's a staple at Squatters Pub in Salt Lake City.

Another favorite office is the Wheat & Rye, just down the road from Detroit's Metro Wayne International. It's still there with over a twenty-year run, although cleaned up or rebuilt since my career's early days riding sideways in the three-pilot Boeing 727. Sure we nicknamed it the *Eat and Die* back then, but we really loved it for their sandwiches that are still feed-the-nation unreal. They're the size of a four-slice toaster. Seriously, the proprietors brag that their stacked ham weighs two pounds. The bread they use has the thickness of a James Michener hardcover. One sandwich will feed the entire crew and then some.

The Slippery Noodle in Indiana-no-place (sorry local Indianapolis residents), with sawdust floors and a labyrinth of rooms that can host more than one band at a time, is a nine-iron away from the aircrew-friendly Omni Hotel. The Slippery Noodle was established in 1850 as the Tremont House, and it somehow survived even before slaves-to-aviation-careers like me came around to support it, but we discovered it as soon as we could—probably about the time that smudge pots lit the federal airmail routes. I have no way of knowing, but it seems likely that my hero Ernest K. Gann may have visited this place after shutting down his DC-2 or DC-3 for the night.

Sometimes I'm lucky and still experience leaving the country on international flights. The Flying Beaver Bar in Vancouver has a view of the seaplane dock in addition to the local mountains and waterways. Their healthy outdoor-loving servers are also easy on the eyes — natural beauties against natural beauty. I don't know what I enjoy more, watching white and yellow Harbour Air float planes takeoff, land, and dock, or the University of British Columbia co-eds circling in holding patterns around the bar. I'd like a wild BC salmon salad with crumbled blue cheese and vinaigrette while I think it over, please.

While stationed in Berlin, Georges Restaurant und Bierkonter wasn't just the office; it was the center of our West Germany-based existence. I can still picture Captain Ken Cook wiping froth off his mustache during my earliest TWA experiences and again during his final days before early retirement and subsequent passing. Punctuated with intricate woodcarvings, it was a place to relax, meet other crews, and listen to the piano bar. By some high-German authority, every kleine bier had to have the appropriate doily around its stem announcing what brand was being consumed.

No trip to Istanbul is complete without seeing the Kapali Carsi (Grand Bazaar), Blue Mosque, Hagia Sophia, and then unwinding at the Sultan Pub. It's a great place to down a Turkish Efes pilsner while shucking pistachios after a day on my feet snapping pictures. Both Istanbul and Cairo remind me of Captain Gid Miller, probably the last person Susanne ever talked to, who I'd flown with to those parts of the world many times and who didn't drink, but instead gave his beer money to street children.

Don't get me wrong; I love to try new things and places. But in a world where foreclosures and chaos are currently the rule, it's nice to step back into old welcoming establishments. They may not know who I am, but I remember them with fondness from my early days.

Although it might seem that the fun-sponge has soaked up the remaining benefits of touring our nation and the far parts of the world for a living, moderation is a good thing. Like gambling, chocolate, fresh seafood, and any other pleasure that tickles our brain, sampling the best of each region when appropriate is still an enticing perk for a job that the traveling public sometimes looks upon as a glorified bus driver. Not many other professions' successes and failures are idolized (*Highest Duty — My Search for What Really Matters*)[12] or vilified (*Flying Drunk: The True Story of a Northwest Airlines Flight, Three Drunk Pilots, and One Man's Fight for Redemption*)[13] the way ours are. Those who no longer venture out to explore their journey's destinations and local flavor are called *slam clickers* by the way they slam their hotel room door and then click the lock as soon as they arrive. As for me, my wanderlust must still be fed. The occasional long layovers are the fun side of the airline business—the balance to the deadly serious side.

Another day
Another five flights
With challenging approaches
Down to the runway lights

Dodging thunderstorms
In an unfriendly sky
And calming passengers
Who are afraid to fly

Avoiding mountains
And high terrain
While navigating
through torrential rain

And mechanical problems
With the plane
There's one thing
That keeps me sane

---

12 Sullenberger, Chesley, and Jeffrey Zaslow. *Highest Duty: My Search for What Really Matters*. New York: William Morrow, 2009. Print.
13 Balzer, Joseph. *FLYING DRUNK: The True Story of a Northwest Airlines Flight, Three Drunk Pilots, and One Man's Fight for Redemption*. New York and California: Savas Beatie, 2009. Print.

Every city that we fly to
Has a special place
Known to every flight crew
As our office space

The Office is our home-away
Picked long ago by our mentors
Some sacred watering hole
With late-night food and beers

37 | HIGH TERRAIN ALL QUADS

Shakin' It in the Dark

"CALL ME MARK, not Captain. That title grabs my immediate attention, and my first question will be, *Where's the emergency?* Save Captain for when an engine fails or we're on fire."

"OK, Mark it is," Dan replied almost reluctantly. I could tell he would be more comfortable with formality. My guess is that he's former military, not a swaggering fighter pilot, but probably someone who flew something heavy like a tanker. Maybe he still serves in the Air National Guard. His short haircut and the deliberate cadence to his speech resemble that of an officer of one of the armed services.

That's part of my canned speech for first officers the first time I fly with them — my own preference that works well for me. Some pilots crave structured hierarchy and are really into their titles. Squatters Pub already claimed *Captain Bastard*, so I stick with Mark. I like to set the tone for a relaxed atmosphere where I can obtain the best effort from my crew by reducing authoritative stress. I know I'm the captain and I don't need to constantly prove it. The four stripes on my shoulders and the star above my shirt wings are more than enough to identify me as the captain to anyone who needs to know. The oak-leaf cluster around my captain's star is a remnant from the six years I served as a check-airman. The St. Louis training center was closed after my airline was bought, but I still live and am based in that city. To passengers, often all pilots are the same. Sometimes we're even perceived to be gate agents when we're standing behind a computer while pulling up our flight plans. They often ask me, "Can you change my assigned seat to an emergency exit?" But our uniforms are distinct, and the subtle differences mean a lot to those of us within the industry. A pair of small diamonds, set on either side of a ruby, within my eagle tie-tack means that I have over twenty-five years of service with my airline — merged time included. There's a lot of information we learn about each other just by observing, even before we officially meet, and well before we climb into the cockpit.

If you have an aisle seat in the cabin when you travel, you're probably looking forward at the bulletproof cockpit door that the pilots hide behind while working our magic that makes the giant metal tube fly. You're putting your trust in two complete strangers to handle everything until you arrive at your destination. When you hear an announcement that invites you to, "Sit back, relax, and enjoy the flight," do you really know what's going on up there behind the cockpit door? You bought a ticket to board, but your flight is the result of a long string of preparation the pilots have performed in order to be seated in our flight deck positions.

The cockpit is small and crammed wall-to-wall — even overhead — with switches, dials, knobs, levers, gauges, placards, and lights. Yet the entire space occupied by pilots feels precision-drafted and then hand-carved by flight-loving craftsmen. Each protrusion has a specific meaning or function, and after thousands of hours staring at the floor-to-ceiling components, we've learned to interpret the subtle things they're trying to tell us.

Looking forward from my seat, the barometric altimeter in the primary instrument cluster in front of me reads 7,320 feet, and so do the other two in the cockpit; yet we're still on the ground at Aeropuerto Internacional Benito Juarez de la Ciudad de Mexico — Mexico City Airport. Almost half again higher than Denver's mile-high, we're near the MD-80 upper limit for takeoffs and landings with a load of passengers and cargo. The high altitude of this airport means thinner air and reduced performance—i.e., less lift and less engine thrust available than the same plane would have at an airport near sea level. And unlike Denver that has mountains only on one side, with long flat terrain to climb out over except to the West, Mexico City sits in a bowl surrounded by high peaks. Internationally recognized as MMMX, I match my flight plan to page one of the route that's programmed into the flight management computer on the pedestal between my copilot and me. Outside the forward windows I can read 5L, meaning *five-left*, painted on the concrete and illuminated by the aircraft landing lights. I match that up with the 5L under the aircraft symbol — that looks like a mini tie-tack of an airplane — on my navigation display screen dead in front of me. I could swear that the runway showed 5I for *cinco-izquierda* the last time I was here. I'm glad the English spelling is being used. Beyond the runway numbers outside I can only see partway down the runway. Visibility is less than a mile with the overcast just a few hundred feet overhead. The important thing is that I'm starting this flight in the right place both in the physical world and in the electronic one loaded into the brains of my aircraft computers.

Dan calls out, "Nav Display?" as I adjust the nose wheel and align the aircraft with the runway centerline. The little symbol that represents our aircraft on the screen also appears to be centered between the two lines representing the runway with a little 5L next to it. As I turn on the EGPWS (enhanced ground proximity warning system), amber blotches appear all around our triangle symbol like we've been packed into the screen with foam peanuts, but what they represent are real rocks of majestic magnitude.

My compulsory response is a little nonstandard: "5-Left in the box with the rocks." This prompts a slight chuckle from Dan because he was expecting, "Checked, Runway 5-Left" — verbatim. I'm really confirming that we're in the right place for takeoff and that I've remembered to turn on the EGPWS. Mountains are hard enough to see at night with their black masses counterpoised against the midnight blue of the sky. But tonight they're shrouded in both darkness and cloud cover. I can sense them hiding beyond my limited view outside, but I have to settle for their painted shapes on my display screen. This aircraft has a worldwide database of mountains and other obstacles programmed into it and will bark at me in English if I try to fly the aircraft where it knows there's something more solid than air. Each pilot's 5x6 inch navigation display paints hazards to navigation on a moving map that's no Xbox or Play Station video game — and there's no instant reset button to start over. We're hemmed by mountains, but by looking at the screen it seems like we're taking off from inside a volcano.

Dan could really be Bill, Ken, Jennifer, Chip, or any copilot — we're trained so that any two pilots of appropriate ranks can fly together the first time we meet, and Dan and I started this trip as strangers. My airline has roughly ten thousand pilots. Based on sheer numbers, every trip there's a good chance it will be the first time the pilots fly together. For that reason I may hear about my nonstandard phraseology later. Creativity is stifled in favor of conformity. We're an amalgam of homogenized uniforms separated by seniority numbers — not actual people in the airline's eyes. I know this, but during the years I taught as an instructor and a check-airman I dissected many procedures into catchy phrases and memory gauges to help the pilots I was training. Sometimes they creep back into my vocabulary at checklist time. Dan snaps me out of my reflective thoughts with the final item that will complete our Before Takeoff checklist, "Nose Lights?"

This time I respond with the standard response, "Bright."

A crackle and then a clear voice announces over our headsets from the primary radio, crackling again after the transmission when the distant microphone is keyed and then unkeyed to frame the controller's words, "Alpha Air 123, maintain flight level two-seven-zero. You are cleared for takeoff."

Dan acknowledges, and then I ease the throttles up partway until both Pratt

& Whitney JT8D-200 turbofan engines are spooled above 1.4 EPR (engine pressure ratio) on the top pair of gauges in the power stack between his and my flight instruments. That means that air is blowing out the back of each engine forty percent more forcefully than it's being sucked in the front. That's just a starting point before engaging the auto throttles and releasing the brakes.

I command, "Auto throttles on," as I quickly scan the other engine instruments to insure normal operation. I push the control wheel forward slightly to maintain pressure on the nose wheel through the early part of the takeoff roll.

Dan complies with the flick of a switch on the glare shield, the EPR needles rise to the preset orange chevrons, and the aircraft lurches forward. The engines are now just about doubling the air pressure they're throwing out the back. The trick is to keep the runway centerline disappearing under my right leg, the one closest to the center of the aircraft, as we roll down the runway. Unlike driving, we steer down the middle of the lane. We accelerate through the thin atmosphere at this high altitude airport and Dan calls out, "Eighty knots." The ambient noise starts to increase as air moves faster right outside our cockpit windows next to our heads.

We are past the point of stopping on the runway except for six specific items: an engine failure, compressor stall, engine fire, other fire or fire warning, windshear warning, or if the airplane is unsafe or unable to fly. In other words, if an electrical, hydraulic, pressurization, or other fault occurs now, we're still going flying and we'll deal with it in the air. As the captain, only I am authorized to make the decision to abort a takeoff. Most abnormalities or emergencies in flight still allow for the input of the crew, but rolling down the runway for takeoff is one time where decision-making is reserved for the pilot in the left seat—the one who has the final authority over the aircraft. Trying to stop a nearly flying aircraft from about halfway down the runway has a lot less chance of success than stopping a barely flying airplane from the beginning of the runway in the designated touchdown zone. Most passengers fear landing the most. Maybe it's the feeling of falling while descending. While landing, we have an abundance of energy and can always go back into the air if something goes wrong. Only during takeoff is the aircraft the heaviest it's going to be for the entire flight, as no fuel is burned off yet, and it's starting from zero energy. I'm not trying to scare you. It's just simple physics—an airplane already flying is easy to fly. Convincing a stationary aircraft to fly is the challenge.

Dan calls out, "Vee-one," indicating that there's no longer enough remaining runway to guarantee stopping anymore, even for those previous six items. We've passed the *Takeoff Decision Speed* and effectively made the *Go/No-Go Decision*. Dan follows up with "rotate" and I gently pull back on the yoke. The nose rises off the ground first. The weight of the aircraft—all 138,000 pounds tonight—transfers from the wheels to the wings, and I can feel it in my seat. We're airborne, and I keep the nose slowly rising to about twenty degrees up. I nuzzle the wedge-shaped aircraft symbol, that looks like an orange stealth bomber in my artificial horizon instrument display, into the magenta flight director command bars that guide me to the proper pitch and bank when the visibility out the window is limited—as it is now.

Dan calls out, "Vee-two," and then, "Vee-two-plus-ten," as our speed increases and I say, "Positive rate, gear up," adding the required supplementary hand signal. The cloud ceiling is low and we're in the soup already. Surrounded by un-seen mountains, I'm now relying solely on my instruments. The physical world is reduced to my interpretation of the digital and analog information in front of me.

As Dan raises the big lollypop handle, three thousand pounds of hydraulic pressure forces the landing gear with its protective doors into the wheel wells for streamlined flight. This whole sequence of heavy moving parts, disturbed airflow under the body of the aircraft, and the rubbing noise of our nose wheel abrading to a stop from over a hundred and fifty miles per hour against a snubber directly under our seats, sometimes unnerves the first-time flyer—but I find it a welcome mechanical symphony. I'm in the air again, and everything is functioning normally.

We're not even a full minute into our flight when the loud popping noises begin and the plane starts shaking.

"Captain, we have compressor stalls in the right engine."

"Auto-Throttles Off," I respond over the unwelcome micro-explosions as I press the disconnect buttons on the sides of the throttles — twice. The first time takes the auto-throttles offline while the arming switch on the glaresh-ield clicks off. The red *Throttle* warning annunciators illuminate briefly, which I extinguished with the second click. I know the auto-throttles are off—I turned them off. This prevents the engines from hunting for their target power setting and making the surges worse.

Dan calls out, "Captain, right engine failure!" as we both watch the EPR needle drop to zero and the aircraft yaw to the right. Only the left engine is now producing thrust, so the aircraft tries to turn away from the source of power. I ease in some left rudder to compensate by pushing on the pedal and manage to keep the aircraft tracking straight. I also twist in about four units of left rudder trim with a dial on the aft center pedestal to take the bulk of the load off my leg. I'm going to be holding this left rudder pressure for what will feel like a long time, so I don't want it to become a squat thrust competition. Managing the adverse thrust of a single pod-mounted engine is just the beginning of my challenges.

My workload just quadrupled. I have a specific vertical profile to fly now, ingrained in me through years of practice. But because of the mountains and high altitude of this airport, Mexico City has its own complicated engine failure lateral route to follow. With only half of its usual power remaining, the MD-80 climbs very slowly on a single engine and the path we have to take is now carefully mapped out. I have to follow this religiously to keep the EGPWS quiet and not become a victim of controlled flight into terrain — a fancy way of saying crashing into a mountain. On top of that, Dan and I have several checklist duties to complete, the first of which will be the Engine Fire/Damage/Separation checklist. And, I have to let air traffic control know we're no longer a routine flight climbing to altitude and eventually the USA — we're stuck at low level and coming back in a big way.

Dan gets right on the radio. "Mexico City Tower, Alpha Air 123 is declaring an emergency. We've had an engine failure and we're returning to land." His voice is very professional. We're often evaluated by the public on how calm we sound under duress, and we know it.

"Roger. ARFF (aircraft rescue and fire fighting) is being notified."

I don't think we left any parts on the runway since the engine failed after we were airborne, so I tell Dan we should stick with Runway five-left because it's already in *the box* — the flight management computer. We wouldn't want to return to a runway that had FOD (foreign object debris) on it that we could run over and blow tires or suck into our remaining engine. He searches through the database and then informs me there's no approach listed for that runway, so we decide on runway five-right — the parallel runway. Dan relays this message over the radio as I call for, "Altitude hold."

Dan presses the button so the flight directors on our artificial horizons, the most prominent instrument in the center of our respective instrument clusters, will guide us through level off as we slowly accelerate.

"Flaps up, max continuous thrust," I say, and Dan complies by moving the appropriate handle. We'll put some of the flaps back out later during our approach, but right now our focus is to gain speed and altitude, and every little bit is priceless. With only one engine pushing us through the air, we need the aircraft as streamlined as possible. We also don't need the remaining engine overheating at the powerful takeoff thrust setting intended just to initially lift the aircraft into the air.

When we reach the proper speed — in this case the best single-engine rate of climb — I call for, "Slats retract, I-A-S, air conditioning to override." Unlike my jovial reply to the Before Takeoff checklist, I'm all business now. My commands and responses are verbatim from our procedures manual to the best of my ability. Our entire authority to fly into and out of this airport is predicated on our aircraft's performance just barely being able to safely complete this worst-case scenario. I know there's little to no room for error.

We continue climbing and I issue two instructions at once: "Dan, set up the inbound turn on my nav radio and open the QRH (quick reference handbook) to the Engine Fire/Damage/Separation checklist."

We need to fly out eight miles and then make a left turn back over the air-port while remaining east of a radial that keeps us clear of some high peaks. Dan is setting up my instruments ahead of the aircraft to keep us on track. I think, *Keep the EGPWS quiet.* That's the modern way of prioritizing: *aviate, navigate, and then communicate.* I can't afford to let distractions cause me to fly into a sudden crunching stop. I have to fly the vertical profile memorized inside my head to get the plane up and on speed, plus I need to fly this special emergency lateral routing that keeps us away from terrain that we could never climb over in this single-engine condition, all while having to shut down the failed engine and its associated systems. All this has to be accomplished while communicating our intentions with a foreign air traffic controller, our flight attendants, and the passengers.

We reach our safe altitude of 8,800 feet and the turn point as Dan starts reading from the checklist and I reply to the first few items. Dan's delivery of each item is deliberate and clearly pronounced. We have to read and respond to each item in order, even if the action has already been accomplished. It's a strict challenge and response protocol. Dan starts with, "Auto-throttles disconnect."

I have to act on or verify each command and then call it done. The auto-throttles are already off so I say, "Disconnect."

Dan reads the next item, "Right throttle close."

I pull the affected throttle back, slowly at first, and watch for any change in thrust. While under the pressure of this emergency procedure, it's just too easy to make a critical mistake by rushing. Finally I pull it all the way back to the stop and reply, "Closed."

"Is fire, damage, or separation suspected?"

"Yes," I say, "forget a restart. It looks like the EGT (exhaust gas temperature) spiked and there's no rotation in the N2 (high pressure) compressor." These are indications that the engine has seized rather than just failed.

"Right fuel lever off, at Captain's command."

Because a mistake here could potentially shut down the wrong engine, Dan puts his hand on what I observe to be the failed engine's fuel lever, and he waits for me to confirm it. Shutting down the good engine is the ultimate sin that all onboard would pay for rapidly and severely.

"Off," I affirm, and he pulls the lever out of its locked detent and selects it off.

"Right engine fire handle pull, at Captain's command." Dan puts his hand on the right fire handle waiting for me to confirm that he has the correct one. If the engine were on fire it would be lit bright red by four high intensity bulbs, and there'd be no mistaking it for the wrong one. It's not on fire so the lights are out, but pulling this handle will secure a lot of items fed off the engine, such as the hydraulic pump, fuel pumps, and an engine-driven generator. It would also shut down the engine if it were running, so it's another killer checklist item not to be rushed through.

After I verify his hand is holding the correct handle, I say, "Pull," and he complies.

Dan continues, "Is an immediate landing planned?"

"Absolutely." His last question is also my clue to divide the labor. We're passed the part where a single mistake can bring down the airplane. I say, "Read and complete the rest of the checklist out loud, but to yourself. I'll handle the radios and fly the plane." At this point we are already committed to returning to Mexico City by following the charted instructions.

Dan starts reducing electrical loads and preparing the aircraft for a single-engine landing, which has its own checklist that we'll have to perform when this one is complete.

We pass over Mexico City Airport while still in the clouds, and I set my own course knob for the outbound radial. Effectively we're making a figure eight — with the airport in the middle — back to the runway that's next to the one where we started. We're level and on speed, so it's now safe to turn on the autopilot. I can now start preparing for the landing and call for the first step, "Below two hundred and eighty knots, slats extend." Dan replies, "Verified," and moves the flap/slat handle. This increase in lift gives us a buffer above stall speed in order to maneuver. After I verify that the autopilot has accepted the aircraft, we're tracking on course, and our airspeed is steady, I select PA on my radio panel. "Ladies and gentlemen, this is the captain. We've had to secure one of our engines as a precaution and so we're returning to Mexico City Airport. We expect to land in about seven minutes. You will see some safety vehicles in position for our arrival. Will the number-one flight attendant please call the cockpit?"

Ding, ding, ding, ding. I switch to interphone and answer the call, "This is the captain."

"Captain, this is Karl your number one." He sounds calm and professional—well-trained.

"Karl, you may have noticed we shut down the right engine. Do you have any additional problems in the cabin to report?" I know he's in the front of the aircraft looking back down the aisle at some inquisitive and probably worried faces of the passengers. He's my eyes and ears back there. I can perceive the aircraft's condition over countless dials and gauges, but my number-one flight attendant is my best source of information for the human element and what's happening beyond the sanctuary of my cockpit. I'm in charge of the whole aircraft from nose to tail. It's important to keep the communication open with him as much as possible without becoming distracted from my primary job of flying the aircraft. Yet another juggling act that I have to manage.

"Just that the engine made a lot of noise right after takeoff," Karl replies. "Passengers are nervous, but nobody is panicking yet."

If the engine had shed parts into the cabin he would have mentioned it, so I assume there's no smoke, fire, or injuries that I need to know about. The compressor and turbine blades inside our engines spin in the tens of thousands of revolutions per minute, and if the engine comes apart when it fails it can become a hand grenade. "OK, here are your TEST items." This is exactly what Karl is waiting to hear. "The *Type* of problem that we've had is an engine failure that started with compressor stalls and it's now shut down. I'm not planning on an *Evacuation* after landing, but if that changes then we'll use the *Easy Victor Signal* over the PA. (We don't have an evacuation alarm on this aircraft.) The *Time* until landing is about six minutes, so do your thirty-second review and be sure you're strapped in. Any questions?"

"No, Captain."

It's now time to make my turn back to runway five-right. Both of Mexico City's runways are over 13,000 feet long. For comparison, they're about as long as Dallas–Fort Worth's parallel runways and almost twice as long as Reagan Washington National's primary runway. I tell Dan, "Set up the ILS (instrument landing system) course and frequency on both of our nav radios."

"Wilco, and the Engine Fire/Damage/Separation checklist has directed me to the Single-Engine Approach checklist. Land with flaps twenty-eight and use flaps eleven if we have to go around." Good, the primary emergency checklist is completed and that's one less thing for me to worry about now. Wilco, by the way, is a contraction—adapted from the military—which means *will comply*.

Dan tunes and identifies the correct frequencies and then compares the Morse code blips and bleeps with the dots and dashes printed on our charts.

As he tunes each nav radio up, I can hear the dit-dit-dahs coming through his speaker that he still has set at a low setting even though we're both wearing headsets. Then he briefs me on the approach: "Set zero-five-three degrees as the inbound course. Set your baro-altimeter bug at 7,600 feet and your radio altimeter at 284 feet. There's high terrain in all quadrants."

I know what I will see by glancing outside but I look anyway—the dark charcoal gray of the inside of an endless stratoform cloud at night. Nothing inside of nothing. "Get the latest weather from the tower," I say, while quietly hoping it's no worse than it was during our recent departure.

He relays the request and the controller reports a ceiling of three hundred feet and a visibility of half a mile. It's going to be a tight single-engine approach right down to minimums.

"Hydraulic pumps, high and on." Dan is reading the first item on our mechanical Before Landing checklist on the center pedestal. It represents one knob, ten lights, and ten toggle switches that passengers see when they look into the cockpit and wonder what everything is for. Dan adds, "Except the right engine pump is off."

"Noted."

"Altimeters?"

I read back, "Set two-niner-niner-four and crosscheck."

He repeats, "Two-niner-niner-four and crosscheck." This part of flying is dry, but the meticulous nature of our checklists has to be followed to the letter so that important information isn't missed. The barnstorming days are long over. Modern aviation is very rule bound. Dan continues, "Flight instruments and bugs?"

"Set at a hundred and thirty-eight knots for a twenty-eight-flap landing and crosscheck. Select medium autobrakes."

"Set and crosscheck. Medium brakes selected. Seatbelt and PA?"

"Complete." I reply. "You do the brace call at five hundred feet." It's required and it gives passengers the best chance of surviving if something goes wrong with the landing. However, sitting in the cabin with no forward view, your head cradled in your arms that are crossed over the back of the seat in front of you while waiting for something to happen has got to be an invitation to panic if ever there was one. That's why we don't tell passengers to brace until just before touchdown, or impact. Making this landing as normal as possible is my job, but I also have my own skin riding on the outcome.

"Roger on the brace call. Tail de-ice is not required. We're down to the gear. Glideslope is alive."

I click off the autopilot and adjust the pitch and rudder trim while getting the feel for the plane again. Every time we change speeds, it needs to be re-trimmed. I wait until the glideslope is one dot away from centering and then call, "Below two hundred and forty knots, flaps all the way to fifteen and gear down." The glideslope is a needle on the side of my artificial horizon and it's my guide for the proper descent path to the runway.

The flap handle looks like a wing, and the gear handle looks like a wheel. I watch Dan move them both and then I call for: "Flaps twenty-eight."

The aircraft is now arranged in our final landing configuration. I confirm the outer marker crossing height, which is co-located with a radio beacon named PLAZA. "PLAZA at 8,755 feet," I intone, verifying we're on the correct glideslope and not a false one — something of an anomaly that's still possible even in our modern aviation environment. I have to follow that little needle to the ground, and I have to confirm that it's not lying to me.

Dan calls out the rest of the mechanical checklist, "Gear?"

"Down and three green."

He confirms, "Down and three green," then continues, "Spoiler lever?"

I pull it up and it locks into place with a clank; then I reply, "Armed." These are speed brakes that will pop up on top of the wings when we touch down to help us stop.

He repeats, "Armed," and adds, "Autobrakes?"

I risk a quick glance at the selector, between and behind us, and then reply, "Medium and armed." The pedals at my feet do three things: steer the plane in the air with the rudder, steer the plane on the ground with the nose wheel, and on top of each pedal is a brake for each main gear. Allowing the plane to auto-brake frees me up to concentrate on steering with my heels still on the floor. Some of our aircraft don't have autobrakes, and I'm grateful this one does.

Dan says, "Flaps and Slats?"

I verify the handle, the gauge, and the slat annunciator before replying in sequence, "Final setting twenty-eight, twenty-eight, land."

Over the radio we hear, "Alpha Air 123 you are cleared to land. Advise if you can clear the runway after landing."

Dan replies, "Negative. We'd like an inspection on the runway before clearing." Then he makes the "Brace, brace, brace" announcement over the PA. All the other work was leading up to this. If we've done everything right, we'll break out of the clouds and land in very short order, and there's very little time to transition from flying on instruments to a visual landing. A single-engine go-around at this elevation, while possible, is all but out of the question. This has to be done right.

Just before our legal limit to descend — as indicated by the settings we previously dialed into all three of our barometric altimeters and both of our radio altimeters — the runway approach lights appear ahead. The temptation is to give up on the instruments and stare outside. I cannot. The runway will only appear in my window a little at a time with this reduced visibility. The view out the front can only become one of the many things I need to scan as we continue. My primary focus is still that little triangular stealth bomber shape in my artificial horizon and the magenta flight director bars. Finally I see those most welcoming numbers painted on the beginning of what I know to be a long straight piece of paved surface, even though I can only see part of the touchdown zone past the white paint displaying 5R.

I know from experience to barely flare when we're just about to touch down on the runway. The ground-effect as we reach half a wingspan above the concrete, plus my subtle back-pressure on the control yoke, are enough to slow our seven-hundred-feet-per-minute descent to about three hundred feet per minute — neither firm nor gentle as we contact terra firma, but right where we need to be in the touchdown zone. I also don't pull off the power until the rubber is on the runway. With an engine shut down, it's too easy to set up pilot-induced problems on short final by over-adjusting the power and wrestling the resulting yaw or turning tendency. In this situation, it's best just to fly the plane onto the runway rather than struggling for a smooth landing.

The tires chirp as they spin up from static to rolling on the runway at a hundred and fifty knots in a split second. The auto-spoilers deploy and the auto-brakes engage. I can feel the anti-skid system release and re-grab the brakes. All I have to do now is carefully lift both engine's throttles into idle reverse and then meter the functioning engine's reverse thrust as necessary while keeping the aircraft's nose on the centerline as we slow down by steering with my feet. Even at idle I can still feel the shudder as the giant clamshell doors open up into the airstream to redirect the engine thrust. I decide not to pull the working engine beyond idle reverse. On this long runway the asymmetric thrust would cause more steering problems than its stopping benefit.

Emergency vehicles with flashing lights pull onto the pavement as I stop the aircraft within the remaining runway and then breathe a sigh of relief. I can feel my sweaty back has soaked through my shirt, and it's sticking to the sheepskin seat cover as a voice comes over the radio, "Alpha Air 123, you have slides deploying and people outside your aircraft."

This is unexpected, and Dan and I look at each other in disbelief. With a glance at my overhead annunciator panel, I can see the door warning lights have illuminated indicating this reported situation is true. Did the passengers start an evacuation on their own? Or is there a new problem in the cabin that I'm not yet aware of? Any crewmember can initiate an evacuation, but only the ranking crewmember can stop one. Because I don't know why this one began, I have to assume there's a new emergency, so I elect not to stop it. I tell Dan, "Evacuation checklist," and he's already ready with the first item, "Parking brake, parked."

I respond, "Parked." He reads the remaining items in order as I reply while shutting down the operating engine. I elect not to configure the flaps and slats to the recommended settings because I don't want to injure passengers who may already be out on the wings. Those controls are operated with three thousand pounds of hydraulic pressure just like the landing gear and could sever limbs. They are meant to be positioned before the evacuation begins.

Dan and I grab our hats so we'll be easily identified as crewmembers and prepare to leave the cockpit when the floor suddenly drops out from under us. Actually, it's the whole cockpit that plunges like an express elevator leaving the top floor. We settle with a dampened thud and the cockpit lights come on. There's a mechanical noise of a gangway being lowered. The view out the front windows disappears. Everything becomes quiet inside the cockpit, and the outside hum of computers can now be heard as the door behind us opens letting in the light of a large room where our cabin should be.

"Good job gentlemen," booms the voice of a man now standing in the doorway.

Bob, a fiftyish graying gentleman with a beaming smile, says, "Our time is up. Grab your crew kits and take a five-minute break. I'll meet you in the debriefing room for a couple of minor discussion items. Overall you both did very well." He's our simulator instructor and has been pulling the strings to create this scenario for the last two hours.

> *The sweat is real*
> *And so is the pressure*
> *The visual seems real*
> *And so does the weather*
> *When an engine fails*
> *We perform the procedure*
> *We're shakin' it in the dark*
> *Up on jacks*
> *We're shakin' it in the dark*

This is where I know I'm going to hear about my nonstandard Before Takeoff checklist response. Bob will probably also have some suggestions for further managing the incredible workload this emergency scenario demands based on his experience of seeing this same Mexico City engine failure procedure many times every month. This was a simulator checkride, but also training. It turns out that the unscheduled evacuation was his way of preparing us for unplanned events, and also a required item to be demonstrated and checked-off on this year's evaluation form. Even though I've been in his shoes before and put countless pilots through similar situations, it's still a stressful jeopardy event when I'm the one being evaluated. An almost overwhelming feeling of relief washes over me when I get to stand up and stretch my legs.

All three barometric altimeters again read 7,320 feet, but I'm leaving them behind as I step out of the simulator and mentally return to the near sea level world of the Flight Academy. The air here isn't Mexico City thin; it's thick and air-conditioned. I breathe deeply and wait for my heart to relax from the adrenaline rush that the check-airman just put me through. A retractable gangplank allows me out of the sweatbox that sits high up on hydraulic jacks designed to mimic three-axis motion plus acceleration forces. I've successfully traversed through the virtual experience of cockpit hell and an auditorium-sized bay in Fort Worth welcomes me.

> *The simulator*
> *Is a pressure percolator*
> *A scenario incubator*
> *And a heart rate stimulator*
> *Pairs of aviators*
> *Try to impress our moderator*
> *Through engine failures*
> *And the loss of generators*
> *Steering clear of windshear*
> *And extinguishing fire indicators*
> *This is what we do*
> *When we're shakin' it in the dark*

As captain, I might tell you as a passenger to "Sit back, relax, and enjoy the flight," but I train every nine months for whatever worst-case scenario our airline's flight department can dream up. With any luck it will be another nine months (some airlines train on an annual basis) before I have to shut down another engine in flight — but you never know. It could happen for real on my very next trip or wait insidiously for me to become complacent right before my next training cycle, or it might never happen at all.

Step on the rudder
Check my fear
Fly runway heading
Pull up the gear
Avoid the hills
Level off when we're clear
We're shakin' it in the dark
Up on jacks
We're shakin' it in the dark

The cause for TWA Flight 800's center tank explosion has never officially been resolved. The passengers and crew onboard that flight never had a chance at survival. Captain Sullenberger and First Officer Skiles successfully landed their Airbus A320 on the Hudson River saving everyone onboard their US Airways Flight 1549 and became well-deserved national heroes. Most aviation accidents fall in between these two extreme outcomes. Above and beyond the training that my airline provides, an opportunity to become part of a groundbreaking aviation safety experiment presented itself. As I continued to fly in the now flattening wake since losing Susanne so many years ago, suddenly I found myself in a position to make air travel a little safer. A member of my aviation tribe invited me to help his Broken Wing experimental aviation team sacrifice an unmanned Boeing 727 in the name of progress. At least on a professional level it felt like an opportunity to finally start moving on.

Time to land
Put down the gear
Fly the gauges
Until we break out in the clear
Land safely
And we're good for a year
We're shakin' it in the dark
Up on jacks
We're shakin' it in the dark
Every year
We're shakin' it in the dark
Until we retire
We're shakin' it in the dark

38 | BIG FLO FLIES NO MORE

Ode to Old Big Flo

I WAS WEARING a green full-length flight suit — the team uniform — in the near-hundred-degree heat while driving a rental car down Highway 5 in the Sonora Desert of Mexico and chasing two parachutes with four parachutists dangling from them. This was part of my duty as a member of the ground support team in the Sonora Desert of Mexico. The copilot and flight engineer had parachuted out the gaping hole in the Boeing 727 aircraft's tail where the airstairs once had been — each making tandem jumps while strapped to their respective jumpmasters. Once I drove as close as the pavement allowed, I pulled off the highway and engaged the four-wheel drive to pick these jumpers up after they touched down on the dry lakebed.

> *Mid-air, Cap'n says it's time to go*
> *All three pilots bail — "Geronimo!"*
> *Chase plane right behind ya*
> *Don't worry, we can find ya*
> *Servos set for remote-controlled pitch and roll*

There was still one pilot onboard, but not for long. After the captain ascertained that the handoff to remote-control flying from the chase plane was successfully coupled, and the commercial jet was established on a long, straight, twenty-mile final approach to the middle of the lakebed (where a nest of cameras awaited within the outline of a runway that was ploughed into the dry mud by a bulldozer), he and his safety skydiver each strolled the length of the cabin and made single jumps out that same void at the aft end of the aisle — leaving behind in the cockpit only a Sock Monkey in the captain's chair, Mr. Potato Head in the copilot's seat, and Wilson the volleyball strapped to the flight engineer station. Whoever said test pilots don't have sense of humor? This is a day that would have made D B Cooper proud and will hopefully spark future advances in commercial air safety.

Big Flo's in position
For her final mission
Will she break up without burning?
Will this lead to higher learning?

So how did I become involved in all of this? Leland "Chip" Shanle, Jr. and I are friends. We've flown together and offered feedback for each other's books. He writes historical fiction and the first book in his WWII aviation series is titled: *Project Seven Alpha*. He's also a former Navy test pilot, Hollywood technical advisor, and the founder of Broken Wing, LLC. When I approached him to write an article about his latest project for *Airways* magazine (where I'm a contributing editor and many segments of this memoir have appeared), he scratched his chin and then replied: "Best way to do an article is to be part of the team." The next thing I knew, Chip, his son David, and I were flying in his Beechcraft Musketeer from St. Louis, Missouri, to Mexicali, Mexico.

"It's pretty hard to hide a plane crash." That's what another friend of mine said over the phone when I told him that unofficial footage of the Boeing 727 experiment I'd been working on had leaked and it was the current headline on the *The Today Show* and CNN. This was early in May 2012, and only a few days after I'd left the faithful three-holer nicknamed Big Flo — a 727-200 that had served with Singapore Airlines, VASP (Brazil), Alaska Airlines, Express One International, AvAtlantic, and Champion Air — in pieces in a dry lakebed south of Mexicali, Baja California, México. Already, YouTube footage, apparently shot by somebody in an area restricted to emergency crews (closer than I was allowed to encroach while picking up the skydivers), was making the rounds on prominent news channels. Yes, it's difficult to hide a commercial jet that's been deliberately crashed.

This exercise by Broken Wing (and sponsored by The Discovery Channel), in an attempt to advance airline safety, may have lacked the secrecy of the Manhattan Project, but as I initially drafted this chapter, details were still closely guarded. A two-hour program titled "Plane Crash" eventually aired on Discovery's *Curiosity* series during the fall of 2012. Safety recommendations revealed by the show then appeared in print in *Maxim* and *Aerospace Test International* (where it was nominated for an international media award), as well as in a four-part series in *Airways* that Chip and I co-wrote in order to provide informed analysis of this historic event. I will share these results in a moment.

How does a small group of test pilots, technicians, and researchers safely crash a commercial aircraft so that the experiment's results can be preserved in order to verify component-based testing and improve survivability?

This isn't the same Chip who I shared a harrowing Egyptian cab ride with before climbing the pyramids in Giza. This Chip spent three years as the Broken Wing team commander responsible for the 727 documentary event, and says that the key to its success was these years of planning and converting a jet aircraft of a previous era into a modern UAV (unmanned aerial vehicle).

And why crash this particular airliner? The 727 is my favorite jet, so I say this with respect, but the reality is that the type has outlived its competitive usefulness, and many examples sit slowly decomposing in desert boneyards. Once the engines, useful instruments, and other equipment are salvaged, 727 hulls become majestic aluminum corpses, with the number of grounded examples far exceeding the inventory of their ever-shrinking, still-airborne siblings. Some former workhorses sit forlorn and idle on ramps and taxiways at secondary airports around the world, resembling broken-down automobiles with their batteries and hubcaps removed. But rather than becoming canvases for graffiti artists, their once-proud tail markings are painted over after their final operator no longer needs them. Some are used as fire and rescue carcasses for aircraft rescue and firefighting training. A lucky few have been converted into homes or hostels. One in Costa Rica, complete with wooden decks built out onto its wings, comes readily to mind. Staying there overnight with someone special is on my bucket list. Finding that someone special isn't my only challenge—it's also going to be difficult fully accepting her. But this journey is not for nothing. We're almost there. Bear with me while I put my aviation legs under me with this safety experiment first, and then work past my finally fading survivor's guilt.

So again, why a 727? "Because essentially it has the same cockpit and fuselage as the most popular jetliner in the world: the Boeing 737," explains Chip. "Thus the experiment had a direct correlation and applicability to current fleets. Data from a controlled impact would not only verify the currently accepted component-based testing procedure, but also provide an immense fund of knowledge for design improvements to increase passenger survivability rates," he adds.

Big Flo was chosen to receive an extensive overhaul and make a final series of flights, terminating in a dry lakebed while simulating an emergency landing intended to be fatal, catastrophic, and survivable all at the same time—but for research purposes only.

First flown in 1963, the Boeing 727 became a bestseller with 1,832 built, and they proudly served hundreds of airlines. With an active fleet reduced to around two hundred near the end of 2012, the type was eased out of service not with the proverbial bang but the equally proverbial whimper.

With two pilot seats, a sidesaddle flight engineer's panel, and an optional two-jump-seat configuration, the 727 flight deck was both the office and classroom in which I had the opportunity to work, teach, and learn for the core of my career. Fond memories of traversing the Berlin corridor with Captain Cook still spring from my memory. It was, therefore, with pride and sadness that I found myself in Mexicali, watching one of the remaining airworthy examples being deliberately flown into the ground.

The 727 was designed around safety, and as you'll remember, its third pilot, or flight engineer, managed the aircraft's complex systems — electrical power, hydraulic pressure, and cabin pressurization, to name a few. This was an aircraft designed in a manual era. Unless you are currently a great-grandparent, you probably can't remember an elevator operator riding with you between the floors of an office building or department store. In times gone by, this person would manually open and close the outer and inner doors for you, as well as select the destination floors. Now, any child can press a button and ride an elevator by him or herself. Likewise, the flight engineer's systems, such as those on the 727, were subsequently automated and moved up front for the pilots to monitor and manipulate, effectively ending the three-person cockpit and saving airlines considerable amounts in payroll costs while cutting down on weight and space requirements.

While post-727 cockpits were becoming smaller, evolution was also playing its part in the powerplant department. Three engines of modest bypass turbofan design, once necessary for performance, gave way to twin configurations. As engines became more powerful and reliable, fuel efficiency also became a priority. The 737, with two pilots and two engines, is the direct legacy of the 727, and newer versions will remain prolific workhorses for decades. Stage 3 noise regulations also had an impact on driving 727s out of service. To remain flying in the 1990s and beyond, they needed to be modified — an expensive option. Some operators added winglets and noise-suppressing exhaust ducts, or hushkits. Others replaced the outer pod-mounted engines with more modern turbofans. But these adjustments merely allowed the aircraft to stretch its useful life until more efficient replacement types could be procured.

Today no U.S. passenger airline uses the 727, and the once one-hundred-strong FedEx fleet of Series 200 freighters dwindled down to half that number in 2012, with the remainder replaced in 2013.

The Boeing 727 faded away one aircraft fleet at a time, joining other proud relics like the Douglas DC-3 and the Boeing 707 in the pages of commercial aviation history. But over its lifespan there were incidents of violent endings. I recall the cover of the Beastie Boys's 1986 debut album, *Licensed to Ill*. When unfolded to its full length, it depicted a 727 in fictitious Beastie Boys livery crashing into the side of a mountain. That was the vision evoked by Big Flo when it was sacrificed in México.

So sorry to see you go, Big Flo
But you'll help us more than you can know
All wired up so we can see
What goes on internally
To study airline crash survivability

While air travel has improved from a dangerous activity of the early twentieth century to a *safer-than-driving* form of modern transport, there is always more to be done. So, the obvious reason for crashing a commercial jet is to improve survivability, through modifying existing models and improving future designs. An obvious analogy is the automotive industry, which smashes newly assembled cars and trucks with such regularity that crash test dummies occasionally serve as animated TV spokespersons, have become a clichéd Halloween costume, and have even inspired the name of a popular modern rock band.

Some early press reports on the Mexicali experiment — showing only the climactic moment of Big Flo's demise — claimed the event was a stunt and that the primary purpose was pure sensationalism. But, "Broken Wing is not a collection of stunt pilots," stresses Chip. "It is a team composed of Members of the Society of Experimental Test Pilots (SETP)." Chip notes that this initial spin also exposed a hole in the news media's logic — larger than Big Flo's cracked-open fuselage — which suggested that only automobiles should be crashed and sacrificed to improve safety, not airplanes.

If we set aside our morbid fascination for car, train, and airplane crashes, and regard the Mexicali exercise as the instructional experience for which it was designed, it would be worth considering that one of the lives saved by Big Flo may eventually be our own. Some of the modern crash test dummies used inside Big Flo were wired to record thirty-two inputs. Cameras both inside and outside the airplane recorded the crash in high definition.

Crash test dummies will see everything
Camera eyes watching nose and tail and wings
Will the overheads fly open?
Will the fuselage be broken?
Will the oxygen deploy when the landing gear's destroyed

As for the lessons learned from this and any subsequent airplane crash tests, we can only hope that we're making a difference and making air travel safer. And what did the research team learn? The Big Flo's unmanned desert crash is not a secret anymore. The *Discovery Channel* footage is fantastic—please see for yourself. At the risk of spoiling the outcome, here are the resulting six major safety recommendations:

In this hard landing scenario, the nose of the aircraft slammed to the ground after impact much harder than the tail of the aircraft (a 12-g force impact up front, 8-g force impact in the middle, and only a few g-forces in the rear). So the first class seats were not the place to be. Passengers in the aft cheap seats —closer to the engine noise and the odor of the lavatories—would have had a higher survivability rate and fewer injuries.

Wear your seatbelt. This should come as no surprise, but for you doubters out there, the internal cameras recorded a crash test dummy that was not wearing its seatbelt submarining under the seat in front of him. We were in Mexico, so we considered this no seatbelt result: a no bueno.

The brace position was embraced by the results. Crash test dummies that were posed in the brace position fared better than similar dummies proximally placed but not braced. So, pay attention the next time your flight attendants demonstrate the pre-takeoff safety demo. The brace position makes the impact punishment easier for your vertebrae, and also protects your head from debris.

Several design improvement recommendations also resulted from this test. Modern planes have emergency escape path lighting, but the amount of dust generated inside the cabin during this crash landing inspires further research. Additional methods need to be developed that will assist passengers to find their way out to safety while experiencing severely reduced visibility.

Passengers are bringing heavier carry-ons onto the aircraft today than when the 727 was first manufactured, and older overhead compartment latching systems may no longer be adequate. The high-speed cameras showed bins opening on impact, creating debris that could harm passengers as well as interfere with an evacuation.

As well as the 727 was designed, fifty years of modification—particularly in the cabin entertainment department — revealed that this additional internal wiring can become a safety concern during an a crash landing. Aftermarket wires and cables spilled from the cabin ceiling and made the aisle a tangle of obstacles. Passengers risked becoming ensnared during the subsequent evacuation.

Sorry to tell you Big Flo flies no more
But she helped us more than you could ever know
All wired up so we can see
What goes on internally
To study airline crash survivability

She kissed the sky then laid her head
In the cold brown earth of a dry lake bed
And now we say farewell to Old Big Flo
Yeah, now we say farewell to Old Big Flo

39 | CATCHING UP WITH CONCORDE

Farewell to Concorde

THERE ARE SOME AIRPLANES that sadly I'll never have the opportunity to fly. One in particular's fate — a type that TWA once had orders for but sadly never took delivery of — was sealed by an explosive engine failure during takeoff. Like paying my respects at Susanne's or Captain Cook's graves, or honoring Big Flo's final moment in words and song, I made a pilgrimage to see the final resting place of one such majestic commercial bird.

I thought her pointy nose would droop at her final resting place within the Steven F. Udvar-Hazy Center of the Smithsonian National Air and Space Museum at Washington-Dulles International Airport. With her head bowed in silence at the end of a proud twenty-seven-year career, it was that unique trick that allowed Concorde pilots to see the runway during her high deck angle on final approach. I remembered her coming in for a landing, looking both regal and predatory, with her head held high and sharp beak pointed earthward as if hunting for prey — her main gear extended talon-like beneath those iconic, swept back delta wings.

Instead, here at the museum, this ex–Air France example is posed to look sleek and streamlined — ready to break the sound barrier. Inside these hangar walls, while surrounded by the most significant aircraft of a century of aviation, I couldn't help feel that Concorde had been stuffed, preserved, and mounted as the ultimate trophy. It's an ironic fate for what was once the world's sole successful supersonic commercial transport — the queen of the skies that from 1976 to 2003 wrote a chapter of tantalizing yet unfulfilled promise in aeronautical history.

The Concorde at the Smithsonian is polished brilliant white. From behind it, you can look into the afterburner (reheat) nozzles on the back of its four Rolls-Royce/SNECMA Olympus 593 turbojets that used to spit fire — literally. Closing my eyes, I put my hands over my ears and tried to imagine the spectacle and roar of raw fuel burning to accelerate this sleek bird twice beyond the speed of sound. I can almost still hear the echo of her sonic boom, feel myself onboard with the lost love of my life, and soak up the rocket-ship ride across the North Atlantic in barely the time it takes to eat a meal and watch a feature-length movie. But when I open my eyes again, I can't help feeling that this imposing bird has been buried alive.

> *I always wanted to go flying on Concorde*
> *But it's something I can no longer do*
> *Because now every Concorde that once flew*
> *   has been grounded*
> *And now within these hangar walls*
> *   they are confounded*
> *Never to fly again*
> *Never to fly again*
> *Never to fly, never to fly again*
> *So bye-bye*
> *Farewell to Concorde*

Early in my airline career, salty captains told me stories of their favorite retired aircraft. They would usually begin with, "Back in the 707 days..." TWA used to send those four-engine narrowbodies around the world in both directions, but they were gone by the time I was hired in 1988. It recently occurred to me that I was now the salty captain when I caught myself saying, "Back in the 727 days ..." I'd flown all three seats of that three-holer and trained other pilots in the simulator. None are still flying at my current airline—the silver fleet that absorbed TWA in 2001 and once had 727s of its own. A look in the mirror also reveals that my dark hair is now turning salty — my preferred pronunciation of gray.

I've been in this game long enough to not only see my mentors retire or expire, but also the airliners in which they taught me. For example, the Lockheed L-1011 TriStar — the final flight of the last airworthy former TWA example was recounted by Ann Meili in *Airways* magazine, May 2010, in her article, "TWA TriStar Returns Home." Thirty-six of them once graced the sky, and I was lucky enough to be a part of that tri-jet widebody history. I was type-rated and flew over five hundred hours as a TriStar first officer back in 1995, and it was one of the finer aircraft of its day. But the retired airplane that truly ended an era is like none other ever built. Commercial supersonic flight came and went with Concorde, finis being written when it flew its last services years ago in October 2003. Sadly, I never flew one. TWA's order for six back in the 1970s was cancelled, along with many others. Only British Airways and Air France ever flew the type with regularity, and Braniff briefly through a lease agreement with two European flag carriers.

> *I used to stop and stare with envy in my eyes*
> *Such a beautiful bird, just to watch it fly*
> *Once this great machine was the envy of the skies*
> *Now I'll never get to ride it before I die*

What I really regret is that I never pass-rode on one either — call me King of the Lost Opportunity. It's a bucket list item never to be crossed off. I once planned the perfect getaway using airline benefits to my maximum advantage: JFK to London-Heathrow on British Airway's Concorde, then back to New York Harbor onboard the RMS Queen Elizabeth 2 (now also retired) combined the ultimate speed with unimagined luxury. *Mach 2 plus the* QE2 was a non-rev travel package that cost only three hundred dollars for airline employees. Even a B-scale airline pilot could have afforded it, but I couldn't find a traveling companion. Maybe I should have showered more — or gone alone. Alas, I let the opportunity slip away.

When I finally did find the perfect partner, Susanne and I considered flying on Concorde for our honeymoon, but we never made it past the planning stage before she died.

> *I always wanted to go flying on Concorde*
> *Because it seemed like just the thing to do*
> *Riding on a Supersonic Transport in the sky*
> *Sipping on champagne and sitting next to you, my baby*

TWA began selling off its 747s after Flight 800, and the proud jumbo — affectionately known as the whale — was soon gone from our fleet. That fateful flight was headed for Charles de Gaulle Airport in Paris, the same city where, four years later almost to the day, Air France lost a Concorde also with fatal consequences after a chain of events including engine failures sparked by foreign object debris. The lifespan of every Concorde was limited after that crash.

In my *Of Mice and Men* moment, I've felt her soft touch and envisioned our dream — clinking mach 2 mimosas while seeing Susanne's diamond ring sparkle, her deep blue eyes and radiant smile, and the curvature of the earth out the window near the edge of space all at the same moment. I can still picture it, and then I find it ironic that Lenny is the shortened version of my middle name, and like Steinbeck's hero, our best vision shall not come to pass but instead live on only in writing.

> *I always wondered what it felt like*
> *To fly faster than mach two point zero four*
> *Sitting on the edge of space*
>   *ten miles up in the sky*
> *Looking down at the world*
>   *while riding next to you, my baby*

My fondest Concorde memory dates from my commuter airline days. Captain Swarner and I were flying a Shorts 330 for Command Airways and following British Airways *Speedbird Concord 2 Heavy* into runway three-one-left at JFK. Captain Swarner had a blonde flattop, and he was a captain I could call by his first name. John was cool. He reminded me of Ice Man from *Top Gun*, and he made the job fun at every opportunity. He kept the power up and the speed just ten knots under the barber pole, as fast as our airplane was allowed to go, which was still slow by airliner standards at barely above two hundred knots. When I asked him why, he deliberately ignored my inquiry. But I knew him well enough to know he was up to something. This is the same aircraft type that the Colonel saved from rolling, and Captain Tony Fine and I tricked Nanette into jumping around in the cabin to make the gear come down. Captain Swarner seemed intent on teaching me a lesson of some kind; I just didn't know if it was going to be practical or comical.

The boxy, twin-tailed, unpressurized Shorts 330 turboprops were made in Belfast — hence the politically incorrect nickname *Irish Concorde*. Sporty, the 330 was not. Concorde and the Shorts 330 represented opposite poles of commercial aviation's sleekness-spectrum. Don't get me wrong; I loved flying the Shorts and logged almost a thousand hours in them. But it just wasn't a beauty contest winner. A favorite joke was: Q: What do Shorts 330s and mopeds have in common? A: They're both fun to operate until your friends see you. It was this stigma that inspired Captain Swarner's high-speed approach, although he was still keeping his expected outcome a mystery from me.

Finally, New York approach called us on the radio: "Command forty-eight twenty-five, you're thirty knots faster than the Concorde ahead, slow to one-sixty knots and contact Kennedy Tower on one-one-niner-point-one."

John pulled the throttles back, looked at me, and a big smile creased his face. Our moped was overtaking the world-champion racing machine.

Shorts Brothers stopped making the 330 in 1992 — so that's another aircraft type I've outlasted. Regional jets have largely replaced turboprops in general within the United States. I can say to my current crews, "Back in the Shorts 330 days ..." but newer pilots would just look at me funny — or funnier than usual. There are a growing number of retired aircraft types in my past, and I still think of my early mentors lamenting the airplanes they used to fly. Progress is unstoppable, but even modern airliners don't fly supersonic anymore — and maybe never will again. The entire age of mach 2 across the Atlantic began and ended with Concorde — and it's over. I was there for it and missed it — except for sharing traffic patterns with them.

> *Well it's famous pointy nose*
> *Now it strikes a permanent pose*
> *In the Smithsonian*
> *Air and Space Museum*
> *Where you can see 'em*
> *On the hangar floor*
> *Never to fly no more*
> *Never to fly again*
> *Never to fly again*
> *Never to fly, never to fly again*
> *So bye-bye*
> *Farewell to Concorde*

(BS AERO SCIENCE – DECEMBER 1985)

When I Look Back at Twenty

THANKS FOR CLIMBING into the cockpit with me for this commercial aviation journey. You can release all the straps from the five-point restraining system of your seatbelt by twisting the large main buckle in your lap. Up here we don't wear a two-piece lap belt. Independent shoulder straps as well as a crotch strap assist the standard connection across each of our waists to keep us in our designated seats.

If this is your first time inside the flight deck, it's no wonder I see the amazement in your eyes as you ponder the vast array of cockpit instruments that frame our small cockpit windows, even though I hope some of this equipment has become a little familiar to you. You have had a firsthand look at how we slip through the clouds for a living. But how we make over a hundred thousand pounds of parts and people fly is only an introduction to the lifestyle and fraternity forged in professional aviation. I still feel airline pioneer Ernest K. Gann's presence when I add the thumbs-up hand signal to my verbal request for my copilot to pull up the landing gear—a remnant from Captain Gann's early days of heavy headsets and loud, unpressurized cockpits.

Just over twenty-five years ago I was learning how to fly at Embry-Riddle Aeronautical University and trying to earn my way into a commercial cockpit. 13,760 Feet is the logbook of my aviation life. I still remember that burning need to earn my wings, from the viewpoint of 20,000 flight hours later.

> *If I was twenty again*
> *And could see me today*
> *Would I be proud of myself*
> *That I'd turned out okay?*

I was hired at TWA as the modern airline boom began. Both luck and timing have a lot to do with career success, but it's important to position ourselves to be lucky. At the end of 2012, the first group of senior airline pilots reached the new mandatory retirement age of sixty-five. Current flight students will see the first wave of major airline hiring since before 9/11/2001. My experience is now a generation old.

When TWA hired me in 1988, I knew my undergraduate education at ERAU had paid off, as well as my persistence while pursuing my aviation goals. Hanging on for the ride at the major airline level has been another story altogether. Flying has been my aluminum parachute throughout my adult life. Since my first solo at age seventeen, and through every brutal milestone up to today — my mother's, my fiancée's, my mentors', as well as my friends' and fellow employees' untimely deaths — flying has been more than just my profession, it has been my lifestyle, my social circle, an ongoing professional challenge, and one of the tent stakes that has kept me spiritually grounded even while I took to the air. I never allow myself to forget that I'm experiencing the career that was my early dream. As a four-and-a-half year-old child, I made that picture out of yarn of a stick-figure guide man — wielding oversized orange wands — as he waved them at a plane with picture windows. Today I sit inside that little airplane, living the career that hand-sewn canvas forecasted.

From Daedalus and Icarus to the most recent Space Shuttle astronauts, we all studied aviation because we didn't want to be ground bound. We took those early lessons for the freedom to move in the three-dimensional space that's offered by an airplane. Aerodynamics, Meteorology, Regulations, and more — there's a lot to study. Most pilots would agree that actually flying the airplane is the easy part of the job — the enjoyable part. There's also an emotional element that's stronger than the science and art of the profession. The allure of the airline industry is a powerful Siren, but total career absorption and acceptance into the informal fraternity of professional pilots is far more demanding than merely moving a control yoke and throttles. The wings we wear on our chest are as much a part of our lives as our heart that beats less than a few inches beneath them. It's almost as if the binding posts of our wings are driven into our hearts when we first earn them. When those wings are torn away, they leave holes, and we also feel hurt with every industry loss.

> *I can still picture classmates*
> *Whose aircraft broke apart*
> *I'm still doing what they loved*
> *And carry them in my heart*

Icarus was the first aviation fatality. The Space Shuttle Challenger, much like TWA Flight 800, exploded offshore shortly after takeoff. Columbia disintegrated on reentry. For all of these disasters, we collectively mourned.

A passenger once asked me where he could get a set of pilot's wings. I told him that we used to give plastic ones out to kids — with peel-off adhesive tape on the back — but as the industry adjusted to economic cutbacks, the airlines discontinued them along with the complimentary decks of playing cards. Then he clarified: "No, I mean real pilot's wings. The kind you wear. Where can I get a set of them?"

Without a moment of hesitation, I answered, "You can't buy them. Pilots dedicate our lives to earning, and keeping them. They aren't souvenirs — they represent our professional commitment and training." What I didn't tell him was: *people die along the way.*

> *When I look back at twenty*
> *Now that I'm forty-five*
> *I think of all I've been through*
> *And that I'm lucky to be alive*

The aviation profession looks different now that I know it intimately rather than idealistically. I worked hard to get here, and moving the heavy metal safely is still rewarding, but I've left a lot of myself behind along the way. The world of commercial aviation has introduced me to struggles I never thought I'd have to face. The fact that Susanne's death happened onboard my airline is the ironic twist that still haunts me. It's the cruelest form of losing the lottery — not holding one of the millions of *not-winning* tickets, but holding the one exact loser with all the aligned wrong numbers. I couldn't have imagined a safer place for her to be than in the hands of my very senior and skilled fellow aviators on a jumbo aircraft that was my ultimate career goal to learn how to operate. But I still have to fly — even without her. I'd rather spin the giant hamster wheel and go nowhere fast, and at least try to move forward, than to take life lying down in failure and nestle in the shredded newspaper underneath the water lick beside the kibble cup.

> *When I look back at twenty*
> *Now that I'm forty-five*
> *The lesson I've learned*
> *Is how to survive*

Sometimes along the side of the road I see crosses, teddy bears, flowers, or photos. I imagine family members and friends are marking the spot where someone they love died in an accident. It's their last living point of contact. In that respect, I sometimes still feel my own connection to Susanne as I climb through 13,760 feet and once again greet that personal marker of my greatest love's short-cut life. Not every flight, but sometimes I do — when I'm looking at the altimeter as it sweeps through that number — if I'm not otherwise scanning the airspeed indicator, or the flight management computer, or the radio frequency selector, or my charts, or a checklist, or one of the countless protruding devices mounted 360 degrees around me that occasionally demand my attention.

My brother Tim now resides in Denver, and although we live eight hundred miles apart, we've grown closer than ever. He's a kitchen manager and oversees the preparation and service of as many as four hundred meals on a busy night. During the summer, I occasionally fly out and we climb a 14er together. Colorado has fifty-three peaks over 14,000 feet, and he wants to conquer them all. I'm not sure my knee — the one without a full meniscus — can handle that lofty goal, but so far we've seen the view from atop Grays Peak, Torreys Peak, and Mount Bierstadt. As a Missouri flatlander, my pace slows to a zombie march above the tree line and my face holds less color than the undead, but I'm too stupid to quit — or maybe I just can't allow myself to let my brother down. Or, maybe I'm driven to pay my respects at 13,760 feet. Susanne died in New York, not Colorado, but it's not her final latitude and longitude where I feel her presence as much as her ultimate altitude. Standing at that elevation isn't quite the same as flying through it, but any fading connection to her still makes me feel alive in her presence. Or maybe it's just my imagination fueled by a lack of oxygen that stirs my emotions. I don't see her there, but I pretend I can feel her, only for a moment, and then I'm back in the real world with a pounding chest, pulsing headache, and colossal breathing while bonding with my brother over our shared accomplishment, hyper aware that I'll need my remaining strength to reverse our course and hike back down before sunset — or before the rain clouds that invariably seem to have been climbing up the opposite mountain face crest the peak, let loose, and envelope our descent as nature's reminder that we are not the boss.

I'm finding new ways through words to focus in the moment, while acknowledging tomorrow is ripe with factors outside of my control. There's plenty of stress in commercial aviation — airline mergers, fleet downsizing, corporate bankruptcies, and much more. Captain Sully's double-engine failure after takeoff defined his career in a single flight, while mine happened on July 17, 1996, without the happy ending—and I'm still here.

And what of that captain who threw me off my post-TWA Flight 800 trip? I held a grudge against him for a long time. On a personal level, what he did really hurt. But with counseling and also my own experience since upgrading to captain, I now know that the pilot in command must carefully manage his own limitations. I have no idea how many close friends he lost on the same flight that took Susanne's life. Now I understand him a little better, and he did what he felt he had to do within his own emotional capacity during a difficult time.

We all take pride in leaving our emotional baggage behind from gear up to gear down. When overwhelming circumstances prevent us from doing that, we need to recognize it in ourselves and in others. We carry hard-earned licenses, and we're part of a professional team that wears our wings with pride. As my Yankee-fan and Zen-master former psychiatrist would say, "Nobody wants a pitcher on the mound or a pilot in the cockpit whose head isn't fully in the game." We also know what else he would say … (and to do it well).

Always I remember that it's not only my job to keep the blue sky clear of angry red and orange—symbolic of disaster when it's not a sunset—but to pass along my experience to you who will follow the Siren's call and dedicate your life to the airborne realm, as my mentors passed their wisdom and advice down to me. Through it all, I will see you in the sky.

And now I look forward
At what's still to be
And when I look back from sixty
I wonder if I'll still recognize me

Thanks for flying with me today. I have one more important person to introduce to you. I appreciate your patience. For the last seventeen years I haven't known where I will go next. My time has finally arrived to move forward. As I leave you with this testament to my past and all who have lived in it with me, I offer you a glimpse of my future—one that only as I write this feels open for the first time.

– CAPTAIN MARK L BERRY

41 | DELIVERY

What Route Do You Fly?

WITH THE REFLECTIVE ORANGE SASH of my overstuffed, newsprint-stained cotton delivery bag slung over my shoulder, I delivered the *Greenwich Time* from 1977 through 1983 — about sixty of them each day for over six years. From the time I was trained — a single day of slinging newspapers from the car of my new boss, a regional circulation manager — I pedaled my red Schwinn ten-speed bike with what looked like ram's horns for handlebars. The rattrap over my rear wheel clamped some of the newspapers, but the weight of many more in that shoulder bag yawed my bike so that I had to lean away from the printed payload in order to pedal straight. Our family pet, a bruiser of a Dalmatian named Domino, escorted me on every adventure, rain or shine.

After a few years, with my small salary supplemented by tip money, I bought a cobalt-blue moped — quite fashionable as the 1980s began, as well as practical for my daily trek through the neighborhood stuffing mailboxes with the latest news. On several occasions the local police pointed out that my motorized transport required a driver's license — something I was still years away from obtaining — and they ordered me to actually pedal that heavy, low-geared, one-horsepower Puch home. I was forced to resume delivery on my red Schwinn for at least a few weeks before I'd sneak back onto the moped again — with Domino chasing me the whole way regardless of my mode of transport. It's not that I didn't have respect for the law; it's just that my memory was short, and their advice was heeded for what felt like a reasonable period of time before resuming my delivery duties in motorized, derelict form.

When I was finally old enough to actually obtain a driver's license, my final year as a paperboy was conducted from behind the wheel of my white, second-hand, Ford Mustang II. With eight cylinders and 302 cubic inches, it drank a healthy portion of my profits in gas as Domino hung his head and drooling tongue out the passenger window and barked at everybody, mostly for attention, while I crisscrossed the backwoods suburban streets. My brother called the slobber that Domino left on the side of my car *Dom Goms*. When Domino's excitement caused a short trumpet burst and a gaseous cloud, occasionally so intense that I had to stick my own head and tongue out the driver's side window and into the fresh airstream, we called these disruptions *Dom Bombs*. Such was the price to pay for having his furry company along for the ride. Did I say *ride* out loud? That word would send his bony tail thumping against the wall, and all things in his way, in the wag of all wags — causing a staccato beat that told one and all he would not let me leave the house without him.

Only rarely was I mentioned within these newspapers that I was delivering. Occasionally one of my baseball teams would be mentioned in the sports pages. One year we (Ronnie's Men's Clothing Store) won the town tournament in the Senior Babe Ruth League. My game stats were mentioned, but that had as much to do with my mom authoring the article as my performance on the field. Nevertheless I had a great attachment to these newspapers that were so much a part of my adolescence, and the daily schedule and route compliance were early training for my future life in the transportation industry.

My final summer working for the newspaper, I signed on to deliver the heavy bundles to other paperboys, in addition to servicing my own route. This was a salaried position and not reliant on tips. My official title as the guy inside the van sorting, counting, and stuffing the bundles was *Jumper*. I had to clock in and clock out with an actual punch card. On the weekends this was an all-night assignment. This turned out to be my earliest preparation for flying redeyes.

As I focused on completing high school and applying to colleges, I considered labeling myself as a circulation expert. I figured that would put me ahead of other applicants who were professional petroleum transfer engineers. Remember when an overall-clad attendant actually pumped the gas into our cars? I remember the sign at our local service station that displayed: *Self-service is 4 cents cheaper per gallon.* The extra money I made working two jobs for the newspaper and pumping my own gas went toward college-bound essentials: I threw a graduation party that left shiny, metallic flip-tops covering my parent's lawn and a trail of discarded, red plastic cups that nearly stretched the length of my paper route. Without ceremony, I handed down my delivery responsibilities — and a green ledger with all my customers' names, addresses, and tipping habits (when Domino decided to mark his territory by lifting a leg on my newspaper bundle before I arrived to deliver them, somebody had to receive the top copy) to a younger neighborhood kid, and then I set off for higher learning.

> *I want to learn this*
> *I want to fly*

I want to see this
World from the sky

What route do you fly?
Where have you been?
Where are you going?
Time and again

For the last twenty-five-plus years I have still been delivering — people instead of newspapers. In the years following those serpentine travels through my childhood neighborhood in my baby-eight powered Mustang, I traded up for wings and became an airline pilot — first in turboprops, then in jets. I still travel for a living — now stopping at airports instead of mailboxes.

Through all the rain
You steer the plane
How do you know
What's far below
Through all the snow
How do you know
How do you see
Where it's safe to be?

What route do you fly?
Where have you been?
Where are you going?
Time and again

My name did appear in Connecticut Newspapers a few times as an adult. My engagement to Susanne Jensen was announced in the *Greenwich Time* back in 1996. Since my mom had passed away by then, I'm not sure who authored that local interest piece. What became a national interest was Susanne's sudden death onboard TWA Flight 800 when all 230 passengers blew up off the coast of Long Island. One of the last photos I took of Susanne — a smiling moment taken on our trip through Belgium the day before I offered her a white-gold diamond ring in Amsterdam — was splashed on the front page for weeks and then moved to internal pages for months as a result of the lengthy TWA Flight 800 investigation.

Thirteen years later, I submitted my first article to Connecticut Newspapers, Inc. about the night I lost Susanne so suddenly. It was appropriately titled, "Thirteen Years Later, He Can Finally Tell the Story of TWA 800," and it marked my emergence as a writer—what turned out to be a serious turn in my life. I was a pilot for TWA, yet Susanne flew as a full-fare, first-class passenger on my airline. Her company, GE Capital, sent her to Paris on business. The irony that she was onboard a fatal flight on my airline was so thick that deeply engrained survivor's guilt ate at me like emotional cancer for over a decade. That eventual *Greenwich Time* article (also syndicated in other Connecticut newspapers) eventually paved my path into creative writing grad school, where I've since completed an MFA at Fairfield University. I now live in St. Louis but was able to attend the Connecticut-based university because they offer a low-residency program hosted twice a year on Enders Island off the coast of Mystic (that includes one-on-one mentorship with a designated professor between each residency).

During both years of grad school, I expanded that initial article while creating an aviation-based thesis about my TWA Flight 800 experience—the rough draft of this book. Along the way more than a dozen chapters have appeared in *Airways* magazine, where I've become a contributing editor. Additional chapters have appeared in nine other publications plus an audio production. Always the survivor's guilt still ate at my core, and the best way for me to dig it out was with a pen. In addition to this memoir, I also wrote a survivor's guilt novel.

Since losing Susanne, fictional characters Billy and Lindy have inhabited my inner world—quite possibly out of the void left by her absence. In my emotional struggle to make sense of life without the person I'd anchored in my heart, I began exploring the extreme, opposing reactions to survivor's guilt and grief. On the one hand, I felt that life is short—play hard. Usually I'd say that with an expletive added. Tomorrow doesn't matter—we only have today. In *Pushing Leaves Towards the Sun*, Billy manifests these clichéd mottos. If my life were a movie, Billy would be the little devil on my left shoulder, prodding me with a pitchfork to do that next thing I just know is wrong but would feel so good. After all, didn't I drive a moped before I was old enough to obtain a license? Clearly I'm capable of more ingenious mischief.

Instead, I let Billy do it. He lives in a world with his own loss—as the author of his story, I put him through his best friend's untimely death—and Billy salves his torn-up emotions with heavy drinking, sexual conquests, reckless driving, and body-painting. OK, I did have to do some research and investigation to be able to write about such things. Truth-be-told, in the early years following Susanne's death I was a total mess, but of course you already know that.

But Billy's misadventures are truly fiction, albeit with threads of my hard years woven in.

On the other hand, there's always an angel on our other shoulder guiding us to do right — at least in cinematic folklore. The other extreme to survivor's guilt is the desire to learn something — to divine from the lesson — and especially the need to help others through similar losses. In my fictional world, Lindy is that angel, as well as a musician, and she feels compelled to make sense of the death of her lover — hers and Billy's best friend Oso — through lyrics.

Of course Lindy's lyrics are my own, often written in the middle of sleepless nights as I wrestled through a world without Susanne. What began as my way to write myself out of a terrible bout with depression became both a prose and a musical companion for anyone struggling with their own survivor's guilt. After fifteen drafts of my first novel *Pushing Leaves Towards the Sun*, Billy and Lindy are now visible and audible by everyone, and I share them with you openly (pronounced, free) in podcast form. Dr. Alison Leston, Christopher Madden, and I recorded my premier novel as an audiobook, and it's available on Podiobooks. com and iTunes > Podcasts (worth mentioning again: for free). It was released on 7/11/2012, less than a week before the sixteenth anniversary of TWA Flight 800.

Recent events in a Colorado theater, where my brother now lives, have reminded me that new people suffer losses every day — either from accidents, ongoing war, natural causes, or in Colorado's case though senseless violence. Once Susanne's services were over and most of her friends returned to work, the loneliness of life without her set in. I remember worrying about wearing out my friends with my persistent lamentation. I read a whole shelf of self-help books on grief and related subjects. They were informative, but preachy. I just wanted to feel normal again.

The spark behind my novel began to grow. I wanted to create characters that would suffer the extremes of survivor's guilt — making every other real-world sufferer feel like their overpowering feelings were normal, or at least that they were not alone. And through the power of music, Billy and Lindy could be with us even when we weren't reading. I wove Lindy's dozen songs into the story, but they can also be heard in their entirety on my website: http://marklberry.com/pushingleaves.

Because my musical skills are not on par with my writing experience, I collaborated with some fantastic musicians worldwide to bring the lyrics I wrote as Lindy to life within my novel, as well as the lyrics for the companion songs within this memoir. Each contributing musician is featured on my website. It's probably bad form to claim a favorite — as I love all of the songs so many musicians have created with me—but for those of you suffering from survivor's guilt, I offer you a chance to hear Lindy's feelings about the world moving on without the one she loved, as expressed in the song: "From a Long Way Away" co-written and performed by Kimi Lyn Smith. This is the first song I ever wrote, and the absolute beginning of my attempt to heal through writing. A snippet of the lyrics reveals:

> *From a long way away*
> *Everything still looks* OK
> *But the sun keeps setting in the middle of the day*
> *I put my tongue on the roof of my mouth*
> *It makes me look like I'm smiling*
> *Day after day*
> *Day after day*

The world has moved on for me, too. I no longer have that reflective orange-sashed newspaper bag. I'm not that paperboy — with the spotted dog and the urge to drive before my time — anymore. Life has dealt me a lot of lessons, and sometimes I've struggled to make sense of them. Sometimes I've lived on the edge and only for the moment — self-medicating with alcohol and chasing sexual satisfaction like my novel's protagonist Billy. If you are there right now, peering into darkness that you never saw coming, please remember you are not alone. My audiobook is free. I hope it brings you some comfort, as well as some entertainment.

In my first Connecticut Newspapers article, I wrote that it took thirteen years before I could tell my story. Now it has been over seventeen. It took me this long to feel open to love again. I'm headstrong and thick-hearted. In emotional matters I'm a slow learner, so I'm confident that everyone reading this will be able to work through your own survivor's guilt far faster than me. That's my hope, at least. Maybe you'll allow Billy and Lindy to help share your journey.

As I mentioned, my audiobook, *Pushing Leaves Towards the Sun*, is co-narrated by Dr. Alison Leston, as well as by lifelong friend Christopher Madden. Alison is not just a friend—she is my new love to whom I have finally been able to open up. As much as I'd love to change the past, I can only change the future. Alison's and my love is a story I am just now beginning to write.

On July 17, 2012 — the sixteenth anniversary of TWA Flight 800 — I wrote an "Open letter to the friends of Susanne," and posted it on Facebook. I explained how I was beginning to feel about Alison and asked Susanne's friends for permission to emotionally move on. That letter has become the Epilogue of my memoir as I attempt to do what the cover of my first novel depicts symbolically with a mighty tree stump sprouting a sapling: regrow a new life after being cut down to my roots. Nearly a hundred friends responded in some way—some of them Susanne's former closest friends. They unanimously offered their support and either think the world of Alison or now imminently want to meet her. And although this special emotional step might be uniquely significant to me, it feels equally as important as asking her father for his daughter's hand—an act I venture many other forty-six-year-olds would have skipped.

Without further adieu, this closing statement is directed to a very special person—someone who has had a difficult time reading about my edgy past and has stuck with me through my emotional struggle to find love again. While some suitors have asked this question on Jumbotrons in stadiums across the nation, an act recently ridiculed in a beer commercial ("We salute you, Mr. Scoreboard Marriage Proposal Guy"),[14] I considered doing my own version in a way that would connect me to my roots, to my family, and to where my own mother used to announce my early accomplishments to my local community— in the *Greenwich Time*. The way that I'm most comfortable expressing my feelings is through writing.

In the end, though, I decided that Alison wanted and deserved her own special moment that was separate from my past, and hers. She also lost somebody in a sudden and dark way that it's not my place to expand upon here. I will only mention that there were criminal trials for the perpetrators — and guilty verdicts—and I supported her though those public reminders of her hardest times. I know the struggle firsthand when dark waters are stirred, adding the pressure of public interest in our very personal moments.

I dropped down to one knee. Writing this book has all been self-preparation for the most important words to come out of my mouth as I begin the rest of my life: "Alison, Alison Leston, will you marry me?"

She said yes, and we are engaged. Hopefully our eventual wedding announcement just might find its way into the mailboxes of some of the people who have been with me through this unpredictable ride of life, although it is doubtful that newspapers are still delivered by bicycle- or moped-riding paperboys anymore.

---

14 Anheuser-Busch InBev N.V. *Bud Light Beer: "Mr. Scoreboard Marriage Proposal Guy"*. Rec. June 2007. DDB Chicago. Radio ad.

EPILOGUE |

OPEN LETTER TO THE FRIENDS OF SUSANNE

Alison

TODAY — July 17, 2012 — is the 16th anniversary of TWA Flight 800 when we all lost Susanne. I remind you of this not to make you sad, but to remind you of a once-amazing lady who is worthy of our occasional continued recognition.

I have lost touch with many of Susanne's friends over the last sixteen years. Some of that was unconsciously intentional in the early years after 1996. TWA offered me a promotion opportunity in St. Louis, and that allowed me to leave the northeast behind — where I grew up, but also a region ripe with daily reminders of the life that would never happen with her.

Some of you might wonder what has become of me and how I'm doing. A lot has changed. My new airline absorbed TWA in 2001. I also went to grad school to become a writer, and as a writer, put my feelings on the page. I'm still flying airplanes, live in a 107-year-old brick house in a hip urban area of St. Louis, and most importantly, I recently celebrated a year with a fantastic gal I hope you all someday have the opportunity to meet. Alison lived seven blocks away from me for a dozen years before our worlds collided and we were set up on a blind date. She's an overachiever with both a PhD and an MD. The joke between us is that I have to call her *Double Doc*, but since earning my MFA in creative writing last January, she now has to call me, *Master*. Musician Das Binky and I co-wrote a song in her honor, "Alison," and he performed and produced it along with singer TFish.

> *Alison, I've tried to let you know*
> *That I am here, I won't let you go*
> *It's taken time for me to see*
> *Everything that you might mean to me*

So much has happened and we'll never know why
But we're not young anymore
Now we've given it a try
Who knows what life has in store

Never a day goes by, when I …
Never a dream I've had, when I …
Always I believe
And never could I conceive, when
I don't think of you
When I don't dream of you
Alison I'll always think of you, and I

A look at you makes my heart soar
You're my sun and stars and so much more
I see my whole life in you
And everything I thought I always knew

Whatever the world might throw in our way
I'll be there to hold you near
When it comes down to it at the end of the day
You're the thing I hold most dear

Alison I'll always think of you, and I
I never knew
What this could be
I never saw
The You in Me

Never a day goes by, when I …
Never a dream I've had, when I …
Always I believe
And never could I conceive, when
I don't think of you
When I don't dream of you
Alison I'll always think of you, and I
Alison I'll always think of you, and I
Alison I'll always dream of you, Goodbye

I look forward to re-establishing our former friendships. I hope everyone is doing well. You can reach me on Facebook or though my website: http://marklberry.com.

As my character Oso (who dies in a motorcycle accident as my novel begins) would say, "Pura Vida."

– MARK L BERRY

IN MEMORIAM OF THE CREW | TWA FLIGHT 800

I NEVER MET Ollie Krick—one of the Boeing 747 flight engineers working TWA Flight 800—but through his close friends Brain Schiff, Paul Epperson, and his father Ron Krick—all former TWA pilots as well—I feel like I have. TWA was such a close-knit family that I feel like I know some of the employees onboard TWA Flight 800 whose paths never crossed with mine.

Ollie Krick was twenty-six years old, accepted by the Missouri Air National Guard for an F-15 fighter squadron slot, engaged, and originally scheduled to fly the Rome flight that cancelled. His entire crew was then reassigned to the ill-fated Paris flight. Two full 747 crews were onboard TWA Flight 800 that evening; that is why so many employees were lost all at once. I can't memorialize them all here individually, but this is what fellow TWA pilot Paul Epperson has to say about his lost friend. Through his reflection, and my memoir, may all the lost family of TWA Flight 800 be eternally remembered.

– MARK L BERRY

"A SHORT TRIBUTE TO OLLIE" BY PAUL EPPERSON

When I read Mark's request for me to write "A Short Tribute to Ollie," my initial response was to walk aimlessly around my house for a while. Many images surrounding 800 flashed through my mind, including the image of a disheveled, unshaven Mark showing up in Building 95 (on the outskirts of TWA's Hangar 12) at JFK. It was the one-year anniversary of Flight 800, and he was there to visit the newly placed memorial. I can still hear the howl of bagpipes coming out of Hangar 12.

When I finally sat down to honor Mark's request, I didn't make it through the second sentence before my emotions got the better of me—all this after more than sixteen years.

There are certain people that everybody likes; it is not something tangible or that can be accomplished by conscious thought or kind words. They have a natural ease about them; they make you feel comfortable even if the situation is uncomfortable; that was Ollie. He was good at anything he wanted to be good at. He had a natural charm about him that made people want to help him, but he didn't take advantage of it. There is nothing he wouldn't do for you if you asked, but you never had to. He was just there with his work gloves on and a couple of pork steaks for the barbeque for when the work was done. He worked hard for what he had, and he played hard, too. In retrospect, he lived hard enough to make me wonder if he knew something. Many people in our lives let us down; Ollie didn't get that chance, and I know with certainty that if he had been given the opportunity, he never would have.

TWA 800 and Ollie's death have had a profound effect on my life. I think most people are familiar with the expression, "Time heals all wounds." I think it would be better said as, "Time makes it hurt less often." I am an only child and I considered Ollie my brother; I still consider him my brother. Ollie's death touched parts of me I didn't know I had. I am not a religious man, but I feel blessed to have had the chance to know him the way I did. I miss my brother.

COMPANION SONGS AND PHOTOS

ALL 34 COMPANION SONGS can be heard in order on my website's main *Memoir* page:

http://marklberry.com/memoir

All of the songs are also spaced throughout the *Memoir Photos* webpage:

http://marklberry.com/memoir/memoir-photos

If you are interested in the lyrics, they are revealed on each song's own page — just click on a song's title wherever it appears on my website. Each musician also has a webpage on my website.

My personal contact info is located on my *About the Author* page. Feedback is welcome. Please also feel free to leave a review for this memoir — or any of my writing — on Amazon, Goodreads, Facebook, Twitter, or wherever you share your reading experiences.

http://marklberry.com/about-author

All words by Mark L Berry unless otherwise indicated. Music and performance credits are listed on my website along with each .mp3 recording. My deepest thanks to all the amazing and talented people who have helped bring this work to life.

ONE MORE STORY | SMOKE IN THE COCKPIT

In Ernest K. Gann's Day

OK, I HAVE ONE ADDITIONAL TALE to tell while I am honoring my family of lost aviators. This one recalls my primary TWA mentor Captain Ken Cook, and the companion song honors the greatest airline pilot/author to ever grace a page with his personal experience: Ernest K. Gann.

SMOKE IN THE COCKPIT

As several of my friends and neighbors sat drinking home-brew around the patio table in my backyard while waiting for steak pinwheels—a rollup of flank, spinach, bacon, and Parmesan—to finish grilling, one of them lit up a cigarette. This is something he wouldn't do if we were gathered inside my house, and couldn't do if we'd met at a restaurant. It's rare that I smell cigarette smoke anymore—local ordinances and state laws have nearly eradicated burning tobacco in any public establishment that I might frequent for a libation or a meal. This is not necessarily a bad thing. I'm a nonsmoker who prefers my clothes and hair to remain nicotine free, my lungs to remain undamaged by second-hand smoke, and my nose to remain capable of distinguishing the subtle aromas of whatever turns up on my plate. But there is one positive thing that wisps of other people's cigarette smoke does provide me on the rare occasion that I encounter it: I'm reminded of another time—specifically of a special trip early in my aviation career. As I sniff the distinctive odor of tobacco, I'm entranced by the swirls of hypnotic, gray smoke as each puff slowly dissipates between my friend's breaths. Soon I'm transported back to 1990, and my first ocean crossing.

There is a constant haze of cigarette smoke in our cockpit, as if we've invited a cloud inside. Each of my two captains—Cook and Ruebler—takes great pleasure in creating potentially carcinogenic clouds while occupying the command seat in our 100-series Boeing 727 cockpit during our multi-leg trans-Atlantic ferry flight. At times, when the other is occupying the forward jumpseat instead of taking his crew rest in the cabin, the combined effort of their cumulative exhalations could signal the election of a new pope.

Most of the round dials and instruments in front of me are as familiar as old friends, but one that's new on this trip inspires my rapt attention. This old Pigship — TWA's nickname for the three-holer — has an INS (inertial navigation system) unit installed where our second ADF (automatic direction finder) control head used to be. The INS can display latitude and longitude, plot a course, reveal the outside wind direction and speed, plus more — all from internal signals without receiving a signal from outside the aircraft. An ADF is a basic device that's merely capable of pointing toward a designated radio station or beacon in the AM (amplitude modulation) band. It doesn't provide distance or wind correction, and its range is limited by the ground station's power. Aircraft dependent on ADF navigation are limited how far they can fly offshore.

Snaking out from the center console between the captain's seat and mine is a long, thick cable that extends through the cockpit door (preventing it from closing) and into first class — where it meets a coffin-sized container that's bolted to the floor tracks. The wide, comfortable seats that have been removed to accommodate the container are stacked back in the coach section for re-installation before returning this airplane to commercial service. Inside this giant box, borrowed from the belly of one of our fleet's long-haul Boeing 747 or L-1011 TriStar aircraft, are the INS gyros that spin in all three axis and combine to provide a single display of inertial guidance as we navigate the Blue Spruce route around the northern rim of the Atlantic Ocean.

The nineties were a time when twin-engine widebody jets such as the Boeing 767 and the Airbus A330 were beginning to dominate the trans-Atlantic oceanic tracks with their proven engine reliability and fuel efficiency. Older-generation airliners with three and four engines were slowly being phased out of favor. The narrowbody, three-engine Boeing 727 was designed for flights within continents, so ferrying one across the ocean was more of a game of hopscotch than the giant leap of the bigger birds. Given our three-to-four-hour range, the northern Blue Spruce route was our only option.

Ernest K. Gann used to navigate this route back during World War II in his c-87 Liberator Bombers and DC-2s and DC-3s with only a single ADF to guide him — that primitive instrument we hoped not to have to rely on. We didn't have an IRS (inertial reference system) with compact laser-ring gyros — the technology that guided the then-modern twin-engine widebodies — or a GPS that's common today, but the single INS unit was enough to land astronauts on the moon, and I was fascinated by its relative complexity compared to the 727's usual reliance on ground-based navigation aids.

Unlike the comfortable summer evening that I was enjoying in my back-yard while reminiscing about my first ocean crossing, this adventure occurred during the icy grip of a particularly cold January. Captain Ken Cook, who had taken it upon himself to become my personal mentor, had selected me to join his crew of five pilots to ferry this Boeing 727 from Kansas City, Missouri, through Goose Bay, Newfoundland, and Keflavìk, Iceland, then on to Frankfurt, Germany, to replace its sister ship that was ready for a periodic maintenance overhaul—what the commercial aviation industry calls a C Check.

We were on the first leg of our journey when Sherry, one of our two flight engineers, passed the Goose Bay ATIS (automated terminal information service —in layman's terms, it's the weather plus specific airport information such as the active approach and runway in use) up to me, sending the cockpit cigarette smoke swirling in a new pattern. My first question after reading the tempera-ture was, "Minus forty degrees, is that Celsius or Fahrenheit?"

She shocked me with her answer: "Yes."

Both Captains Cook and Ruebler began laughing between puffs, and then taught me that's where the two temperature scales meet. It was a lesson I was never going to forget once I stepped outside of the airplane at our first, frigid, fuel stop.

I thought this would be the year I won the lottery, as Hell had surely frozen over and we'd landed in the inner ninth circle. While we taxied to our assigned spot on the ramp (there was no Jetway parking), either Sherry or Connie—our other flight engineer—announced that the APU (auxiliary power unit, or the little engine in the tail that provides heat and electrical power on the ground between flights) wouldn't start. It was cold-soaked, and both Captains Cook and Ruebler considered leaving the left engine running while refueling—a nonstan-dard procedure they preferred to shutting completely down and then waiting for spring to defrost us so we could depart. But after several attempts, the APU reluctantly spun back up to life.

It was so cold at this icy airfield that Connie and Sherry split their preflight duties and each inspected half of the airplane. They left the forward boarding door together, ran down the portable stairs that were mounted on the back of a truck that was probably left idling from fall until spring, and then split up. They each ran a different direction around the airplane to the tail—inspecting their respective wing along the way. I opened the rear entry door for them when I heard their winter boots pounding up the aft air stairs.

Then it was my turn to race to the terminal with the two captains. I was the sole first officer on this long trip serving as a relief pilot. We had to locate a landline so that we could call our dispatch office for the next flight plan on to Keflavìk — something that would appear on curly, wax fax paper if we were lucky — and pay for our jet fuel. I just wanted to see something of this remote airport as I suspected my visits here would be few and far between, if ever again.

When I stepped out of the aircraft, I never had time to get cold. Any exposed skin quickly transitioned straight from warm to numb, and the rest of me wasn't far behind. I immediately felt that I was wearing my face like a mask. I pre-wound my Olympus Stylus camera so it was ready to shoot — it used film; remember that stuff? — and the race to the terminal began. I stopped my sprint only long enough to pose for a quick *I was here* snap, then handed my compact camera to Captain Cook who successfully depressed the shutter button through his thick gloves. His raw, frosty breath was as clearly visible as if he was still smoking a cigarette, only this time his exhalations sank like bruised clouds to the frosty tarmac. My fingers — already frozen though my own inadequate gloves — were in no condition to wind the film for a second outdoor photo. The *National Geographic* Polar Adventure Team would not be calling me for its next expedition.

Once inside the terminal, my face hurt as it warmed up. The itch and sting was a surreal experience, like freezing to death in reverse. Only now, with the warm terminal air burning life back into my flash-frozen body, could I say that I'd experienced minus forty degrees.

I found the gift shop, which was more of a static display. A few racks contained postcards, iron-on T-shirts, and an honesty box for leaving payment. I couldn't imagine who would want to be stationed here to man this kiosk. I dropped a U.S. $5 bill in the slot — I didn't have any Canadian currency — and procured round "CYYR" stickers (with "Goose Bay" in small print underneath) for each of our flight bags. I definitely wanted something tangible to remind me of this place, even though it was frost-burned into my skin.

Despite our short stay, our already-cold-soaked engines needed coaxing back to life. We addressed our inanimate machinery with universal aviation chants to enhance our efforts: "Come on baby, you can do it," and, "Just a little more now, just a little more," were typical G-rated examples. Finally we powered up, pointed into the Arctic wind, and launched — leaving Goose Bay with goose bumps and a combined sigh of relief.

Keflavìk is the largest airport on the island nation of Iceland. When the weather zeroes out there, the nearest diversion field can be at the end of an impossibly long flight to either mainland Europe or Greenland. With full tanks when we departed Goose Bay, we carried holding fuel, but realistically we were committed to landing somewhere on Iceland even if we had to find it by feel.

As we began our descent toward the ocean's volcanic oasis — a land of black lava—Connie handed us the latest weather that seemed to be holding steady at quarter-mile visibility—less than our promised forecast, and right down at our landing minimums. Captain Cook smiled and said, "Mark, this is as good of a time as any to learn how to fly a Category II approach." He was having fun with this trip, but this was my first ocean crossing and so much was new to me that I felt like a freshman in a senior-level class.

It was policy for the captain to fly Cat II approaches on revenue flights. We all trained for these low-visibility landings in the simulator, but the boss had to do it when the actual rubber was going to meet the road with passengers onboard. But this wasn't a revenue flight, it was a reposition ferry flight, and Captain Cook was a check-airman—he was certified to train our airline's pilots. The responsibility of flying us down to 100 feet above the runway—for real—intimidated me, but Captain Cook's confidence was unflappable. Through steady puffs of his ever-present cigarette—the smoke between us gave him the aura of a genie that had just escaped from his enchanted lamp—he explained, "There is so little time after the aircraft breaks out of the cloud deck that you don't have time to screw up the landing. As long as you fly a tight approach on the instruments, the runway will magically appear right in front of your face—and then just as you flinch, it's already time to gently flare."

Captain Cook pointed out every minor deviation while I flew so that I could make timely corrections. He closely monitored his own gauges while I tracked the localizer and glideslope, and maintained the proper approach airspeed. Finally, I couldn't help smiling when he said, "100 to go," then, "Runway in sight dead ahead," and then, "Minimums." As I looked up, his cockpit cigarette smoke seemed to dissipate along with the cloud deck outside my window. I saw the first third of the runway lights and gently applied a little backpressure to the yoke. The main wheels touched down with a satisfying squeak. I lowered the nose wheel to the pavement and pulled up on the three reverse levers. Captain Cook deployed the spoiler lever, and he allowed me to steer with the rudder pedals while I braked to a full stop before he took over to taxi the aircraft to our parking spot. I think he had taken control after landing before I realized we'd both been holding our collective breaths though all the excitement.

Captain Cook and I had flown together before—it was, after all, his invitation that had recruited me for this ferry-flight assignment—and I had both admiration and respect for him. I didn't dare utter a word about his in-flight smoking, even though I felt like the visibility was IMC (instrument meteorological conditions) inside the cockpit much of the time. In fact, in those days it wasn't uncommon for captains to smoke. Later that same year, 1990, the first smoking ban passed for domestic flights of two hours or less. It wasn't until

1998 that flights six hours or less joined the smoking ban. Only in 2000 were the cabin no-smoking signs fully deactivated as all U.S. domestic flights became smoke-free by law.

There wasn't much to see of Iceland in darkness and a mere quarter-mile visibility, but I was glad to be here. The terminal, as a primary gateway for Iceland, was far more modern than Goose Bay, and hosted a lot more passenger traffic—even in the middle of the night. I think there was a Hard Rock Cafe right inside the terminal, but we were focused on our mission and didn't stay long enough for sit-down dining. Many years later I would return as a non-revenue passenger on Icelandair (one of TWA's marketing partners), tour the city, stay out all night with the locals until breakfast, and swim off my hangover in the world-famous hot springs of the Blue Lagoon. Then I'd feel like I'd really been here. But on this trip, Iceland was just an Atlantic-rim fuel stop for an aging Boeing 727 modified for a special trans-Atlantic journey.

After the frozen-field experience in remote Newfoundland, and the foggy landing lesson in Iceland, the third flight to Frankfurt seemed routine—the way most flights are meant to be. That night, in the German suburb of Weisbaden, we toasted our successful mission with liters of Warsteiner bier while the captains puffed away. The smoke was part of their aura. They belong to an era that has been relegated by regulation—a time when I was a rookie at the edge of the frozen and obscured corners of the world. I almost miss their smoke.

As the memories of that sacred mission wound down, my mind slipped back through my captains' cigarette fog to my neighborhood celebration — safely home again in my own backyard, with charred, pinwheeled meat ready to be removed from the grill. Perhaps I'm an old-school pilot now — defined as one prone to reminiscing. Adventurous sailors used to get tattoos to mark their visit to the Arctic or Equator. As an aviator, I instead marked my flight bag with a sticker, and sent my uniform to be dry-cleaned.

IN ERNEST K. GANN'S DAY
(a tribute to the greatest aviator/author who ever lived, flew, and wrote)
Words by Mark L Berry & Music by Mike Skliar
Performed by Mike Skliar

http://marklberry.com/memoir/in-ernest-k-ganns-day

In the thirties and forties
His flights were called sorties
In Liberator Bombers
And DC-2s

He earned his wings
Beside Captains like Kings
The High and the Mighty
Made him pay his dues

Then war brewed in Europe
So he went and signed up
To help out our country
In the Air Transport Command

He earned a promotion
To fly 'cross the ocean
Now as a captain
With a steady hand

Ernest K. Gann
Wore epaulets
And flew across the ocean
Well before jet

But Fate is a Hunter
A blood-thirsty butcher
And every pilot
Was all too aware

It took skill and luck
To fly through the muck
And with wings full of ice
Just to stay in the air

That was before radar
But still he found Gander
And then on to Greenland
With barely a map

Bluie West One
Was never any fun
Tucked into fiords
As a dire one-way trap

Ernest K. Gann
Wore epaulets
And flew across the ocean
Well before jets

Then on to Iceland
A dark lonely island
With no navaids to follow
He dead-reckoned his way

On my first ocean crossing
I can't help but thinking
How much has changed
Since back in his day

Without laser-ring gyros
Those pilots were heroes
They crossed the cold ocean
Without GPS

Those early days of aviation
Have my admiration
Because every flight
Was a lethal game of chess

Ernest K. Gann
Wore epaulets
And flew across the ocean
Well before jets

In the thirties and forties
His flights were called sorties
In Liberator Bombers
And DC-2s

A pilot, an author
A gentleman of adventure
There was never a man
Like Ernest K. Gann

THANKS FOR JOINING ME on this aviation journey. For more of my work, look for me in *Airways* magazine. I also hope you will enjoy my other books and audio. For a small sample, here is the first chapter of my novel *Pushing Leaves Towards the Sun*. It's a survivor's guilt story that develops a dozen original songs.

   – *Pura Vida*, MARK L BERRY

NOVEL PROMO

PUSHING LEAVES TOWARDS THE SUN
   http://marklberry.com/pushingleaves

CHAPTER 1 | CURB HOPPING

[Billy]

I'm holding the report but can't get my eyes to focus on the words — they scatter in tiny optical windows like the view from a low-budget science fiction fly's-eye view. The pulse in my temples is pounding with the echoes from my heartbeat — boom, boom, boom from my chest, and then tap, tap, tap in my skull. My eyes finally focus, and the word jumble snaps into a single orderly paragraph. *The chain struck the headlight and rode up the quarter fairing, cleared the top of the tinted Plexiglas with a snap, and connected under Roberto Acevedo's chinstrap, fatally separating the rider from his motorcycle.* This is as far as I get before dropping the report.

Nobody calls him Roberto. The words don't feel real without *Oso* on the page. But looking over at Lindy, I know it's real. She's slumped in a metal folding chair next to Oso's parents with her face in her hands. Her long hair is held back in a clip. Tears are slipping through her fingers, which are covering her eyes, and run down her smooth tan arms. I watch one drop hang from her elbow in an elongated drip, threatening to jump the gap to the floor.

What if I didn't have to cover those extra shifts? I should have told Derek to find somebody else to work because I already had weekend plans, damn it. If only I'd kept my promise and driven Oso to the lake in my Jeep. If only Oso had gone straight to the cabin instead of coming to visit me. Or, what if he had just stuck to the streets? Damn, he only learned to ride on the ragged edge because of me. I'm the one who taught him how to shortcut over curbs and cut through parking lots. Why had I done that? Because I'm an asshole, that's why. Making him race me for a burger — fuck, fuck, fuck! I can't shake it out of my head. I can't keep my guilty conscience from replaying my character-corrupting, condemning behavior only hours earlier.

I stomped on the brakes and my tires screeched as Oso pulled up behind me on his bumblebee-yellow BMW motorcycle. I still almost clipped that oversized giant as I panic-stopped my dark red Jeep. "Hey, dumbshit," I yelled over my shoulder. "Now I see why you painted that bike so bright. You're one lucky S.O.B. that I didn't back right over your ass. This is an off-road vehicle, after all."

"I was just swinging by to see you," Oso told me in his characteristically unfazed tone. "I got my personalized plate — PHX. Thanks for looking up the three-letter airport identifier for me, 'cause *Phoenix* wouldn't fit."

"No sweat. You did raise that bike back from the dead. You're quite the grease monkey. I could use your help keeping this machine running. I barely got it started, and I need to get it up to speed in order to recharge the battery with the alternator."

"No problemo, amigo," Oso said. "I skipped breakfast and I'm starving. Got time for an early lunch?"

"Sure thing, if we hurry. I've got just a little time to kill before heading into work for a short shift before our weekend. I'll race you to Kassi's Diner. Loser buys."

"I could use one last free hot meal before camping tonight. This glorious machine has cleaned out my wallet, but it's sooo worth it."

I watched Oso pat his gas tank with pride while I turned the wheel and eased in front of his meticulous motorcycle, facing the lawn that was way overdue to be cut, weeded, or attended to in any way.

"OK, three-two-GO!" I shouted, as I hit the gas and cut across the grass to begin the race with an unfair head start. In my mirror I could see Oso answering my getaway by revving his engine up to at least 5000 rpm and then letting go of the clutch. His knobby rear on/off-road tire spun before digging in, spraying a rooster tail of grass and dirt. The sudden release of power and torque caused his BMW R80 G/S to lurch sideways as it accelerated on the edge of control. Oso swerved out onto the road and grew bigger in my mirror a couple of turns later when I became stuck behind a car at the first stoplight. He pulled up next to me and laughed. Pointing an accusing finger, he boasted, "No way is that beach buggy of yours going to beat my bike, even though you're cheating."

I was smiling, but he wasn't finding this funny. "If you're not cheating, you're not trying," I said as I tried to look him in the eye through his tinted helmet visor. Oso has seen my mischievous smile before. I could tell he really wasn't amused when he stated, "No more games, and no more shortcuts. This is a race, not a chase. Let me know if my taillight is working after the street light turns green." He knew he could work his bike up through the gears faster than I could work my Jeep's lanky stick shift and propel the heavy all-terrain frame.

I looked for pedestrian traffic while devising a plan to challenge Oso's over-confidence. "You ain't seen nothin' yet. I hope you brought a credit card."

I turned the wheel hard and drove my right two tires up over the sidewalk, squeezed past the car in front of me, and made a right turn on red. Next, I accel-erated through the speed limit just as fast as my six cylinders allowed with the pedal to the floor. I could hear the pistons knock and the frame shake. My Jeep could almost climb walls, but it wasn't made to be a speed demon. I was trying to teach it a new trick.

I needed to keep Oso in my mirror where he belonged—behind me. Oso fol-lowed by hopping up on the curb slowly, using both feet for balance, and then racing down the sidewalk after me. The startled driver who was still waiting for a green light just stared. I turned to watch over my shoulder while plowing ahead at full bore. Oso stood on the pegs as he hopped off the curb. He looked tentative and challenged. He shifted up to speed once he was back on the road and tried closing the gap between us. Now we were both racing like Gene Hackman in *The French Connection*. I tipped my Jeep up onto two wheels several times while swerving to keep him from passing, and worried that my roll bar might need to live up to its name, not that it would do any good without my seatbelt fastened.

At last, Kassi's was coming up on the left and Oso wasn't going to have enough time to pass. He must have realized he was going to have to solve his problem geometrically, and my shortcutting strategy across the lawn prob-ably served as his inspiration. He turned early—into the lot of a small group of stores. He had one more curb to hop, as the lot to Kassi's was not directly connected. He hit the curb fast and almost spilled the bike, but somehow man-aged to keep it upright. He stopped right in front of the entrance. I was slow to jump from my Jeep as I ground it to a stop with the parking brake pedal—still stunned by his new balls-out performance.

"I win," I tried to lie. "I made it into the lot before you did, even with your death-defying entrance."

Oso dropped the kickstand, hopped off his bike, and opened the door for me. Then he blocked me with one of his rhinoceros arms and proclaimed, "The first one inside is the winner, mi loco amigo. This is going to be the best burger I've tasted all year, mostly because you're buying it."

I felt miserable losing our bet, so I poked Oso in the chest. "Where did you learn to hop a curb like that? I thought you were going down for sure. Blood and teeth wouldn't make a very good meal."

Oso let me follow him in the door, turned, and then patted me on the shoulder while replying, "I've done a lot of riding, mostly bicycles and mini bikes as a kid, but those were the first curbs that I've hopped on Phoenix. I really have no money, so I had to beat you. You're the one who made this an adventure race rather than a speed run."

I can still hear him saying that. Those last words still echo in sync with my pulsing heart and temples.

You're the one who made this an adventure race rather than a speed run.

You're the one who made this an adventure race rather than a speed run.

It only made things worse when I remembered that I'd told him, "I'll race you back after we eat to see who's buying the beer for the lake." What if I hadn't been such a competitive asshole?

What ifs weren't helping my pulsing head, but my mind wrapped around them like a python on prey. I kept chewing on the seemingly normal decisions made over the course of an ordinary day — the smallest chain of events that had such punishing ramifications at that parking lot chain. Oso's last day kept playing like an unstoppable roller coaster in my subconscious. Oso is gone, while I live on—a new life-changing detail that will last forever. My first taste of survivor's guilt burns like broken glass marinated in battery acid. I can already feel that it's just a sample of what will become a full indigestible meal.

MARK IS A PILOT for a major airline with twenty-five years of seniority and he's also a contributing editor for *Airways* magazine. He earned an MFA in creative writing from Fairfield University where he was also a managing editor for *Mason's Road* literary journal. His work, including excerpts from this memoir, has appeared in *4'33"*, *Aerospace Testing Int'l*, AOPA *Flight Training*, BMW *Owners News*, Connecticut Newspapers, *Epiphany*, ERAU *EaglesNEST*, *Graze*, *LIFT*, *Mil-Speak Memo*, *Port Cities Review*, *Rogue*, SO...STORIES, *The Stoneslide Corrective*, *The Story Shack*, TARPA *Topics*, *Under the Sun*, and *Write This*. He lives in St. Louis, Missouri near the big staple in the middle of the USA map. Locals call it: The Arch.

www.ingramcontent.com/pod-product-compliance
Lightning Source LLC
Chambersburg PA
CBHW022113080426

42734CB00006B/116